Gendered Institutions and Women's Political Representation in Africa

Africa Now

Africa Now is published by Zed Books in association with the internationally respected Nordic Africa Institute. Featuring high-quality, cutting-edge research from leading academics, the series addresses the big issues confronting Africa today. Accessible but in-depth, and wide-ranging in its scope, Africa Now engages with the critical political, economic, sociological and development debates affecting the continent, shedding new light on pressing concerns.

Nordic Africa Institute

The Nordic Africa Institute (Nordiska Afrikainstitutet) is a centre for research, documentation and information on modern Africa. Based in Uppsala, Sweden, the Institute is dedicated to providing timely, critical and alternative research and analysis of Africa and to co-operation with African researchers. As a hub and a meeting place for a growing field of research and analysis the Institute strives to put knowledge of African issues within reach for scholars, policy makers, politicians, media, students and the general public.

www.nai.uu.se

Forthcoming titles

Stephen Marr and Patience Mususa (eds),
Practice and Politics of DIY Urbanism in African Cities
Cecilia Navarra and Cristina Udelsmann Rodrigues (eds),
Transformations of the Rural Spaces in Mozambique
Laura Stark and Annika Teppo (eds),
Power and Inequality in Urban Africa

Titles already published

Jesper Bjarnesen and Simon Turner,
Invisibility in African Displacements
Fantu Cheru and Cyril Obi (eds),
The Rise of China and India in Africa
Ilda Lindell (ed.),
Africa's Informal Workers
Iman Hashim and Dorte Thorsen,
Child Migration in Africa
Prosper B. Matondi, Kjell Havnevik and Atakilte Beyene (eds),
Biofuels, Land Grabbing and Food Security in Africa
Cyril Obi and Siri Aas Rustad (eds),
Oil and Insurgency in the Niger Delta
Mats Utas (ed.),
African Conflicts and Informal Power
Prosper B. Matondi,
Zimbabwe's Fast Track Land Reform
Maria Eriksson Baaz and Maria Stern,
Sexual Violence as a Weapon of War?
Fantu Cheru and Renu Modi (eds),
Agricultural Development and Food Security in Africa

Gender and representation scholars have been good at explaining why some African countries are among the top-ranked in the world when it comes to the high levels of women elected into elected offices. Are you interested in some in-depth insights into the mechanisms and dynamics of countries lagging behind their more well-known neighbours, this is the book for you to read.
–Ragnhild Muriaas, Professor, University of Bergen

This book is an important and interesting contribution to the literature on women in politics in Africa. It provides a rare collection of rich case studies from eight African countries of how informal institutions in numerous ways work to exclude women from political spaces.
–Vibeke Wang, Senior Researcher, Chr. Michelsen Institute

Gendered Institutions and Women's Political Representation in Africa

Edited by Diana Højlund Madsen

ZED

Gendered Institutions and Women's Political Representation in Africa was
first published in 2021 by Zed Books Ltd,
Bloomsbury Publishing,
50 Bedford Square, London, WC1B 3DP

www.bloomsbury.com

Copyright © Diana Højlund Madsen, 2021

The right of Diana Højlund Madsen to be identified as the editor of
this work has been asserted by them in accordance with the Copyright,
Designs and Patents Act, 1988.

Typeset by Integra Software Services Pvt. Ltd.

Printed and bound in Great Britain

A catalogue record for this book is available from the British Library

ISBN: HB: 978-1-9134-4120-3
           PB: 978-1-9134-4121-0
         ePDF: 978-1-9134-4119-7
         ePub: 978-1-9134-4117-3

Contents

List of Illustrations

Figures

Tables

Author Biographies

Amanda Gouws is Professor of Political Science at the University of Stellenbosch, South Africa. She holds a PhD from the University of Illinois in Urbana-Champaign in the USA. Her specialization is South African politics and gender politics. Her research focuses on women and citizenship, the national gender machinery and women's representation, and she has published widely in these areas. In 2017 she published a co-edited book with Joy Watson, *Nasty Women Talk Back* with Imbali Press. She was a Commissioner for the South African Commission for Gender Equality from 2012 to 2014. She is currently a Distinguished Professor, holding an NRF Research Chair in Gender Politics. Her e-mail is: ag1@sun.ac.za

Asiyati Lorraine Chiweza is Associate Professor in Public Administration in the Department of Political and Administrative Studies at Chancellor College, University of Malawi. Her main research interests are in gender, local governance, development and political economy analysis. Dr Chiweza has been the principal researcher and coordinator of several international collaborative research programmes including the following: *Democratisation, Political Participation and Gender in Malawi (2014–2016)* and is currently working on a collaborative project with University of Bergen on *Money Talks: Gendered Electoral Financing in Democratic and Democratising States.* Her e-mail is: achiweza@cc.ac.mw

Catherine Cymone Fourshey is Associate Professor of History and International Studies and Acting Director of the Griot Institute for Black Lives and Culture at Bucknell University, USA. Her work focuses on histories of gender, hospitality, migration, agriculture and intersections of environment, economy and politics in pre-colonial eastern and east central

Africa. Fourshey's publications include a co-authored book *Bantu Africa* and numerous articles. She is currently working on a book entitled *A (Re)Turn to the Girl: Feminist Girlhood Studies and Development in East Africa*. Her e-mail is: ccf014@bucknell.edu

Diana Højlund Madsen is Senior Gender Researcher at the Nordic Africa Institute in Uppsala Sweden and Research Fellow at the University of the Free State, South Africa. She holds a PhD from Roskilde University in Denmark on gender mainstreaming processes in Ghana. Her specialization is on women's political representation, gender and democratization, gender mainstreaming and gender and conflict especially with a focus on Ghana and Rwanda. She is the coordinator of the projects *Gendered Institutions and Women's Political Representation in Africa* and *Global Talk Local Walk – the Translation of the Women, Peace and Security Agenda into Practice in Africa*. Her e-mail is: diana. hojlund-madsen@nai.uu.se

Mandiedza Parichi is Lecturer at the Peace Department, Midlands State University in Gweru, Zimbabwe. She holds a PhD in Media and Gender. She also holds an MSc in Gender and Policy studies another MSc in Peace, Leadership and Conflict Resolution Degree and an MSc in Media and Society Studies. Her research interests include gender equality politics, media, development studies, democracy, youth and peace. Her e-mail is: mazvitadawn@gmail.com

Marla L. Jaksch is Associate Professor of Women's, Gender, & Sexuality Studies, with affiliations in the African American Studies Department and the Department of International Studies, in the Africa concentration, at The College of New Jersey. Her interdisciplinary research interests include neocolonialisms, development and digital cultures; science and technology studies in sub-Saharan Africa; and transnational feminisms and girlhood studies. Her current research project is a co-authored book entitled *A (Re) Turn to the Girl: Feminist Girlhood Studies and Development in East Africa*. Her e-mail is: jakschm@tcnj.edu

Maude Dikobe is Senior Lecturer, Department of English, University of Botswana. She is a Fulbright scholar and holds a PhD in African Diaspora

Studies from UC Berkeley with a focus on performance and gender. She is an educator, researcher, consultant and gender activist. Her primary research interests include gender studies, literature and the expressive arts of Africa and the African diaspora, prison writing and third world cinema. She is involved in many national and international networks aimed at promoting equality and women's empowerment.

Monica Adele Orisadare is Senior Lecturer in the Department of Economics, Obafemi Awolowo University, Ile-Ife, Nigeria where she obtained a PhD, MSc and BSc in Economics. She is the current Acting Director at the Centre for Gender and Social Policy Studies, Obafemi Awolowo University. Her research area is in Gender, Development Economics and Public Finance, where she has published widely in reputed international journals. Her e-mail is: mdare@ oauife.edu.ng

Sethunya Tshepho Mosime is Senior Lecturer in the Department of Sociology, Faculty of Social Sciences, at the University of Botswana and holds a PhD. She has a multidisciplinary background in sociology, political science, social anthropology, cultural studies, media and communication. Her research and teaching interests are around the rights of political and social minorities across ethnicity, gender and sexuality, African social thought, sociological theories and methods, gender and the criminal justice system, communication for development and media-military relations. She is a gender activist who has been a member of the Botswana women's movement since the late 1990s. Her e-mail is: mosimest@mopipi.ub.bw

Shillah Sintoyia Memusi undertook her doctoral research at the University of Bayreuth's International Graduate School of African Studies (BIGSAS), Germany. Carried out within the framework of the 2010 Constitution of Kenya, her research focused on public participation by Maasai women in Kenya, with respect to gendered politics of appropriateness within the community. She currently works as a research consultant on governance and institutional development. Her e-mail is: shillah.memusi@mailbox.org

Introduction

The book explores the complex processes of gendering institutions and the interaction between formal and informal institutions in the different African case studies (Botswana, Ghana, Kenya, Malawi, Nigeria, South Africa, Tanzania and Zimbabwe). While much focus has been on both the macro-level in terms of women's political representation (e.g. types of regimes or patriarchy) and the micro-level (e.g. women's individual capacities), perspectives on the meso-level and the role of formal and informal institutions have not received much attention – especially in an African context. Combining the analytical perspective on gendered institutions with the topic of women's political representation provides new perspectives on the African empirical case studies and takes the analytical development of the 'institutionalist turn' further as the book speaks back to the approach of feminist institutionalism with its African perspectives. The book addresses pertinent questions such as: Which formal and informal institutions are influencing women's political representation in an African context? Why have women's political representation developed so unevenly on the African continent? And which role do the formal and informal institutions play in explaining this uneven development in Africa?

The book is inspired by 'feminist institutionalism' taking its point departure in that institutions are gendered rules, norms and processes (Krook and Mackay 2011). In an African context, politics and processes of political representation are characterized by not only formal but also to a large degree informal institutions making the study of these processes from a feminist institutionalist perspective highly relevant for the understanding of the specific case studies. Institutions are defined as 'rules and procedures (both formal and informal) that structure society by constraining and enabling actor's behaviour' (Waylen 2014: 114). The focus on gendered institutions implies that gender constructions are intertwined and embedded in the logic of political institutions – often with a male bias. Waylen (ibid) defines informal institutions as 'socially shared rules, usually unwritten, that are created, communicated and enforced outside of officially sanctioned channels' in opposition to formal rules defined as 'rules and procedures that are created, communicated and enforced through channels which are widely accepted as official'. In aiming to explain why informal rules exist, 'some hypothesize that informal rules emerge when formal institutions are incomplete; when actors prefer, but cannot achieve, a formal institutional solution; or when actors are pursuing goals that are not publicly acceptable, either because they are unlikely to stand the test of public scrutiny, or will attract international condemnation' (Krook and Mackay 2011: 11). This suggests that informal rules will often work against or parallel with formal rules, as they often attempt to preserve the status quo and maintain existing power structures and therefore work against more women in politics and/or substantive changes in a more gender-friendly direction.

The book aims at exploring newer developments on women in politics both from countries which are not usually dealt with in the debate on women's political representation, for example, Botswana, Ghana, Malawi, Nigeria with low representation of women in politics as well as some of the more well-known 'success cases' like Kenya, South Africa, Tanzania and Zimbabwe. In their 2003 work Goetz and Hassim are comparing the 'success cases' Uganda and South Africa. With their 2006 book on women in African Parliaments, Bauer and Britton focus mostly on the success stories on the African continent, for example, Rwanda which is on a 'fast-track' to political representation with its adoption of institutional reforms in the form of quotas. In addition, newer work (Tripp et al. 2009; Tripp 2015) demonstrates how many post-conflict African countries, for example, Liberia, have a higher representation in politics. As post-conflict settings are characterized by a political vacuum, it can work as a window of opportunity or a political opening for women in politics caused by the need for a reconfiguration of power. During conflicts, women's organization have often had a role in peace resolution at an informal level just like gender disruptions have taken place at the local level. In the aftermath of a conflict, global and African gender norms on women's political representation are also influential due to the presence of international actors. More recently, a number of countries, for example, Kenya, have adopted legislative measures to increase the representation of women in politics – a 'second-wave' movement of quota related to broader constitutional reform processes. However, even the 'success cases' in this book (Kenya, South Africa, Tanzania and Zimbabwe) are dealt with from a different perspective than hitherto adopted in other research within this area.

The book is an outcome of a two-day workshop 'Gendered Institutions and Women's Political Representation in Africa' on the 12–13 December 2018 at the Nordic Africa Institute in Uppsala, Sweden. Most of the authors of the book participated in the workshop. For this book, it has been of importance to ensure that the majority of contributions are written not just about African case studies but also by African researchers themselves. The aims of the workshop were: (1) to present selected case studies from the African continent and analyse how gendered institutions influence women's political representation; (2) to present new knowledge on feminist institutionalism and its use for understanding formal and informal institutions influencing women's political representation and (3) to share lessons learnt and strategies for promoting more women in politics from the African continent.

Measuring success – substantive representation in the 'success-cases'?

Traditionally, women's political representation is measured in terms of descriptive representation (numbers) and substantive representation (policies). Often women's descriptive representation is expected to bring about changes in women's substantive representation. However, for women's descriptive representation to bring about change in a more women/gender-friendly direction female politicians should 'have distinct views on women's issues, bring a women's perspective into political decision-making, or bring a different style and set of role expectations to politics' (Bauer and Britton

2006: 4 – with a reference to Joni Lovenduski). As such, women are not automatically or in terms of their numbers *per se* regarded as bringing about change.[1]

The case studies in this book from the quota 'success cases' in eastern and southern Africa (South Africa, Kenya and Tanzania) question any automatic linkage between descriptive and substantive representation and the extent to which the introduction of quotas has brought about transformation for gender equality. The adoption of the SADC (Southern African Development Community) Protocol on Gender and Development in 2008 aiming for a fifty-fifty representation has been important for the adoption of quota in countries such as Tanzania, South Africa and Zimbabwe.[2] Gouws accounts how South Africa has undergone 'state capture' and dismantling of the national gender machinery with the help of compliant women from the ruling party, the ANC. South Africa introduced a quota after the end of apartheid in 1994 and now ANC has a 50 per cent quota. In her chapter, Gouws further elaborates how women in politics have become instrumental in the upholding of the ruling party and with loyalties rather towards the party than a pro-gender equality agenda with the reference to the (ANC) 'Women's League' syndrome, with its rather conservative focus on women as being wives or mothers of the nation. 'Slate politics' and the deployment of caders play an important role in this negative development.

From another angle, Memusi in her study of the ethnic community Maasai in Kenya illustrates how the introduction of a quota in 2010 with a female representative from each county in parliament (forty-seven) has not led to any substantial changes in the Maasai community. Memusi pinpoints the importance of looking beyond the national level and of reflecting on intersecting categories such as gender and ethnicity / gender and age. In her chapter, Memusi states that the affirmative action policy adopted also has had negative consequences as women limit themselves to these special seats and that politics is (still) dominated by political patronage involving huge costs for women. In the dominantly Maasai counties one female parliamentarian is in place although they are entitled to more (eleven). Memusi demonstrates through specific examples at community level how Maasai women are marginalized in political decision making due to informal institutions working against women's political representation despite the fact that the quota also applies at the local level.

In Tanzania, a quota of 30 per cent women was adopted in 1985. Fourshey and Jaksch argue that the picture is mixed as the parties control the system for allocating special seats making room for a menu of manipulation including sexual corruption and opens up questions of loyalty towards the party or a women's constituency. In addition, Fourshey and Jaksck indicate that these special seats are viewed as inferior and opponents of affirmative action have called for the abolishment of these special seats with the argument that it was supposed to be temporary measures. However, Fourshey and Jaksck also note that the introduction of affirmative action and related an increase in numbers have changed the attitude towards women in politics, the passing of some pro-women legislation and improved interaction between female and male politicians. They also emphasize that despite the introduction of quota male dominance in party politics persists.

The case study from Zimbabwe by Parichi analyses the representations of (former) ZANU PF (Zimbabwe African National Union – Patriotic Front) Vice President Joice Mujuru in the Zimbabwean media. The case study illustrates how the media downplay her political credentials and thereby attempt to undermine the position of Joice Mujuru with headlines questioning 'How did they arrive at the 30 per cent quota system? The fuzzy math of SADC'. The media analysis reveals how ZANU PF is portrayed as scoring cheap political goals with the introduction of quota and how 'fuzzy maths' becomes 'fuzzy female Vice President'.

However, the Nigerian case study illustrates an extreme case in relation to the introduction of quota as the military regime led by Babangida introduced a quota for women in 1983 in the form of a directive stating that there should be one woman appointed as a member of the Executive Council in each state. These women served as token representatives in an otherwise masculinist institutional environment and may serve to legitimize the regime in the form of 'flirting' with women's representation.

The experiences from Kenya, South Africa, Tanzania, Zimbabwe and Nigeria underline that the adoption of affirmative action measures or quotas is not an end goal in itself but there is a need to move 'beyond numbers' with a popular slogan. Focus should be on their actual translation in practice at both national and regional levels including the control of the processes of selecting women and related their possibilities for adopting a pro-gender agenda within a masculinist institutional context. However, the latter should not be the sole responsibility of the women in politics but also their male counterparts. Similarly, the media and their representations of female MPs play an important role. The book identifies a need for moving beyond a polarized debate pro or against affirmative action and rather focuses on the variations and workings of affirmative action in specific African contexts. However, in some of the case studies with a low number of women in parliament the adoption of affirmative action is still seen as an end goal (e.g. Botswana, Ghana and Nigeria). Mosime and Dikobe put forward how one of the earlier presidents of the Botswana Women in Politics Caucus Moggie Mbaakanyi advocated for the introduction of quota. Madsen analyses the process of trying to introduce an affirmative action bill in Ghana and the patriarchal arguments and institutional inertia associated with this process. However, she also writes about the need to address informal institutions even beyond the adoption of an affirmative action bill to ensure that women do not remain at the margins of politics in Ghana. In the concluding part of the case study on Nigeria, Orisadare states that Nigeria is far from achieving global measures on affirmative action calling for the government to live up to its international obligations.

The role of informal institutions

A number of the book chapters highlight the importance of informal institutions as a potential way of reducing uncertainties and creating some form of predictability (Bjarnegård 2015). As stated earlier, informal institutions often exist when formal institutions are weak and other ways are needed to accomplish the targets, when formal institutions do not provide any proper answers or when the answers sought are not formally acceptable within the institutional framework (ibid). Potentially, informal institutions can work both for and against women's political representation. However, most of the examples point out how informal institutions are rather distorting or subverting formal rules (see also Waylen 2014) or effectively introducing new 'rules of the game' aiming at excluding women from political office with no apparent sanctions for non-compliance. The hidden life of informal institutions makes them difficult to identify (Waylen 2017). It is the aim of the book to uncover the hidden life of the informal institutions in an African context at a national and regional level and in political offices and the media.

In the case of Malawi, Chiweza illustrates how informality in different stages of the election processes in 2014 and 2019 has led to the exclusion of some female candidates as the formal rules (which were only transmitted orally to the female candidates and in this process left some room for interpretation) were disregarded in favour of male candidates. Chiweza describes how the selection and identification of delegates were side tracked with sudden changes and new delegate areas and mobilization to promote their male candidate in a chaotic election. She also describes how female candidates have deliberately been kept out of the loop for crucial information on times, dates and venues in relation to the election process. Furthermore, Chiweza accounts of how the preferred male candidate was declared a winner by influential local political decision makers despite evidence to the contrary. This is illustrative of how formal institutions are not always very formalized and can be sidelined and undermined by informal rules through tactics and strategies used by male political networks.

A number of the case studies (Botswana, Ghana, Kenya, Malawi and Nigeria) emphasize the monetarization of politics and elections including patronage networks or clientelism as a barrier for women's political representation due to their (often) disadvantaged economic position. In a case study from Ghana, Madsen explains how the expenditures have increased 90 per cent from the 2012 to the latest 2016 election including some unaccounted 'other costs'. Women have to negotiate with their husbands over funds, use their professional and private networks to fundraise, take loans and receive gifts (often with the expectation of favours once they get into office). She further elaborates how an informal rule – reduction of the filing fee for female candidates – works as an acknowledgement of the disadvantaged economic position of women and the need to build their financial muscle, and it is an example of an informal rule adopted by the two major political parties working in a pro-women/gender equal direction. However, Madsen states that it is too little as the big spending is in the election process. In the case study on Malawi, Chiweza accounts of how the female candidates had to spend a lot of money on transport and catering for having people in place where the polling was done. In Malawi, the chairperson was withholding information about the venue of the primary elections preventing the female candidates from participating as the money had already been spent once. The first-past-the-post electoral system or 'the winner takes it all' in the five countries mentioned increases the monetarization of politics and is rather excluding for newcomers in politics including women.

Other informal institutions working against more women in politics are the gender stereotypical representations of prominent female politicians in the media. Parichi identifies how the prominent Zimbabwean politician Joice Mujuru has been trapped in a catch twenty-two in the portraying of her. Particularly, Parichi identifies different double binds like 'sinner/saint', 'the female freak' and 'wifehood/motherhood' representations despite Joice Mujuru's professional record of accomplishments.

The book also provides some contributions to the emerging body of literature on gendered perspectives on electoral violence. Madsen emphasizes how a 'politics of insults, ridicule and rumours' prevents and excludes women from political offices. She describes how insults have become a part of the working of Ghanaian politics and particularly affects women in a negative way with verbal abuse relating to gender/sexuality, name-calling, and cartooning. In addition, Madsen outlines how women are affected by rumours about sexual relations and trapped in a catch twenty-two when they engage with the dominantly male political networks and male supporters. In the Maasai communities in Kenya, Memusi accounts of how women are expected to respect men (enkanyit) and not demonstrate any opposition and how a lack of enkanyit invites physical abuse at the domestic front and public shaming or shunning. The case of the Maasai in Kenya also highlights how the first female Maasai MP has overcome threats, alienation and curses from Maasai elders. In the case of Malawi, Chiweza illustrates how the primary elections in some constituencies were characterized by electoral violence as some male opponents deliberately brought in unknown candidates to stir up the process preventing the primary elections from taking place in a peaceful manner. Whereas the cases of Ghana and Kenya are examples of violence against women in politics in the forms of psychological, sexual and physical violence, the case of Malawi rather illustrates how violence in politics generally has negative effects on female candidates. However, more research needs to be conducted with an explicit focus on violence against women in politics in an African context. All these informal rules and norms aim at silencing women and exclude them from political offices.

The methodological approaches adopted to identify the informal institutions and their relations to the formal institutions differ. But a number of the case studies adopt what could best be described as variations of 'political ethnography' with a focus on localized versions of 'the informal' using qualitative methods such as participant observations, semi-structured interviews and extensive field research in different African contexts over a longer period of time to establish the needed familiarity, relations and trust. Some of the authors have an insider – outsider perspective being observers but maintaining a critical distance. Harding speaks of 'strong objectivity' understood as 'strong objectivity requires that the subject of knowledge be placed on the on the same, critical plane as the objects of knowledge. Thus, strong objectivity requires what we can think of as 'strong reflexivity" (Harding 2004: 136). Her concept of 'strong objectivity' includes that the subject of knowledge (the researcher) will be scrutinized as much as the object of knowledge throughout all phases of the research process or 'to be a necessary object of critical causal – scientific – social explanations' (Harding 2004: 137). Harding presupposes a feminist political position as she states: 'Strong objectivity requires the scientists and their communities be integrated into democracy-advancing projects for scientific and epistemological reasons as well as moral and political ones' (Harding 2004: 136). More broadly, the 'political ethnography' work has taken place within the framework of a feminist epistemology guiding the case studies in the book and the overall research questions asked.

Gouws has followed the work of the South African national gender machinery from both an insider and outsider perspective as a former commissioner for the Commission on Gender Equality and a researcher on gender and politics and has used these different experiences in her book chapter. Memusi has with her own background in the Maasai community also been able to draw on an insider and outsider perspective in her analysis of the women's political participation in Maasai communities in Kenya and she too had to comply with the gendered informal rules and norms in the local setting. Madsen has embarked on multiple extensive field works in Ghana with a focus on the parliament in Ghana and actors working on gender and politics. Particularly, she has used participant observation in fora on women's political representation including policy dialogues organized by women's organizations and donors with the presence of a number of female candidates, and at different informal settings in parliament. She has also conducted interviews with female MPs and members of the Committee on Gender, Children and Social Protection as well as the Department of Gender, Children and Social Protection in Ghana.

Other methodological approaches have been media analyses in the Zimbabwean case study. Through an extensive analysis of three different newspapers and their representations of high-level female politician, Joice Mujuru, Parichi demonstrates how she is type-casted in stereotypical ways. The focus on media widens the scope of the book to include insights on the informal institutions at play and the need to include perspectives on broader societal representations of women in politics.

Gender and institutional change

As institutions are gendered, they can also be re-gendered. Bearing in mind the section above this should include informal as well as formal institutions. In their work, Mahoney and Thelen (2010) introduce different strategies for changing institutions in a more gender friendly direction. The strategies are 'layering' (when new rules are attached on top of existing ones), 'displacement' (replacement of existing rules with new ones), 'drift' (when rules remain the same but their impact changes due to external factors) and 'conversion' (when rules remain but institutions designed with one set of goals in mind are redirected to other ends). Whereas these strategies have proven useful for identifying different types of changes (see, for example, the debate (Gouws) on whether the changes in South Africa could be labelled as 'drift' or the debate (Madsen) on the introduction of affirmative action as displacement as sudden or gradual), it will be important for future research to identify more/different strategies based on the African experiences. Furthermore, gendered institutional changes may not necessarily 'move forward' but may also be a 'step backwards' like the concept of 'institutional nestedness' coined by Mackay (2014) indicates that institutional changes may be oriented either towards something 'new' or something 'old' due to the stickiness of old formal and informal rules. According to Mackay 'nested newness is a metaphor used to capture the ways in which the new is embedded in time, sequence and its institutional environment' (Mackay 2014: 552). There is a need to identify strategies of resistance against institutional changes for more women in politics. The focus on informal institutions contributes to the visibility of these strategies of resistance. However, further research needs to be done both on strategies for changing institutions in a more gender friendly direction and to identify strategies of resistance towards these changes.

Traditionally, within feminist institutionalism focus has also been on the institutional spaces for voicing women's claims at the state level in the form of national gender machineries or gender committees. Some of the case studies on South Africa (Gouws) and Ghana (Madsen) address the questions of whether these feminist institutions are actually working effectively to address women's claims for political representation – descriptively as well as substantially. Both authors conclude that these feminist institutions are not working effectively for different reasons. Gouws accounts of how the South African national gender machinery with the integrated set of structures never quite materialized and that institutions have been closed down under Zuma and what was left lumped together under an umbrella of victimhood including 'women, children and people with disabilities'. She emphasizes how a state capture of these spaces has taken place by a masculinist state and the dominant political party hereunder, the compliant women hampering their transformative potential.

Madsen also points out how the national gender machinery in Ghana is not in a favourable position to spearhead the process of introducing the affirmative action bill. She states that the national gender machinery has been lumped together with an isolated focus on care work under the labelling 'gender, children and social protection', suffers from a long-to-do list and serious underfunding and staffing. In addition, an internal power struggle seems to have taken place. Madsen also puts forward the Committee on Gender, Children and Social Protection is a partisan institution with especially members of the opposition party questioning the strength of the leadership and the role of committee. Generally, there seems to be need for capacity building within the committee. Both Gouws and Madsen indicate that although institutions matter, gender-sensitive women or femocrats within institutions also matter – especially in weak institutional spaces. Gouws points out the changes with the compliant women replacing other more inclined women within the state and Madsen the role of the individual members of the Committee on Gender, Children and Social Protection as gender ambassadors.

Towards an African feminist institutionalism

Much of the work on feminist institutionalism has roots in Western contexts and related Western concepts (e.g. most of the chapters in the book by Krook and Mackay (2011)). Recently, more work has been published within the 'feminist institutionalist turn' with case studies from other geographical contexts in Asia (e.g. Bjarnegård 2015; Nazneen 2017)) and Latin America (e.g. Franceshet 2011 and 2017; Piscopo 2017)). However, very little research has been carried out combining feminist institutionalism, women's political representation and African perspectives (e.g. Bjarnegård 2016 on Tanzania is an exception). As such, the book is an attempt to launch research, which is based solely on African case studies on women's political representation analysed through a feminist institutionalist lens inspired by earlier work on women's political representation in Africa (e.g. Bauer and Britton 2006; Goetz and Hassim 2003; Tamale 1999). As it has been illustrated in earlier sections of this introduction, the approach on gendered formal and informal institutions has proven to be highly relevant and useful for analysing women's political representation in different African contexts. The following is a first attempt to identify how an African feminist institutionalism could be characterized(?) And in which way it differs from other versions of feminist institutionalisms(?)

Re-excavating the past – beyond the colonial

The first element towards an African feminist institutionalism is the *re-excavating of the past moving beyond the colonial* analysing the negative influence of colonization and colonial institutions on women's political representation and searching for alternative reference points in pre-colonial female political icons and institutional arrangements working in a pro-women/gender-friendly direction. A number of the authors (Orisadare, Fourshey & Jaksch and Memusi) engage in 'memory work' from the perspectives that the past, present and future are interlocked and recovering the past provides an opportunity to understanding the present and regendering the institutions in the future to strengthen women's political representation. The cases demonstrate that the rules and norms imposed by white male colonizers had very little to do with the realities in the African contexts where women played significant roles in governance during pre-colonial times and in the liberation movement.

In her chapter on Nigeria, Orisadare is inspired by feminist historical institutionalism and accounts of how women in pre-colonial times had political powers. She underlines how the women carried out separate complementary functions in the society and that 'seniority' was more important than gender in this period similar to the Kenyan case. Orisadare brings forward the examples of Queen Amina from the city of Zaire in the Kaduna state who protected the city from invasion, extended it beyond its boundaries and transformed it into a prominent commercial centre. Similarly, the women in ancient Yoruba land the Oba (King) ruled with the help of eight ladies of the palace hereunder the amazon Moremi of Ile-Ife. In the Igbo culture, the women exercised traditional measures to ensure that their decisions were obeyed.

Both Memusi and Orisadare account of the processes of colonization through which respectively Kenyan and Nigerian women were stripped off their powers. Memusi accounts of how colonialism influenced the Maasai communities and women's political representation with the indirect ruling allowing the male leaders to redefine relationships and roles. As such, women were excluded from the political space but also subordinated in the domestic realm. Memusi pinpoints how male political authority and economic control were reinforced through new bases of power and control over land for agriculture and cattle. Orisadare elaborates how the colonizers introduced European patriarchal perceptions to Nigeria expecting women to be subordinate to men confined to the home with child rearing and domestic chores in line with Victorian ideals.

Several of the case studies (Ghana, Nigeria, Tanzania) account of how women engaged in fighting against the colonial powers. Madsen focuses on how the queen mother Yaa Asantewaa from Ejisu organized to fight a siege in Kumasi and protect the golden stool. In present politics 'Yaa Asantewaa' is used mockingly to refer to women in politics who are outspoken and fighting for women's rights and gender equality. Orisadare elaborates how the Nigerian women did not accept this setback without a fight, and a series of protests took place including the anti-colonial Aba riots with a focus on the role of the warrant chiefs against the restricting of the role of women in government leading to an inclusion of women in the native courts. Fourshey and Jacks focus on the legacy of women's agency in colonial rule and forwarding pan-African political struggles with the example of Tanzanian Bibi Titi Mohamed who has been neglected in the history of liberation. As a leader of the women's section of TANU (Tanganyika African National Union), she mobilized Tanzanian women and later became the only woman in the government of Julius Nyerere and the leader of the women's organization Umoja wa Wanawake in Tanzania.

African feminisms and institutionalisms

The second element towards an African feminist institutionalism is *the role of African feminisms in reshaping patriarchal institutions and identifying new versions of institutionalisms*. In their chapter on Tanzania, Fourshey and Jaksch emphasize how especially nego-feminism understood as the 'feminism of negotiation' and 'no ego' feminism linked to African cultures of compromise and balance is useful as an analytical tool to renegotiate and regender Tanzanian institutions and the building of institutions – not just how women are limited and shaped by existing institutions. With their contribution, Fourshey and Jaksch pinpoint and question definitions of 'the feminist' in 'feminist institutionalism' in different contexts emphasizing specific African forms of feminism.

However, Fourshey and Jaksch question not only the 'feminist' but also 'institutions' and launch a form of 'feminist institutionalism' which they label as 'feminist symbolic institutionalism' with a focus on sites of commemoration and the role of female political icons like Tanzanian Biti Titi Mohamed and the recognition of her and other women in the liberation struggle. They argue that symbols matter in acknowledging not only the easy visible action, rhetoric and thinking behind independence struggles and nation building but also the less easily seen but equality important work of women. Besides, from a focus on these sites of commemoration Fourshey and Jaksch also focus on African women's knowledge systems demonstrating women role as political actors in awareness raising, political archive and legacy building and as nego-feminism – the traditional art form of women's clothing the khanga which also is used as a weapon of political struggle.

In their chapter on training programmes for female political candidates and empowerment in Botswana, Mosime and Dikobe also refer to nego-feminism as a source of inspiration for describing women's agency in their more practical work. Their training programme with the non-governmental organization Letsema supported female political candidates in their preparations for campaigning not only for elections but also for broader perspectives on political empowerment and negotiation of opportunities outside the formal political sphere.

Potentially, other versions of African feminisms can be explored in a similar manner. African feminisms have emerged as a counter-reaction against the dominance of Western feminist thinking, which are not designed to understand the realities of African women and promote exclusionary practices where men are classified in a binary construction as 'the enemy' and questions of race silenced with historical trajectories erased (Nkealah 2016: 62). The development of African feminisms is drawing on local African knowledge building, which should address feminism from 'an African cultural perspective, an African geo-political location and an African ideological viewpoint' (ibid). Thus, the focus within African feminisms is on 'inclusion, cooperation and accommodation' (Nkealah 2016: 63).

One approach related to 'nego-feminism' is the 'snail-feminism'. Nkealah (2016) mentions that 'snail-feminism' may be specific for the Nigerian context and focus on the negotiation around multiple systems of oppression such as patriarchy, cooperates with potential male allies and avoids confrontation. The version of African feminism labelled 'womanism' applies to black women globally and relates to multiple forms of domination and discrimination when confronted with culture and colonialism (Nkealah 2016: 62). Another version of African feminism is 'motherism' and emphasizes the female-shared experiences of motherhood with a particular emphasis on the role of rural women in caring for the citizens of the nation due to her role in production and reproduction. Stiwananism on the other hand is more firmly rooted in the experiences of African women based on the continent. However, whereas thee 'womanism', 'motherism' and 'stivanism' address some global power dynamics between Western and African feminism, they also produce other types of exclusions based on location (rural/urban and African women on the continent/African women in diaspora) and questions of sexualities with the lack of queer perspectives (Nkealah 2016). This may limit their usefulness for regendering masculinist institutions in an inclusive and intersectional manner.

African concepts and feminist institutionalism

A third element towards an African feminist institutionalism is the *development of specific African concepts* on gendered institutions and women's political representation. In her contribution about South Africa, Gouws refers to the 'Femocracy' and 'First Lady' syndrome (originally coined by Amina Mama in 1995) referring to the role of these high-level women based on their personal ties with men in power rather than personal achievements as leaders. The phenomenon is coined after the Nigerian first lady Mrs Mariam Babangida who launched her Better Life Programme and managed to get access to government funding and gain a lot of publicity in the name of promoting women's interests.

In the case of Nigeria, the national gender machinery was also taken over by the first lady. Often these first ladies and their organizations ended up serving the ruling party mobilizing support from the female voters, entertaining and serving at the party rallies. Gouws nuances this African concept and account of how different first ladies in South Africa have in most cases stayed out of state politics but had a political project on their own. However, during the ruling of the former president these women have been part of his patronage network and group of compliant women.

In the chapter on Ghana, Madsen identifies a 'politics of insults, ridicule and rumours' preventing women from seeking office and working to undermine and silence women's voices in the political sphere with a reference to former work (e.g. Tamale 1999). She elaborates how women are exposed to different forms of violence including being labelled and targeted based on their gender and sexuality and as having masculine traits if they are very outspoken and assertive on women's rights and gender equality. Further work could explore more African concepts related to feminist institutionalism.

The book chapters are organized according to geographical regions – southern (South Africa, Zimbabwe, Botswana and Malawi), eastern (Kenya and Tanzania) and western (Nigeria and Ghana) Africa. The case studies constitute a first attempt towards the development of an African feminist institutionalism based on the three elements described above. Inspired by different versions of feminist institutionalisms the African case studies contribute empirically, methodologically and theoretically to the field of feminist institutionalism and women's political representation. In the concluding remarks, some policy recommendations are made.

Notes

1 However, the focus on symbolic representation (impact) at societal level could also be of importance.
2 It should be noted that Botswana has not adopted the SADC Protocol on Gender and Development even though it is a member of SADC and that Kenya is not a member of SADC.

References

Bauer, G. and Britton, Hannah E. (2006): *Women in African Parliaments*. Boulder London: Lynne Rienner Publishers.

Bjarnegård, E. (2015): *Gender, Informal Institutions and Political Recruitment – Explaining Male Dominance in Parliamentary Representation*. New York: Palgrave Macmillan.

Bjarnegård, E. and Zetterberg, P. (2016): 'Gender Equality Reforms on an Uneven Playing Field: Candidate Selection and Quota Implementation in Electoral Authoritarian Tanzania', *Government and Opposition*, Vol. 51, No. 3, 464–86.

Dahlerup, D. and Freidenvall, L. (2003): 'Quotas as a 'Fast Track' to Equal Political Representation for Women', Paper presented at IPSA World Conference, Durban, South Africa.

Franceshet, S. (2011): 'Gendered Institutions and Women's Substantive Representation: Female Legislators in Argentina and Chile', in M. L. Krook and F. Mackay (eds) *Gender, Politics and Institutions – Towards a Feminist Institutionalism*. New York: Palgrave Macmillan.

Franceshet, S. (2017): 'Disentangling Informality and Informal Rules: Explaining Gender Inequality in Chile's Executive Branch', in G. Waylen (ed.) *Gender and Informal Institutions*. London: Rowman & Littlefield.

Goetz, A. M. and Hassim, S. (2003): *No Shortcuts to Power – African Women in Politics and Policy Making*. London and New York: Zed Books.

Haraway, D. (2004): 'Situated Knowledges: The Science Question in Feminism and the Privilege of Partial Perspective', in S. Harding (ed.) *The Feminist Standpoint Theory Reader*. New York and London: Routledge.

Harding, S. (2004): 'Rethinking Standpoint Epistemology: What Is 'Strong Objectivity'?', in S. Harding (ed.) *The Feminist Standpoint Theory Reader*. New York and London: Routledge.

Kenny, M. (2015): 'Gender and Institutions of Political Recruitment: Candidate Selection in Post-Devolution Scotland', in *Gender, Politics and Institutions – Towards a Feminist Institutionalism*. New York: Palgrave Macmillan.

Krook, M. L. and Mackay, F. (2011): *Gender, Politics and Institutions – Towards a Feminist Institutionalism*. New York: Palgrave Macmillan.

Lowndes, V. (2019): 'How Are Political Institutions Gendered', Political Studies, 1–22 August.

Mackay, F. (2014): 'Nested Newness, Institutional Innovation, and the Gendered Limits of Change', *Politics & Gender*, Vol. 10, 549–71.

Mackay, F. and Waylen, G. (2014): 'Introduction: Gendering 'New Institutions', *Politics & Gender*, Vol. 10, 459–94.

Mahoney, J. and Thelen, K. (2010): *Explaining Institutional Change – Ambiguity, Agency and Power*. Cambridge: Cambridge University Press.

Nazneen, S. (2017): 'Negotiating Gender Equity in a Clientelist State: The Role of Informal Networks in Bangladesh', in G. Waylen (ed.) *Gender and Informal Institutions*. London: Rowman & Littlefield.

Nkealah, N. (2016): '(West) African Feminisms and Their Challenges', *Journal of Literary Studies*, Vol. 32, No. 2, 61–74.

Piscopo, Jennifer M. (2017): 'Leveraging Informality, Rewriting Formal Rules: The Implementation of Gender Parity in Mexico', in G. Waylen (ed.) *Gender and Informal Institutions*. London: Rowman & Littlefield.

Tadros, M. (2014): *Women in Politics – Gender, Power and Development*. London and New York: Zed Books.

Tamale, S. (1999): *When Hens Begin to Crow – Gender and Parliamentary Politics in Uganda*. Colorado and Oxford: Westview Press.

Tripp, A. M. et al. (2009): *African Women's Movements*. New York: Cambridge University Press.

Tripp, A. M. (2015): *Women and Power in Post Conflict Africa*. New York: Cambridge University Press.

Waylen, G. (2013): 'Gender and the Hidden Life of Institutions', *Public Administration*, Vol. 91, No. 3, 599–615.

Waylen, G. (2014): 'Informal Institutions, Institutional Change, and Gender Equality', *Political Research Quarterly*, Vol. 67, No. 1, 212–23.

Waylen, G. (2017): *Gender and Informal Institutions*. London: Rowman & Littlefield.

1

Feminist institutionalism, women's representation and state capture: The case of South Africa

Amanda Gouws

Introduction

By now, women's descriptive representation has increased by leaps and bounds because of the acceptance of quotas for women. Globally it is a success story, as well as on the African continent, with Rwanda at 68 per cent, the highest in the world, and by 2009 twenty-eight countries in Africa had some form of quota (Tripp et al. 2009), with varying impact on political Policy making. Whether this can be considered substantive representation is, however, contested. There is a tenuous relationship between women's substantive representation and feminist institutions. While theories of feminist institutionalism are quite robust, they cannot be applied to Africa without revision, even substantial revision, because of the particularity of African liberation struggles, weak political institutions, the impact of nationalism and patriarchal cultures in post-colonial contexts.

Weak African state institutions pose not only significant challenges, but also specific problems for women's substantive representation. Where women's institutions or national gender machineries exist they lack the authority to influence ministries, and where they are embedded in ministries they seem to deal with social welfare issues and community development. Often their mandates are unclear, they lack staff capacity, are under-resourced and where they are able to influence policy it is often devoid of feminist content (Tripp et al. 2009: 178–9). Issues of party loyalty, patronage, clientelism and, in the South African case, state capture, where institutions are repurposed to serve the needs of a corrupt elite, endanger electoral processes, women's substantive representation, as well as feminist institutionalism.

In this chapter, I explore feminist institutionalism in South Africa by analysing political conditions which contribute to undermine women's substantive representation and feminist institutionalism such as state and party fusion; slate politics and cadre deployment; state capture and women's compliance with and complicity in patronage relationships.

Illustrating the problems of feminist institutionalism in Africa I focus on the challenges of patronage, clientelism and women's compliance to the extreme form of the hollowing out of the state, called state capture, in the South African context. If state feminism is based on an understanding of how the state functions, it is undermined when a shadow state is ensconced for which the rules are not known, women are excluded from male patronage networks or are made compliant in order to enter these networks. In these conditions, they become beholden to the goodwill of men who repurpose the objectives of the state for their own gain and therefore deeply damage feminist institutionalism as well as women's substantive representation. For this purpose I draw on secondary literature and participant observation.

Feminist institutionalism

The inclusion of feminist perspectives contributes to an understanding of a dynamic relationship between gendered institutional architects, gendered institutionalized subjects and gendered institutional environments, involving strategic and creative action combined with calculated self-interest (Hay and Winnicott in Mackay et al. 2010). Mackay (2014) warns that institutional blueprints need to be put into practice and institutionalized and that gender reforms are vulnerable to regress. Where new institutions become embedded in old ones, they are exposed to the 'stickiness of old rules' (Mackay 2014: 551) or the continued reliance on 'the old and forgetting the new'.

New institutions require active maintenance, especially where they become linked to different kinds of older institutions. As Mackay (2014: 554) indicates the importance of 'attending to the ways in which gendered institutions are enacted and instantiated in the post-design phase by *gendered* actors using formal and informal rules and norms and new and old institutional elements' (her emphasis), especially where there are processes of contestation and shifting coalitions of actors over time. She calls this the 'liability of newness' (2014: 565).

Transitional processes open spaces for institutional renewal or the creation of new institutions to perform functions that were not required under previous regimes. How these institutions are shaped and used contribute to the legitimacy of new governments. The winning transitional coalitions take on board gender equity concerns and make space for gender entrepreneurs. The transition to democracy in South Africa presupposed the engineering of new institutions to protect a very progressive Constitution and to give effect to the requirements of equality, including gender equality (see, e.g., Waylen 2007). These institutions in South Africa, the National Gender Machinery (NGM), were not encumbered by being nested in old institutions, nor the stickiness of old rules.

Feminist institutionalism produces certain path dependencies over time, as well as what Chappell (2006: 225) calls 'the logic of appropriateness'. These routines and practices are enforced through informal means (varying from disapproval, social isolation, threats and even violence) (Lowndes 2014). The logic of appropriateness constrains some types of behaviour, encourages others and is perpetuated by institutional actors (Chappel 2006).

Chappel (2006: 224) draws on Beckwith's notion of gender as a category and gender as a process, which is 'the differential effect of apparently neutral structures and policies upon women and men actors'. Norms of institutions may appear gender neutral, while they are deeply gendered, most often to the benefit of men. How these norms shape and influence policies, legislation and rulings is important to understand, as well as how they produce and reproduce gender. Where liberal democracies prevail, we expect responsive governments; yet, actors behave in certain ways that may promote gender outcomes or inhibit them. Institutions also create formal and informal rules, and as Waylen (2014) remarks it is important to understand how these rules are gendered. This is especially necessary when the rules are created in the murky world of patron–client relations.

Feminist institutionalism cannot be separated from women's representation in government and women's participation in politics. Globally women's quotas have ensured the entry of more women into legislatures. In African countries, quotas have also made a great difference, with Rwanda now having the highest number of women in a legislature in the world with 68 per cent. Greater descriptive participation leads to expectations of greater substantive representation that can be facilitated through a working relationship between women in government and the women's movement to get important issues onto the legislative and policy agendas (Stetson and Mazur 1995).

While these predictors of substantive representation are important, there are other issues in the political context in African/developing countries that need to be considered. In this regard, the research of Bjarnegård (2009), Wängnerud (2009) and Ahikire (2018) is important. All these authors focus on the male dominance of legislatures and the late entry of women into legislatures. Wängnerud (2009) distinguishes between two kinds of divisions between men and women where first kind relates to formal power and second to policy areas. Women seem to be more left on the political spectrum and women prioritize other policy issues as men – such as social policy, family policy and care issues. It also seems that women members of legislatures prioritize issues that are prioritized by women voters. According to Wängnerud (2009), preconditions for substantive representation are the existence of gender differences in the public opinion between men and women that influence the political culture and the presence of women in the executive. The best electoral system to get women in remains closed list proportional representation (PR) systems, but parties remain the biggest gatekeepers in the recruitment process.

Bjarnegård's (2009) research on men in politics in Thailand makes an important contribution because she brings in issues of clientelism, corruption and homosocial capital. While these issues are prevalent in developed countries, they have a more damaging effect on developing countries where political stability is often fragile and oversight mechanisms are weak. Political context plays a very important role; because where clientelism is rife, it influences and constrains the majority of people, because it targets communities and exercises influence through service delivery or the lack thereof. Elections and electoral support are also influenced through vote buying.

The important point that Bjarnegård (2009) makes is that women have a different relationship to state patronage than men, because they are excluded from many political arenas and networks. These networks are constituted through what she calls 'homosocial capital' – how men relate to each other in tight networks based on patronage that exclude women. Male dominance is achieved through different means such as compliant men (and women), as well as traditions, culture and institutions, so that power is dispersed and exercised beyond the legislature. Neopatrimonialism and patronage networks form the political culture with the effect of reproducing patriarchy. It also translates into parliamentary seats, especially in PR list systems where male party bosses draw up the final lists before elections.

Political ideology is made subservient to particularist and personal politics. Bjarnegård (2009) argues that male networks do not necessarily keep women out because they are women, but in order to protect men. In this way, male dominance is reproduced. The accumulation of homosocial capital produces predictability because without it some men may never get into positions of political power. What she argues, importantly, is that women benefit more from heterosocial capital because including men may benefit them, while men benefit more from homosocial capital, because of perceptions that men are successful, having authority and privilege. The traits that are often authoritarian and paternalistic are viewed as competence that women do not have. What is also important about Bjarnegård's contribution is showing that when formal institutions are weak, informal institutions play a very important role. It shifts the demands on the formal system to the informal system. In countries with high levels of poverty, people cannot wait for the formal system to deliver but rely on clientelism. This is a way of reducing the unreliability of formal institutions. It also bolsters the behaviour of parties that start to rely on informal networks rather than formal rules. In the Ugandan case, for example, Ahikire (2018: 10) shows how women have to 'innovate' to win over the goodwill of men in patronage networks.

Stensöta et al. (2015) show in a thirty-country study that women's impact on corruption is greater in the electoral arena than in the bureaucracies or civil service. Women are more visible in the electoral arena where they can also make a stand on values (such as anti-corruption). In bureaucracies, there are rules and procedures that degender experiences that will prevent women from having an impact on corruption. Where bureaucratic organization is weak there may be opportunities for women to influence corruption. Their study bears out these assumptions. However, the argument is based on the notion that bureaucracies have strong rules and procedures. In countries like South Africa where a middle class is grown through the civil service, the impartial rules of bureaucracy are often devalued to suit the purposes of self-enrichment through, for example, procurement fraud. There is a need to understand how women become co-opted.

Feminist institutionalism in Africa

Feminist institutionalism has been weak in Africa, operating mostly through Women's Ministries that have ghettoized women's issues in one place without mainstreaming gender throughout government. While women's representation in Africa has increased, it seems that the structures that were created to include feminist issues in the state never materialized, but femocracy, understood as the First Lady Syndrome and the Women's League Syndrome, works against the positive outcomes of women's representation. Mama (2000) argues that state structures in Africa became involved in mobilizing women for nation building, which means support for the status quo. As she argues, the structures of national machineries function in isolation from each other, reflecting the low status of women in society, and are in general under-resourced. In her view, national machineries have only achieved the most modest liberal goal of giving women a space in the state. In many countries, there are or were only one structure such as a Ministry for Women, or a Department of Women's Affairs, rather than a set of structures (see also Gouws (2008) and Tripp et al. (2009: 169–72) for a comprehensive table of National Gender Machineries).

More recent literature has shown more positive results about women's quotas in Africa, for example, a study on Uganda found no evidence that quota women are more likely to be party loyalists than any other representatives or that party loyalty comes at the expense of women's interests. Quota women who are party loyal will also attempt to put women's issues on the political agenda (O'Brien 2012). In the case of Rwanda the impact of the quotas was wide and deep, because it went beyond government to change perceptions of gender equality in society, even though it did not contribute to more transparent democracy or changed the legislative process because legislation starts in the executive branch (Burnet 2012). In the case of Morocco, however, a study has shown that even when women are educated and politically active, the source of their political success is allegiance to political leaders and their efforts to create gender equality are often far removed from the reality of women and that these women remain non-receptive to gender reforms (Sater 2012).

Amina Mama (2000) pointed out the influence of African first ladies in matters of the state. This does not refer to feminist influence (the femocrat phenomenon), but to the influence of wives of African leaders as a result of them being close to power. A 2018 First Lady database that was compiled by Van Wyk and her co-authors shows that first ladies create a dynamic in which political space is appropriated and abused by the wives of presidents for personal gain (Van Wyk et al. 2018).

In African countries such as Chad, Uganda, Eritrea and Zimbabwe, first ladies have captured certain institutions because of their proximity to power, but not in a way that promote gender equality, but rather to promote the First Lady's own interests (see Van Wyk et al. 2018). South Africa, in this regard, has been one of the exceptions. Since 1994, South African first ladies have been visible, but as independent politicians in their own right or women who have their own political projects. After Nelson Mandela got divorced from Winnie Mandela (who was a struggle activist in her own right), he married Graca Machel, the former first lady of Mozambique.[1] She was seen by his side but never interfered politically, while often travelled to represent a political project of her own. For example, she has been appointed by the UN as an expert to chair a study on the impact of armed conflict on children. Zanele Mbeki is one of the founders of South African Women in Dialogue (SAWID) in 2003 that is platform for women to make their voices heard. It has a strong socio-economic focus and is still operating today.[2]

The only exception was the four wives of Jacob Zuma, who is in a polygamous marriage. Some of these wives often appeared by his side or were invited to events as first ladies, but they never interfered politically. However, they are deeply implicated in his patronage networks and corruption. Gloria Bongi Ngema Zuma was involved in a project of the Gupta family whose corruption is at the centre of state capture in South Africa (Twala 2012). The Nkandla saga in which Zuma upgraded his own private homestead with taxpayers money to the amount of R248 million benefitted all the wives who live at Nkandla on a regular basis.[3] Scandal also surrounded one wife, Nompumelelo Ntuli-Zuma, who is alleged to have tried to poison him[4] and was banned from Nkandla. Zuma's ex-wife, Nkosasana Dlamini-Zuma (not one of the current four), however, is a minister in the executive and who held different portfolios. She is currently the Minister for Cooperative Governance and Traditional Affairs. She was also the chair of the African Union.

Another challenge is what Geisler (2004) refers to as the 'Women's League Syndrome' in Africa with its conservative influence of perpetuating the idea of women's first obligation to the nation as being wives and mothers, in this way mobilizing support for ruling regimes. Very often women who are members of women's leagues promote very conservative gender politics that undermine struggles for gender equality. The ANC Women's League (ANCWL) in South Africa is no exception (see Hassim 2014), but is very influential in making sure their members get into influential positions in government (to be discussed later).

Hern's (2017) research in Zambia on the United National Independent Party (UNIP) Women's Brigade has shown that rather than getting women to participate it managed to alienate women and demobilize political participation among women because its policy content locked women into the roles of mothers and caregivers, rather than challenge gender hierarchies.

National Gender Machineries in Africa also contributed to a deep rift between women in institutional settings and existing women's movements. Women's organizations often do not trust women in government and are therefore often not being consulted on policy issues by women in government. In some African countries women's organizations claim that national machineries work actively against them (Tripp et al. 2009: 180). Where ministries have developed national gender policies they cannot enforce their policies, because they have 'no carrots or sticks' and thus their policies remain on paper, enforcing women's organizations' beliefs that they do not care about gender equality (Tripp et al. 2009: 179).

The South African context

South Africa is often hailed as the success story of transition from apartheid authoritarian rule. One of the main dimensions of the transition to democracy was the inclusion of women's equality onto the transformation agenda. This was a process driven by the Women's National Coalition (WNC) (Hassim 2006).

At the time of transition, feminist activists and academics mobilized a campaign to include a range of structures in the state that would have been responsible for promoting gender equality (Albertyn 1995). This campaign led to very integrated NGM that compared very well with machineries in the global North. It included an Office of the Status of Women in the Office of the President, a Joint Monitoring Committee on the Quality of Life and Status of Women (that monitored all state departments), a Women's Empowerment Unit in the Office of the Speaker, a multi-party gender caucus in parliament, gender desks in all civil service departments (on national and provincial levels) and the autonomous Commission for Gender Equality, protected in the Constitution (Gouws 2006). Feminists vehemently resisted the ghettoization of women's issues in a Women's Ministry. South Africa, however, has lost all its policy structures in the last ten years (except for the Commission for Gender Equality) when they were systematically dismantled and replaced with a Ministry for Women, Youth and People with Disabilities from 2009 until 2017, and then replaced with a Ministry for Women in the Presidency up to the present.

In the first five years of the South African democracy, a strong relationship existed between women members of parliament (many of them entering parliament as feminist activists in the women's movement on a 30 per cent quota of the ruling party, the African National Congress (ANC)). The most progressive and comprehensive women-friendly legislation was made during this period. This started to change during the presidency of the second president, Thabo Mbeki, due to his authoritarian leadership style, his AIDS denialism and his sidelining of women's issues and action against feminist members of parliament.[5]

Denise Walsh (2012: 128–9) shows how women's counterpublics that were founded during the first parliament started to decline, together with a decline in debating conditions. Women's voices and their capacity to intervene in policy became constraint because they had to tow the party line. As the ANC continued to centralize decision making in the presidency and cabinet party loyalty replaced healthy contestation and contributed to the exit of feminists. This led to them being replaced by women who thought of themselves as professionals, not activists (Britton 2005). The departure of feminists led to a decline in substantive representation.

The transition to the Jacob Zuma presidency in 2007 aggravated already very tense relationships between government and feminists. The ANCWL played a key role in securing majority support for Zuma, despite the fact that he went through a rape trial in which he was acquitted in 2006, but that exposed him as a philanderer and a man of low moral standards (see Hassim 2009). The ANCWL is a party auxiliary that was formed in 1913 as the Bantu Women's League with the aim to give women a voice in the ANC. It changed its name in 1923. While it never was a feminist organization, it played a key role in mobilizing women in the liberation struggle (to include the struggle for gender equality into the struggle for non-racialism) and to negotiate a 30 per cent quota during the political transition, as well as being key in the formulation of some gender-friendly legislation. The ANCWL has always had a nationalist focus and mobilized on a (nationalist) platform of motherism (mothers as reproducers of the nation). Post 1994 it has become a very conservative but powerful organization that get their members into key political positions and which supported Zuma throughout his tenure, despite serious corruption allegations against him (see Hassim 2014; Makhunga 2014).

It was also the slow start of the period of the hollowing out of the state by Zuma's patronage networks, which finally culminated in what is now called 'state capture' in the South African context. Different commissions of inquiry into state capture, such as the Zondo commission and the Mokgoro inquiry, have exposed the depth and breadth of state capture,[6] leaving the South African state on the verge of bankruptcy.

If feminist institutionalism means spaces in the state where women can insert women's interests and needs, we need to understand what state capture does to the feminist project. In the South African context, gender research from this perspective has not been done yet. Below follows an attempt to do so.

The impact of state and party fusion on women's representation/feminist institutionalism

The ANC in 2019 is a party that is fused with the state. This party/state fusion started under Mbeki, but it has escalated significantly under the Zuma presidency. African liberation movements are well known for the challenge of changing from liberation movements to political parties. The ANC is no exception, but given the party's change over the last twenty years, especially under Zuma, there was a development into a party that views the state as its personal fiefdom (Booysen 2015). It opened the door to self-enrichment of politicians through the state. In this process of hollowing out institutions, the conflict of succession battles is paramount and factional mobilization is rife. Factionalism and splits within factions play themselves out in ANC nominations during elections, on regional and provincial levels, with changes to the executive and parastatal organizations at the order of the day to ensure loyalty to one faction or another during the Zuma regime. As Booysen (2015: 29) puts it: 'This has far-reaching implications for governance and the fiscus. They protect their executive political handlers – keeping them out of court, shielding them from uncomfortable questions, moderating succession contests.' Booysen (2015) also argues that there are privileges beyond the formal rules of the state for those who operate on the right side of the ANC President (Zuma), especially if they helped to protect him over time. For women to survive in parliament they had to calculate their self-interest for which joining a faction was often very attractive, preventing them from prioritizing gender equality issues. In this regard, they have the same vested interests in their careers as men (Gouws 2011). It also means that their positions on party lists during elections depend on these men.

The party became a highly structured mass party under factional leadership with a group of loyalists exercising control through the branches and regions. Booysen calls this the ANC 'elite beneficiation machine' (Booysen 2015: 31). A system of patronage, tax evasion, defrauding social grants and corrupt tenders has contributed to the failure of state institutions in a process of state capture. Parastatal organizations such as the electricity provider, ESCOM, the South African Broadcasting Corporation and South African Airways were especially vulnerable to crony politics.

State capture

Chipkin and Swilling (2018) distinguish corruption from state capture with corruption focusing on individual action, while state capture is systemic and well organized by people who have an established relationship with each other, with repeated transactions on an increasing scale. Whereas corruption bypasses rules, state capture aims to change the formal and informal rules, legitimizing them and opening the way for those who are allowed to play the game. Chipkin and Swilling (2018: x) call this the 'repurposing the institutions of state' in a way that institutions are structured, governed, managed and funded which give them different purposes from their formal mandates. One of the intended outcomes of state capture is that a symbiotic relationship develops between the constitutional state and the shadow state (2018: xi). The shadow state is the network of corruption that ties people to each other. The symbiosis between these two types of states is the agenda of rent-seeking elites.

Through this symbiosis unelected individuals get access to decision-making power (such as the Gupta family that even instructed President Zuma whom to appoint as ministers). One of the root mechanisms is clientelism through which goods and services are exchanged for political support in a way that erodes electoral processes and the integrity of elections.

At its core, state capture is a political project 'to repurposes state institutions to suit a constellation of rent-seeking networks that have constructed and now span the symbiotic relationship between the constitutional and shadow states' (Chipkin and Swilling 2018: 31). Tender rigging is an important mechanism to sustain the shadow state with the proliferation of government departments on national and provincial levels in order to extend patronage networks with the decentralization of financial accountability to departmental heads (chief accounting officers).

Since 2009, the role back of women's gains accelerated under Zuma, with the systematic closure of institutions of the NGM and replacing feminist-inclined women with compliant women (women who form part of patronage networks or the Zuma faction). The creation of a Ministry of Women that lumped issues of women, children and the disabled together has repurposed the national gender machinery. The purpose of the NGM was to facilitate and promote gender equality through an integrated set of structures that had access to the legislative, the executive and different tiers of government, including national and provincial levels. The dispersed nature of the architecture would allow women access to different sites of power in government. By ghettoizing women's issues in the Women's Ministry, feminists' worst fears were realized if judging by the lack of delivery on policy and legislation and the lumping of women, children and people with disabilities. However, even worse is the lack of understanding of the urgency in dealing with matters such as gender-based violence, reproductive health and poverty. The repurposing meant that state resources became more readily available for purposes that they were not intended for.

It also shows the repurposing of ministries to be compliant with the state-capture process. Since 2009, under Zuma's regime there have been four Ministers of Women, all of them viewed as compliant with the demands of the Zuma regime. The second minister, Lulu Xingwana, was supposed to establish a Council on Gender Based Violence in a context of escalating sexual violence against women. There was a demand by civil society for this council after the brutal gang rape and disembowlment of Anene Booysen in 2013. Xingwana did not manage this; neither did her successor, Susan Shabangu, as Minister of Women in the Presidency.[7] The fourth minister, Bathabile Dlamini, is one of the most disgraced ministers, who was retained in cabinet by Zuma's successor, Cyril Ramaphosa, as Minister of Women, after serious allegations of incompetence as Minister of Social Development. Women in civil society called Dlamini's appointment as Minister of Women a disgrace.[8] After the 2019 election, she was left out of cabinet and resigned, but another inappropriate appointment was made to the Ministry of Women. The new minister, Maite Nkoana-Mashabane, has never been involved in women's affairs, but was the Minister of Foreign Affairs.

The Commission for Gender Equality (CGE), an autonomous oversight body protected in Chapter 9 of the constitution, has also become beholden to the ANCWL (Hassim 2014). Even though the CGE Act of 1996 requires commissioners to be independent and non-partisan, the majority of women commissioners during the period 2012–14 were members of or loyal to the ANCWL. While their affiliation to the ANC Women's League affected the CGE in different ways, the most problematic aspect was the refusal to criticize the incumbent President, Zuma, making the whole commission compliant to the presidency.[9]

The ANCWL's complicity with men in the party extended to marches in honour of Zuma with slogans such as 'Hands off our President!' under Bathabili Dlamini's chairpersonship.[10] Conflict between the ANCWL and women's organizations that work with gender-based violence was rife, because of Zuma's rape court case and his constant philandering (see Motsei 2007).

Slate politics and cadre deployment

The proportional closed list system that was negotiated during the transition to democracy was aimed at including smaller parties in parliament, but also once a women's quota was in place combined with a zebra list (alternating the names of men and women on the list) it would give women access to parliament. One of the important aims of the electoral system was therefore the promotion of gender equality. The ANC, the ruling party in South Africa, has a 50 per cent party quota with 44 per cent women in parliament and 50 per cent women ministers after the 8 May 2019 election (Gouws 2019).

Yet, as the history since 1994 has shown this type of electoral system has a serious deficit when it comes to accountability because political candidates become accountable to party leaders – those who put them on the list, rather than the members of their constituencies. It also gives party leaders an enormous amount of power to manipulate the process of putting lists together (Booysen 2015; Calland 2013).

Where crony politics and patronage networks are strong, it opens spaces for the manipulation of lists to ensure loyal and compliant 'cadres' that will fall in line behind party leaders' projects – how nefarious these may be. This can be men and women, but given the existence of male-dominant politics at branch level, it makes it so much more difficult for women to pursue politics that will have women's interest at heart. Women can also get onto the lists through the ANCWL, but then they are beholden to it (see Gouws 2011).

One of the most notorious practices in the ANC is that of 'slate politics'. A slate is a list of candidates to be considered for nomination by a party for election to party positions. However, as Setati (2012: 2) points out, from an ANC perspective it is a 'list of candidates to be nominated by particular factions for appointment into the top leadership positions of the party'. It is driven by factional politics and are hotly contested and enmeshed in self-interest. Slate politics has nothing to do with wanting to serve the citizens, but everything with career ambitions and getting the spoils of patronage. As Butler (2015) argues, the ANC exerts control through a mix of procedural manipulation, patronage, co-option and invented tradition. The party, therefore, has become a stepping stone for personal gain. Membership increases are directly linked to political competition in factional struggles, rather than recruitment planning, with many branches being in total disarray.

In a damning investigation requested by the National Executive Committee (NEC) of the ANC about widely disputed candidate processes for the 2010 local government elections, a task team investigated departures from the guidelines and manipulations of processes to get predetermined outcomes. Its work was comprehensive and the investigation looked into the preparations of branch meetings, screening committees and public consultation meetings in 419 wards. They interviewed regional and provincial list committees, as well as regional and provincial executive committees (Butler 2015).

Damning findings showed that properly reached nominations were overturned while deep-seated factionalism, tribalism, regionalism, gatekeeping and the bulk buying of membership were rife. It also showed that provincial leaders failed to supervise registration and verification processes and ignored illegitimate participation from outside branches and accepted other forms of manipulation (Butler 2015). While this investigation took place in relation to local government elections, the same problems exist with national and provincial government elections, just on a larger scale.

Slates are predetermined lists of candidates of those members who fight the hardest to be on the slates, who will turn a blind eye to manipulation. However, this also determines the processes of how women will get onto the lists, through the branches or the ANCWL. Whatever process is followed women can only make it onto the lists if they are connected and compliant and do not challenge these deeply flawed processes, but benefit from the homosocial capital derived from this type of politics. As Booysen (2015: 31) puts it, 'The ruling party became a highly structured, measured mass party under factional leadership, the president [Zuma] and his regiments of loyalists exercising control through commanding the branches and the regions.' The ANC prioritizes political connections over principles of impartiality, fairness, accountability as well as the effective use of resources (Southall in Tsheola and Nkuna 2014).

When patron–client relations determine governance, there is a lack of transparency by which to measure policymaking. Zuma governed through kitchen cabinets, sets of advisors whose decisions were not necessarily discussed with each other. Booysen (2015) notes that the multiple coexisting kitchen cabinets have constituted different networks of influence and co-optation. Most of these relationships are opaque to any outsider. What was actually clear was that competency in senior appointments in government was not a priority. Cabinet appointments foremost were related to loyalty to the president – Zuma's men and women.

A compliant state is created through the re-engineering of institutions. Under the Zuma presidency government departments were constantly redesigned. There was the creation of inter-ministerial committees to deal with intractable policy problems. While new departments were created and portfolios regrouped to improve functionality and efficiency, it did not necessarily contribute to better policy outcomes. One such case was the grouping of Women, Children and People with Disabilities into one Ministry (Booysen 2015). As already pointed out, this Ministry was totally inefficient, with policy foci scattered among three 'vulnerable groups' – a discourse that assumed a lack of agency and permanent victimhood on the part of women, young people and people living with disabilities.

Another important mechanism of the ANC to protect interests in state structures, ensuring access to power and resources and to prevent opposition parties from gaining ground, is cadre deployment (Booysen 2015). This means that those loyal to the president is sent to spaces, for example, in provincial governments to protect their own interests and the president's patronage networks. Rural provinces are especially tied to patronage networks, with three premiers of the provinces of the Free State, Mpumalanga and North West, called the Premier's League, provided a united front to protect Zuma's networks at the time. They were influential in, for example, getting Bathabile Dlamini elected as the chair of the ANCWL.[11] Where there was a greater gender balance of premiers under Thabo Mbeki, only one woman premier out of nine was elected in 2007 when Zuma came to power. She was the premier of an economic marginalized province, the Northern Cape. Very often cadre redeployment prevents women from gaining access to certain spaces or they are not promoted into spaces where deployed cadres reside.

Compliant women and collusion with men

The role of the ANCWL is key to the creation of compliance of women in government. Makhunga (2014: 34) points out how the League uses key state resources 'to reproduce a conservative, anti-transformative and nationalist political narrative and nationalist gendered political narrative on the ruling party's behalf'. As with many other post-colonial African countries' women's auxiliaries, the ANCWL is complicit in the patronage networks of the conflated party/state relationships. This is done by using patronage to entice the leaders of organizations to ensure that they could make personal gains, rather than acting in the interest of citizens (Tripp in Makhunga 2014). Depending on how the patronage is used, gains for gender equality can be made as was the case in the first democratic parliament in South Africa. However, as the ANC started to factionalize patronage became a method used to buy loyalty to one faction or another, or to negotiate certain deals, for example, the Women's Ministry at the Polokwane conference of 2007.

The ANCWL also views itself as carrying on the struggle narrative. In order to do this the League has to 'hijack' events where it appropriates state resources, such as Women's Day's events or the Women's Parliament (Makhunga 2014). This often involves providing those who attend with T-shirts or other ANC paraphernalia (such as skirts with Jacob Zuma's face on it), bussing in attendees or treating those to lavish meals. The opening event and dinner of the Women's Parliament of 2013 were held in the Mount Nelson Hotel in Cape Town, one of the most expensive hotels in the country.[12] This gives the ANCWL a distinct advantage over opposition parties which cannot access resources for gender struggles through the state.

The ANC legitimizes power using the Women's League that will mobilize women according to the ruling party's struggle narrative that it reproduces. It is harking back to the liberation struggle and what the League did for women then. It also keeps the gender narrative alive (women as caregivers and men as protectors) in order to create the impression that the party cares about gender equality. The ANCWL positions itself as the saviour of powerless and socially excluded women. The main mechanism to foster cohesion is loyalty to the party (Makhunga 2014). As Makhunga (2015) points out, the internal political culture of the ANC is conducive to facilitating patriarchal bargains that would politically empower women as a group, but individually advance their careers through patronage that would imply a conservative, nationalist gender agenda.

One of the ways in which Jacob Zuma rewarded loyalty was to appoint his allies as members of his Cabinet. Under his presidency South Africa had one of the biggest cabinets in the world with thirty-five ministers and thirty-four deputies at the beginning of his second term.[13] This increased over time to seventy-two altogether. While many of the ministers in his cabinet were women, many of them were compliant with the demands of the president, for example, Batabhile Dlamini, Faith Muthambi and Nomvula Mokonyane. Zuma's power resides in the executive, which means that he needed compliance in the executive, but it also made the legislative subordinate to the executive, something that erodes the separation of powers. As president, he demanded absolute loyalty from ministers, and if he did not get it, he reshuffled his cabinet. In his term of nine years he reshuffled his cabinet eleven times to include loyalists.[14]

The gendered implications of the repurposing of state institutions

The repurposing of state structures shows how informal rules have the power to circumvent the purposes of the original architecture, formal rules as well as the policy intent of institutions. Feminist institutions are very vulnerable to repurposing because they are institutionalized through the good will of male-dominated governments. In the case of South Africa, it is the Women's League of the ruling party that is deeply complicit in the systematic closing down of the NGM.

If we accept that a shadow state operates next to a constitutional state and that feminist institutionalism takes place in the constitutional state according to formal rules, women are excluded from the spaces of power in the shadow state where many important decisions are taken or if included it is not on their terms. The lack of attention to women's issues therefore manifests as a lack of 'political will'. There is no political will to engage with the issues put on the agenda by women committed to gender equality in these institutions or that are being demanded by women voters. That is why many proposals initiated and mobilized for by women's organizations do not succeed to get onto the 'real' political agenda of the repurposed state. The logic of appropriateness disappears when the state is captured. The relationship between structure and agency also disappears, if we accept as Mackay et al. (2010) indicate that there is a dynamic relationship between institutional architects, institutional subjects and institutional environments with agency being strategic, creative and intuitive action. Where state capture is rife, most action takes place in a clandestine way.

South Africa would mostly likely fall in the category of 'institutional drift' where institutional arrangements are neglected or co-opted. I am reluctant to use the concept of 'drift' because I am of the opinion that with state capture it is not only drift that occurs, but it is the wholesale usurpation of intended path dependencies for purposes that serve corrupt male actors and compliant women in such a way that institutional spaces in the constitutional state become dysfunctional. This usurpation manifests itself as a 'lack of political will'.

As Cellis (2008) has argued, 'context is crucial' when it comes to gender politics. South Africa may be an extreme case because of the ingenuity with which state capture has been implemented; yet, it is doubtful that it does not happen elsewhere in Africa or in the global North. The difference in the global North is that states are stronger and monitoring mechanisms are harder to circumvent.

Conclusion

This chapter has shown the gendered nature of state capture and its implications for feminist institutionalism in South Africa. The consequences are dire and manifest themselves as the lack of political will to deal with serious political problems such as gender-based violence. We need a better understanding of how institutional rules are created in post-colonial states that take over Westminster arrangements, such as South Africa. What develops is a hybridity of institutional norms, gendered norms and rules of which patronage and patron–client relations form part. For too long we have superimposed analytical models develop in the Global North on post-colonial societies, where structure and agency are fraught with complexities. Many of these complexities are related to loyalties that were cultivated during liberation struggles by monolithic liberation organizations and perpetuated after liberation.

Context and history play important roles in understanding how power is concentrated in the hands of some and at the cost of some with strong gendered consequences. What this chapter shows is how the development of state capture in a specific political context under the rule of a powerful personality has managed to make the logic of appropriateness of constitutional institutions in general and feminist institutions in particular disappear with the help of compliant women.

Notes

1   https://www.sahistory.org.za/people/graca-simbine-machel (accessed 30 October 2019).

2   http://dev.starshipsystems.com/sawid2/index.php/86-about-us/103-introducing-jsn-pixel (accessed 30 October 2019).

3   https://mg.co.za/article/2016-06-27-da-demands-zuma-pay-back-100-of-nkandla-funds-as-concourt-deadline-looms (accessed 30 October 2019).

4   https://www.news24.com/SouthAfrica/News/Zumas-wife-ousted-over-plot-to-poison-him-report-20150222 (accessed 30 October 2019).

5   See, for example, the memoirs of one of the leaders of the WNC and remarkable feminist activist who resigned from parliament in frustration with Mbeki and because he made it impossible for her to stay, Pregs Govender, *Love and Courage,* 2007/2018.

6   https://www.sastatecapture.org.za/ (accessed 24 February 2019).

7   https://genderjustice.org.za/project/policy-development-advocacy/stop-gender-violence-national-campaign/ (accessed 24 February 2019).

8   https://briefly.co.za/9404-bathabile-dlamini-a-disgrace-women-south-africa.html#9404 (accessed 24 February 2019).

9   The author was a commissioner for the CGE during this time.

10   https://rekordeast.co.za/69629/ancwl-wants-hands-off-our-president/ (accessed 24 February 2019).

11   https://www.dailymaverick.co.za/article/2015-09-07-ancs-leadership-race-the-rise-of-the-premier-league/ (accessed 26 February 2019).

12   The author attended this function. The wasteful expenditure was shocking.

13   https://en.wikipedia.org/wiki/Second_Cabinet_of_Jacob_Zuma (accessed 24 February 2019).

14   https://mg.co.za/article/2017-10-17-president-jacob-zuma-implements-his-12th-cabinet-reshuffle (accessed 28 May 2019).

References

Ahikire, J. (2018): 'On the Shifting Gender of the State in Africa: Reflections from Uganda's Experience', *Politeia*, Vol. 37, No. 1, 1–15 (first article in Vol. 37).

Albertyn, C (1995): 'Mainstreaming Gender: National Machinery for Women in South Africa', Centre for Applied Legal Studies, Occasional Paper, 24.

Bjarnegård, E. (2009): *Men in Politics*. Unpublished PhD Dissertation, University of Uppsala.

Booysen, S. (2015): *Dominance and Decline – The ANC in the Time of Zuma*. Johannesburg: Wits University Press.

Britton, H. E. (2005): *Women in the South African Parliament*. Urbana: University of Illinois Press.

Burnet, J. (2012): 'Women's Empowerment and Cultural Change in Rwanda', in S. Franceschet, M. L. Krook and J. M. Piscopo (eds) *The Impact of Gender Quotas*. Oxford: Oxford University, pp. 190–207.

Butler, A. (2015): 'The Politics of Numbers: National Membership Growth and Subnational Power Competition in the African National Congress', *Transformation*, No. 87, 13–31.

Calland, R. (2013): *The Zuma Years*. Cape Town: Zebra Press.

Cellis, K. (2008): 'Studying Women's Substantive Representation in Legislatures: When Representative Acts, Contexts and Women's Interests Become Important', *Representation*, Vol. 44, No. 2, 111–23.

Chappell, L. (2006): 'Comparing Political Institutions: Revealing the Gendered "Logic of Appropriateness"', *Politics & Gender*, Vol. 2, No. 2, 223–35.

Chappell, L. (2014): '"New," "Old" and "Nested" Institutions and Gender Justice Outcomes: A View from the International Criminal Court', *Politics & Gender*, Vol. 10, 574–94. https://www.researchgate.net/publication/280233720_New_Old_and_Nested_Institutions_and_Gender_Justice_Outcomes_A_View_from_the_International_Criminal_Court

Chipkin, M. and Swilling, M. (2018): *Shadow State*. Johannesburg: Wits University Press.

Geisler, G. (2004): *Women and the Remaking of Politics in Southern Africa*. Uppsala: Nordic Africa Institute.

Gouws, A. (2006): 'The State of the National Gender Machinery: Structural Problems and Personalized Politics', in S. Buhlungu, J. Daniels, R. Southall and J. Lutchman (eds) *The State of the Nation 2005–2006*. Cape Town: HSRC Press, pp. 143–66.

Gouws, A. (2008): 'Changing Women's Exclusion from Politics: Examples from Southern Africa', *African and Asian Studies*, Vol. 7, 537–63.

Gouws, A. (2011): 'Women's Representation in Government: Quotas, Substantive Equality and Self Interested Politicians', *Transformation*, No. 77, 80–99.

Gouws, A. (2019): 'The Gender Gap and the 2019 Election', in C. Schulz-Herzenberg and R. Southall (eds) *Election 2019 – Change and Stability in South Africa' Democracy*. Sunnyside: Jacana.

Govender, P. (2007): *Love and Courage – A Story of Insubordination*. Johannesburg: Jacana.

Hassim, S. (2006): *Women's Organizations and Democracy in South Africa – Contesting Authority*. Scottsville: UKZN Press.

Hassim, S. (2009): 'Democracy's Shadows: Sexual Rights and Gender Politics in the Rape Trial of Jacob Zuma', *Journal of African Studies*, Vol. 68, No. 1, 57–77.

Hassim, S. (2014): *The ANC Women's League*. Sunnyside: Jacana.

Hern, E. (2017): 'The Trouble with Institutions: How Women's Policy Machineries Can Undermine Women's Mass Participation', *Politics & Gender*, Vol. 13, 405–31.

Lowndes, V. (2014): 'How Are Things Done around Here? Uncovering Institutional Rules and Their Gendered Effects', *Politics & Gender*, Vol. 10, No. 4, 685–91.

Mackay, F. (2014): 'Nested Newness, Institutional Innovation, and the Gendered Limits of Change', *Politics & Gender*, Vol. 10, No. 4, 549–71.

Mackay, F., Kenny, M. and Chappell, L. (2010): 'New Institutionalism through a Gender Lens: Towards a Feminist Institutionalism', *International Political Science Review*, Vol. 31, No. 5, 573–88.

Makhunga, L. (2014): 'South African Parliament and Blurred Lines: The ANC Women's League and the African National Congress' Gendered Political Narrative', *Agenda*, Vol. 100, 33–47.

Makhunga, L. (2015): 'Elite Patriarchal Bargaining in Post-Genocide Rwanda and Post-Apartheid South Africa: Women Political Elites and Post-Transition African Parliaments', Unpublished PhD. University of the Witwatersrand.

Mama, A. (2000): *National Machinery for Women in Africa: Towards an Analysis*. Ghana: Third World Network-Africa.

Motsei, M. (2007): *The Kanga and the Kangaroo Court – Reflections on the Rape Trial of Jacob Zuma*. Johannesburg: Jacana.

O'Brien, D. Z. (2012): 'Quotas and Qualifications in Uganda', in S. Franceschet, M. L. Krook and J. M. Piscopo (eds) *The Impact of Gender Quotas*. Oxford: Oxford University Press, pp. 57–71.

Sater, J. N. (2012): 'Reserved Seats, Patriarchy, and Patronage in Morocco', in S. Franceschet, M. L. Krook and J. M. Piscopo (eds) *The Impact of Gender Quotas*. Oxford: Oxford University Press, pp. 72–98.

Setati, G. (2012): 'Through the Eye of an ANC Slate', *Mail & Guardian Thought Leader*, 4 December, https://thoughtleader.co.za/garethsetati/2012/12/04/through-the-eye-of-an-anc-slate-2/. Accessed 24 February 2019.

Stensöta, H., Wängnerud, L. and Svensson, R (2015): 'Gender and Corruption: the Mediating Power of Institutional Logics', *Governance: An International Journal of Policy, Administration, and Institutions*, Vol. 28, No. 2, 475–96.

Stetson, A. and Mazur, D. M. (eds) (1995): *Comparative State Feminism*. Los Angeles: Sage.

Tripp, A. M., Casimiro, I., Kwesiga, J. and Mungwa, A. (2009): *African Women's Movements – Changing Political Landscapes*. Cambridge: Cambridge University Press.

Tseola, J. and Nkuna, N. (2014): 'The African National Congress' Post-Apartheid Politics: Prominence of Individual Personalities above Communications', *Mediterranean Journal of Social Science*, Vol. 15, No. 5, 630–7.

Twala, C. (2012): 'The Road to the Mangaung (Bloemfontein) National Elective Conference of the African National Congress in December 2012: A Political Challenge to the Jacob Zuma Presidency', *Journal of Contemporary History*, Vol. 27, No. 1, 213–31.

Van Wyk, J.-A., Muresan, A. and Nyere, C. (2018): 'African First Ladies, Politics and the State', *Politeia*, Vol. 37, No. 2, 1–20 (second article in Vol. 37, since all articles start on p1).

Walsh, D. (2012): 'Party Centralization and Debate Conditions in South Africa', in S. Franceschet, M. L. Krook and J. M. Piscopo (eds) *The Impact of Gender Quotas*. Oxford: Oxford University Press, pp. 119–35.

Wängnerud, L. (2009): 'Women in Parliaments: Descriptive and Substantive Representation', *Annual Review of Political Science*, Vol. 12, 51–69.

Waylen, G. (2007): *Engendering Transitions*. Oxford: Oxford University Press.

Waylen, G. (2014): 'Informal Institutions, Institutional Change, and Gender Equality', *Political Research Quarterly*, Vol. 67, No. 1, 212–23.

2

Confronting the double-bind dilemma in the representations of Joice Mujuru in Zimbabwean newspapers between 2000 and 2008

Mandiedza Parichi

Empowerment of Zimbabwean women in the post-independence era

After independence in 1980, the new Black Nationalist government introduced a raft of measures intended to improve the lot of women in the country. These included pro-women legislation, such as inheritance laws that protected the interests of widows, domestic violence law, affirmative action measures such as maternity protection under the Labour relations Act that gave preferential treatment to women and girls in educational institutions and the labour market, and gender mainstreaming in most sectors of the economy (Parpan 2011). In 1997, Zimbabwe had ratified and signed the

Southern African Development Community (SADC) Declaration on Gender and Development, thus committing itself to achieving a target of at least 30 per cent in the promotion of women's access to resources and their empowerment through increased representation in political and decision-making structures by 2005. The period 2000–8 witnessed contested elections that showed significantly polarization of the Movement for Democratic Change (MDC) and the Zimbabwe African National Union Patriotic Front (ZANU PF). A number of disgruntled sections within these political parties, such as women, war veterans, the youth, academics and workers unions, are evident This period was also characterized by the controversial fast-track land reform programme which attracted international media attention. The government was pressured to appoint women because of the changing political terrain in Zimbabwe. Female Zimbabweans were appointed to senior positions in government and the civil service, such as ministers, Senate President, police commissioners and state vice president. Other women also rose on their own in their various career paths. The more prominent ones include the Managing Director of Nicoz Diamond Insurance Company, Grace Muradzikwa; prominent business woman, Jane Mutasa; Judge President Rita Makarau; and University Vice Chancellors, Hope Sadza and Primrose Kurasha. The media has thus played a key role in developing conceptual tools to apprehend the condition of women and men in Zimbabwean society (Bhebhe 2016).

Despite the ascension of a number of women to prominent positions of power, the percentage of women occupying influential positions in Zimbabwe remained lower in comparison to their male counterparts. The conditions of Zimbabwean women at the turn of the century can be attributed to a century of rapid socio-cultural transformation under various political regimes from the colonial era to the post-independence dispensation. For instance, the majority of senior managerial positions in both the private and public sectors are still occupied by men, thus limiting the capacity of women to influence Zimbabwean society (Parichi 2017). Women held only 22 per cent of the Zimbabwean cabinet posts by 2014 (*Herald* 29 January 2015). Despite the fact that a substantial number of women were now educated, women remained excluded from positions of influence through the patriarchal systems of governance that are controlled by men (*Herald* 29 January 2015). In ZANU PF, only a few women were in the top echelons of the party. Zimbabwe's seventh parliament ensued from the March 2008 elections that led to the country's Government of National Unity (GNU) incorporating ZANU PF and the two MDC formations in place then. Over time, women joined a number of non-governmental organizations and those within the ZANU PF party began to protest about the situation (Mashingaidze 2003).

Zimbabwean female politicians and the double bind

Regardless of their history and achievements most Zimbabwean female politicians are consistently exposed to a double-bind situation. This article analyses cited examples of double-bind constructs of female politicians in the media from particularly the two Zimbabwean main political parties of the MDC and ZANU PF. Stories about female politicians in all the analysed newspapers used gendered labels in the form of nouns and nominal groups. Analysis of the black female politicians – Dr Joice Mujuru, Mrs Sally Mugabe, Mrs Julia Zvobgo, Mrs Ruth Chinamano, Margaret Dongo, Pricillah Misihairambwi, Cecelia Gwachiwa among others – just after independence has images from the media that point to the use of a double-bind notion through their representation. For instance, *Kwayedza* story of 13–21 August 2008:11 carries a story titled '*Danho remadzimai muchimurenga*' (the role of women in the liberation struggle) which emphasizes the catch twenty-two situation Zimbabwean female politicians are subjected to. In the article Ruth Chinamano is represented more in terms of her association with her husband's success, '*mudzimai wa Josiah Chinamano*' (Josiah Chinamano's wife) even though the article goes on to report that she was a champion of the liberation struggle in Rhodesia and as a politician too. However, the title Mrs is but a loose approximation of the Shona *Mai*. A strong hint of the difference between Mrs and *Mai* is that whereas convention dictates that the English Mrs is only affixed to surnames (or surname preceded by first name), as in Mrs (Sarah) Jones, Extract 1 uses the title *Mai* with the subject's first name only – '*Mai*

Sally' – while elsewhere in the story the title is used to qualify her surname – *Mai* Mugabe. The availability of the Shona *Mai* to accompany a woman's first name alone suggests that the word is strongly linked to motherhood than it is to a woman's marital status. Thus, even though *Mai* is generally used to refer to married women, it would seem that this label constructs marriage as inherently connoting procreation. The collocation of the formal title '*Mai*' with the heroine's first name, as in the article, suggests naturalizing a social role that mirrors the close bond between a mother and her children. The use of these women as mothers and wives in politics cues the reader to judge them as mothers who are in politics in terms of their ability and willingness to be the pacifiers and caregivers who can easily and naturally sacrifice their political career if they must choose between their families and politics. Female politicians who depart from the gendered constructs of wife and mother may be stigmatized by *Kwayedza* as inadequate and unfit for public office or written out of the publication's narratives about politics and society in general. Two very similar *Kwayedza* stories about two female members of parliament (MPs), one from ZANU PF and the other from the MDC, who defrauded their respective constituencies of money collected for the purchase of fertilizer, also point to this double bind. They are titled *Gwachiwa mudare* (my Translation: Gwachiwa appears in court; *Kwayedza*, 4–10 December 2008:9) and *MP onenedzerwa nyaya* (my translation: an MP stands accused of fraud; Kwayedza 10–16 December 2000:7), respectively. This is indicated by the emphasis of the wifehood and motherhood roles within the story.

However, despite these challenges calls to include women in political positions became much more pronounced in the 1990s, which culminated in the promotion of Joice Mujuru to the vice presidency of both ZANU PF and the state in 2005. This book chapter explores the way women, in particular Joice Mujuru, are represented in the election years between 2000 and 2018.

Joice Mujuru double-bind unpacked

Like most of the female politicians in Zimbabwe since 1980, there seems to be a deliberate intention to draw attention to Joice Mujuru's motherhood and/or status as a married woman more than her role as a successful politician. The double bind for female politicians in Zimbabwe particularly for Joice Mujuru can be explained through by the controversial issues around her ascension to the vice- presidency position. Her promotion is questioned through the stories from the *Financial Gazette* newspaper of 15–22 January 2005 titled 'ZANU PF'S latest Gimmick: women', and that of 13–19 January 2005 titled 'Just how did they arrive at the 30 per cent quota system? The fuzzy maths of SADC'. The story queries the ascension of Joice Mujuru to the post of vice president of ZANU PF and Zimbabwe in 2005. Misihairambwi and Kwinjeh (2005) say of Joice Mujuru,

> She has been propelled to the party's top most position precisely because she poses no threat to any of the distinct factions engaged in a bitter power struggle within ZANU PF. These include the ZAPU faction, Emmerson Mnangagwa faction and of course the Mujuru faction led by her husband, Solomon.

The story also distils Mujuru's credential to just one attribute which is her marriage to Solomon Mujuru, former ZANLA commander, former Zimbabwean army commander and retired commander of the armed forces turned millionaire businessman and highly influential ZANU PF power broker. Thus the story underscores its argument that on her own Joyce Mujuru is not worth much as a politician. This is despite Joyce Mujuru's well-documented military exploits as a ZANLA combatant and military officer during Zimbabwe's liberation war as well as that she is one of the selected few ZANU PF politicians to consistently hold a ministerial position from Zimbabwe's independence to the date of publishing of the story examined here. A quick survey for most of ZANU PF female politicians suggests similar double-bind discursive practices. These include the late first lady of Zimbabwe Sally Mugabe who was born Sarah Francesca Heyfron in 1931. In 1968 she was the deputy secretary for women's league. She was elected secretary general of the ZANU PF women's league and was actively involved in the Akina Mama waAfrica, a London-based organization for African and UK women. Julia Zvobgo was born Julia Tukai Whande. She became a member of ZANU PF in 1963 and was elected as Zvishavane MP at independence in 1980. She was elected secretary for publicity and information in the women's league in 1984. Julia Zvobgo was a member of the central committee for the first ten years after independence. In 1985 she was re-elected as a member of parliament for Zvishavane. Julia Zvobgo was wife to prominent parliamentarian Eddison Zvobgo. Ruth Chinamano was born Ruth Nyombolo in 1925 *Josiah Chinamano*. She joined the National Democratic Party in 1960. She was the secretary of the Salisbury district of the Zimbabwe African Women's Union. She became an MP in 1980 and was last elected to parliament in 1995. All of these prominent women are explained in terms of their motherhood and wifehood roles despite having taken part in the liberation struggle.

Thus because of that notion she is set up to fail as a politician. This is captured by the statement, 'It must first be understood that Mujuru is only acceptable to President Robert Mugabe as his Vice President because she does not threaten his hold on power either nationally or within the ruling party'.

The assumption of their power being associated with the patriarchal power is validated by the events that transpired after the demise of Joice Mujuru's husband popularly referred to as the King Maker in Zimbabwe and ZANU PF politics. In the absence of her perceived source of power she was shamed and demoted by the patriarchal strongholds within the ZANU PF party. The demotion of Joyce Mujuru from the select class of the *amai* is reflected in the fact that Grace Mugabe labels Joyce Mujuru a 'baby' '(*mwana*)' that can be dumped by its (political) parents, the president and Grace Mugabe, because of its alleged misbehaviour (*Daily News* 21 October 2014). In response, Joyce Mujuru defends herself by casting herself as President Mugabe's 'daughter' as a way of claiming the political legitimacy that derives from Mugabe's name and stature within ZANU PF.

While this book chapter does not necessarily focus on the representation of male politicians, it draws attention to overt differential representation of male and female politicians in the media. Male politicians are not exposed to the same familial/politician double bind. In *Kwayedza*, for instance, female Vice President Joice Mujuru is consistently referred to as *Amai* (a noun meaning mother) while the male president of the country was labelled *Mutungamiri wenyika* (a nominal group meaning leader of the country), thus constructing Mujuru in terms of the private domain of interpersonal family relations and

Mugabe in terms of his official public office. This is illustrated in the story *Mai Mujuru vanopedza zvidzidzo zvavo payunivhesiti* (translation: Mrs Mujuru completes her university studies; *Kwayedza*, 25 December 2005). The statement *Mutevedzeri wemutungamiri wenyika Mai Mujuru svondo rakapera vakapemberera kupedza zvidzidzo zveBachelor of Science Degree in Management and Entrepreneurial Development izvo vakaita neyunivhesiti yeWomen's university in Africa* (translation: Vice President Mrs Mujuru last week celebrated the successful completion of her Bachelor of Science in Management and Entrepreneurial Development degree studies, which she did at the Women's University in Africa).

This is true of the story 'Losing ZANU PF candidate punishes voters' published in *The Standard* on 30 March to 6 April 2005, which critically assesses the behaviour of female ZANU PF election candidate, Sithembiso Nyoni, in the aftermath of her loss to the MDC's David Coltart in the 2005 legislative elections. Subtle discursive strategies that suggest an implicit double bind between feminine and masculine characteristics are employed by the reporter. Throughout the story, Nyoni is represented as heartless, a characteristic not ordinarily associated with femininity and/or motherhood. This is despite the fact that male counterparts such as Nyoni's rival David Coltart are not subjected to such crippling expectation in politics. In other words, the newspaper works for a stereotype of woman as mother and expects the woman politician to be motherly and kind rather than practise real politics which is presumed to be a man's game.

This book chapter focuses on Joice Mujuru as the only female politician to be consistently elected to ministerial positions in the Zimbabwean parliament since 1980 until her demotion in 2013. She is also the only female politician to have assumed the prestigious position of vice president in the history of Zimbabwean politics. As vice president, she was strategically positioned to take over power from the president in the event that he left office under whatever circumstance. In comparison to other female politicians, the media also focused more on Joice Mujuru's career. Besides the above feat, Joice Mujuru was a celebrated war hero who had held influential positions during the Liberation Struggle of Zimbabwe, having accomplished, among others, the unprecedented feat of downing a Rhodesian Air Force aircraft.[1]

The double-bind paradox

This book chapter tests the applicability of the double-bind theory to Joice Mujuru's political career during electoral years from 2000 to 2017. The double-bind term and theory were first used in Bateson et al.'s (1956) *Toward a Theory of Schizophrenia*, which focused on schizophrenic patients. In their description of the double-bind theory, Bateson et al. (1956) argue that it is 'a situation in which no matter what a person does, he [*sic*] can't win'. Gender stereotypes do not fall off easily but continue to pose challenges for women. It is embedded in the constructs of patriarchy. It is against this background that the book chapter investigates how media representations have created a double-bind dilemma, which is also often termed the catch twenty-two situation to shape societal public opinion about women. Power relations that are embedded within discourse point to the power of the definer within the selected media constructs. Systems of the double bind produce conflicting situations which bring challenging dispositions for the victim. This situation is often related to power dynamics and in many societies enshrined in patriarchal ideology.

Evidently, double binds work well with stereotypes (Bhabha 1994; Irvin 2013). Multiple scholars have written extensively on the socialized stereotyped roles of men and women (Durkin 1985a). One assumption and stereotype that has been overstretched in narratives is that women are naturally less able leaders than their male counterparts; yet, in reality what may differ are leadership styles (Eagly et al. 2000). The basis of leadership and management roles and activities is primarily to execute, monitor, subordinate, gather and disseminate information. Men and women therefore can be different in their execution of these duties without meaning that one gender is inferior to the other (Eagly 2009). Managers may be friendly or more remote, exhibit much or little excitement about future goals, consult few or many colleagues about decisions, provide extensive or limited mentoring of subordinates, and so forth (Podsakoff et al. 2000).

The double bind therefore seems to be a terrible conceptual trap in the hands of the media. For the female politicians, it is the proverbial 'catch twenty-two' syndrome, a 'lose-lose' scenario. In that respect, they are either unable or popular but never both. The challenges to the dilemma are that the victims of a double bind are destined to fail regardless of the choices they make. This is aptly captured within the Catalyst Report (2007) which describes the situation for women in leadership positions as 'damned if you do, doomed if you don't'. The two options penalize the person that is being offered the choices. The idea places expectations and condemnations together so that to fulfil expectations is also to inevitably attract condemnation (Johnstone and Swanson 2003: 244). In this book chapter, Bateson's double-bind theory (1956) is used as the basis to apprehend gender non-conforming identities. For instance, a double bind occurs when women have to choose between being liked but not respected, or being respected but not liked. In such situations, women in leadership positions face complex political dynamics that do not necessarily affect men. The result in most instances is that the subject struggles to find solutions to the double bind and may become paranoid. Sometimes affected women are forced to conform to all gender expectations, which discourage independent thinking (Tracy 2004). Cook (2009) outlines four prominent areas of double bind, to which women are subjected to such as womb/brain and femininity/competence. Elsewhere the Catalyst Report (2007: 7) also presents three common double-bind dilemmas, which are 'extreme perceptions: too soft, too tough, and never just right; the high competence threshold: women leaders face higher standards and lower rewards than men leaders; competent but disliked: women leaders are perceived as competent or likable, but rarely both'.

The dominant idea that is tested in this book chapter through the double-bind theory is that women can never be adequate or good enough in whatever position they find themselves. In this respect the position and experiences of Joice Mujuru as politician, wife and mother within the domestic space against her role in politics will be interrogated. The idea of the double-bind theory is interrogated in this book chapter because of its deliberate manipulation of images of female politicians by sections of the media with the intention of setting up some women to fail in the leadership and political environment (Johnstone and Swanson 2003; Malcom et al. 1976). The popular patriarchal assumption pushed forward in numerous narratives especially media is that women are naturally born to take care of the home or any private spaces while men control the public domain (Lovenduski 2002). Stereotypes work well with the double bind to create misleading perceptions in terms of leadership, concerning taking care and taking charge of behaviour traits.

Media representation of female politicians

In many societies from a tender age, narratives particularly media socialize women to be feminine, relationship-oriented and more or less homebound and men to be masculine, macho and oriented towards results and controlling public institutions, which include embracing politics (Fowler and Lawless 2009; Ryan 2013). According to Markstedt (2007: 4), 'Today, female politicians remain restricted not by their sex but by their gender, which is constructed through the representation of women in public discourse.' As a result, society is conditioned to assume that men and women have different genetic compositions that naturally make men and not women leaders (Holt 2012). This media discourse strategy is summarized by Brooks (2010: 2), who argues that 'the conventional wisdom is that female politicians are greatly constrained by a toughness-related double bind: if a woman fails to demonstrate toughness, she confirms a stereotype that women are not strong enough to lead; yet if she demonstrates toughness, she will be disliked for violating gendered expectations'. Media representations of both men and women in leadership positions are thus much more simplified than the reality represented (Markstedt 2007: 4). Empirical evidence through existing literature has indicated that ordinarily there is hardly any difference between the leadership styles of males and females. False perceptions that portray men and women as 'worlds apart' are created through stereotypes in numerous subjective narratives (Catalyst Report 2007: 4; Eagly et al. 2003). Stereotyping results in women having to do more than their male counterparts to be noticed and acknowledged. Success however makes a woman less likeable and thus creates a further complication through double bind (Sools et al. 2007). However, being weak at workplaces is also treated as incompetence. This challenge and complication is often referred to as 'ambivalent sexism' (Bhabha 1994; Glick and Fiske 2001). Such pressures by both society and media have detrimental consequences for women empowerment (Brooks 2010). Carter (2011: 24) contends that 'stereotypical depictions of women in the rigid sex roles of wife and mother' manifest as the most prominent and well-known double-bind dilemma faced by women.

Braden (1996: 1) argues, 'More than a century later women politicians are still discovering what (Susan B.) Anthony had learnt that journalists often ask female politicians questions they don't ask men.' The reporters describe women politicians in ways and with words that emphasize women's traditional roles and focus on their appearance and behaviour. Consequently, they perpetuate stereotypes of women politicians as weak, indecisive and emotional. In the process, female politicians are held accountable for the actions of their children and husbands, though they rarely hold men to the same standards (Braden 1996: 1).

Most scholars argue that the media remains sexists in its representation of female politicians (Georgia Duerst-Lahti 1997). Males competing for parliament are often referred to as eligible bachelors to downplay the feminine traits that compete for politics. This marginalization is also mirrored in the organizational structures of the most newsrooms. In many media organizations, female journalists are expected to cover soft news that are often welfarist or related to home economics while hard news such as politics, military and finance remain a privy for male journalists (Braden 1996). This mode of representation marginalizes female politicians through focus on marital status, appearance, education and healthcare issues. In terms of ministries, the Military and Finance Ministries are often considered too masculine for female politicians to tackle.

The gendered coverage has had adverse effects on female politicians' careers (Ryan 2013). She further argues that, women continue to be downgraded through structural, societal and institutional spaces. Consequently, gendered coverage by the media remains one of the major barriers of female politicians' success in politics. Thus for many societies the glass ceiling is still firmly in place. There is still a marked difference in the way female and male politicians are represented. As Mayer (1999: 2) points out, 'Despite its rhetoric of equality for all who partake in the "national project", nation remains, like other feminized entities – emphatically, historically and globally – the property of men.' Female politicians are distinctly viewed first as women and then as politicians (Ross 2002). For that reason they are given more pressure than males to perform in leadership positions to put it in Garcia-Blanco and Wahl-Jorgensen (2012: 435) they had to be 'whiter-than-white'. Elsewhere Mawarire (2009) contends that media is generally dominated by male patriarchal thinking, to the disadvantage of women. Critical analysis on media is instrumental as it shapes the public opinion through the images generated concerning female politicians. This book chapter through qualitative analysis thus interrogates the discursive practices that are used by the media in the representation of female politicians through the selected newspapers.

Methodology

The study made use of qualitative methodology, which takes an interpretive outlook to explain the language experience through content analysis of the selected newspapers. Content analysis was used to determine the presence of certain words, concepts, themes, phrases, characters or sentences within texts or sets of texts and to quantify this in an objective manner. To minimize subjectivity the book chapter made use of three newspapers that belong to two different steads of the public and the private media of Zimbabwe that are highly polarized. The major assumption was that Zimbabwean female politicians are marginalized through the news media regardless of political divide and newspaper. In this respect, the researcher is aware that the etic and emic components of qualitative research might have made the research subjective. The book chapter coded stories, which fall under the double-bind theme. Though the focus was on Joice Mujuru, analysis of the representation of other female politicians could not be completely avoided. Excerpts of selected stories were used to demonstrate and illustrate the development of the double-bind construct of Joice Mujuru. This increased the reliability, validity and trustworthiness of the research. The study analysed a corpus of thirty newspaper articles about Joice Mujuru from the three newspapers within the electoral periods between 2000 and 2018. The sample was made up of eighteen stories that were selected from the three newspapers.

Motherhood and wifehood stereotype

A number of stories that were analysed indicated the mother and non-mother double bind. In most of the stories, Mrs Mujuru is represented in familial terms, which emphasize the social spaces of both motherhood and wifehood. Let us take, for instance, these two stories: *Mai Mujuru vanopedza zvidzidzo zvavo payunivhesiti* (translation: Mrs Mujuru completes her university studies; *Kwayedza*, 25 December 2005) and *Musangano wekuratidza kudya kwechivanhu wakabudirira* (my translation: Traditional African food fair was a success; *Kwayedza* 14–20 January 2005: 5). These stories report on Vice President Joice Mujuru's graduation ceremony and her attendance at the Traditional African Food Fair respectively. Each of the four times that she is referred to by name, the title adjective *Mai* is affixed to her name as in '*Mai Mujuru*'. This is unlike the other politicians mentioned in the story who are referred to as either Cde or Dr Cde (short for comrade), comrade being a Marxist revolutionary title associated with all ZANU PF militants and leaders regardless of gender. The use of the adjective '*Mai*' (literally, mother) attributes to the subject two social statuses: wifehood and motherhood. Since, traditionally, motherhood is linked to marriage, and since men traditionally marry women in order to procreate, to be called '*Mai*' is to be constructed in terms of both those social functions. It seems, therefore, that gives prominence to the notions of natural (biological) and nurturing functions in its representation of Mrs Mujuru. This is despite the fact that Mrs Mujuru has a well-documented list of public domain accomplishments spanning the military, political and academic spheres. The notion of wifehood cues the reader to construct the adult female subject as a being whose persona is completed by the presence of a husband in her life. Whereas the familial or relational term *Mai* (Mujuru) is generally used as an equivalent of the English title Mrs, it also connotes that Joice Mujuru is wife of Mujuru, mother of Mujuru's children or both. Bias towards the said connotation is suggested by the context in which the term is used in the story. For instance, if, in a story, all women who are married are referred to as *Mai* and the Shona title *Va* (Mr) is affixed to all men, then there might not be an intention to highlight the motherhood or marital status of a particular woman or group of women. In the case of the extract examined above, there seems to be an intention to draw attention to Joice Mujuru's motherhood and/or status as a married woman. This cues the reader to construct her persona in terms of those themes, thus building up a married mother/politician double bind with the conflicting expectations of good motherhood and political success. The motherhood theme seems to draw the reader's attention to Mujuru's domestic roles and functions and yet what makes her newsworthy is her status as the leading Zimbabwean female politician and liberation struggle icon. The stories associate the two most powerful women in Zimbabwe, Grace Mugabe and Joice Mujuru, with motherhood. The stories use motherhood and wifehood to redefine the status of a female politician to her disadvantage. A feature of the story that casts female politicians as a social category that must be seen primarily as mothers is the use of Joice Mujuru as a substitute for Mrs.

These sentiments are also found in negative stereotypes developed in the story from *Financial Gazette* of 13–19 January 2005 titled 'Just how did they arrive at the 30 per cent quota system? The fuzzy maths of SADC'. The story queries the ascension of Joice Mujuru to the post of vice president of ZANU PF and Zimbabwe in 2005. Makuni, who is a woman, dismisses the 2005 promotion of Joice Mujuru to the vice presidency of ZANU PF as well as the State as undeserved and shows ZANU PF's propensity to abuse the SADC protocol on gender equity to score cheap political goals. Makuni cues the reader to also trivialize Joice Mujuru's credentials as a politician and her suitability for the lofty position of vice president. To the journalist, the 'fuzzy maths' of the SADC female quota decision becomes a metonym for the 'fuzzy female Vice President' Zimbabwe gets as a result of that policy.

To use British voices to validate Mujuru is the height of mischief since she is the second most powerful leader of a party that has thrived on anti-British rhetoric particularly in the era of the Fast Track Land Reform Programme (FTLRP) proximity to the 2008 general elections pitting Mujuru's ZANU PF against MDC suggests the story's mischief. Association of Mujuru with the British is tantamount to labelling her an ally of the MDC and their alleged British sponsors. Such 'mischief' can, however, be expected of a sophisticated publication whose owners have a stake in ZANU PF politics. To use a military decision to exclude female soldiers from combat to support the claim that Joice Mujuru is inherently pacific contradicts the well-documented military and political history of Mujuru. It may be intended to set her up to fail as a leader of a party whose historical bedrock is its militancy and espousal of violence as just means to attain and defend revolutionary ideals.

This is a war hero around whom her own party has developed a myth of courage, violence and ruthlessness. For instance, she chose for herself the nom de guerre '*Teurai Ropa*' (spill blood) during the liberation war, implying she espoused bloodshed and violence as core values in the struggle to liberate Zimbabwe. Her well-documented conduct and beliefs thus contradict Makuni's claim that women are inherently uneasy about using violence as a conflict resolution strategy. Indeed, Mujuru's ZANU PF party has prolonged that struggle into the twenty-first century in the form of the FTLRP and yet it is for adopting the FTLRP's violent methods that Madzongwe, a loyal party activist, is condemned in the article examined above. Makuni's story about Mujuru is thus clearly based on a lie, which shows that the overriding intention is to develop the woman/female freak double bind that sets up ZANU PF female politicians to fail regardless of the side of the bind they find themselves.

Makuni casts Mujuru's non-violence as 'unusual', thus continuing to build up a discourse of Mujuru's difference started by the caption beneath a picture, a discourse which justifies the messianic traits attributed to Mujuru in the title of the story. That difference is enhanced by her participation in an inter-denominational prayer for peaceful elections: 'By taking the trouble to show up for this important prayer meeting and speaking out against violence and vindictiveness, Mujuru has brought a special and different dimension to her office.'

Repetition of the adjective 'different' drives home the notion that Mujuru is a saintly woman in the midst of evil. The clause 'by taking the trouble to' suggests the incongruity of Mujuru in a Christian prayer meeting for peaceful elections. Desperation for creating a scoop story causes Makuni to exaggerate the nature and value of the participation of Mujuru, whose membership of the Salvation Army Church is well known. That exaggeration includes the dubious claim that Mujuru 'led [the] national prayer service', which contradicts the notion of her 'taking the trouble to show up' at that prayer meeting. It extends to the attribution of femininity to Mujuru alone in a prayer 'organised by women': 'By coming forward to join other women as an ordinary Christian, Mujuru has added a special feminine touch to the anti-violence campaign.' The story's overarching discourse strategy is therefore unequivocally to construct Mujuru as the ideal woman, mother, Christian and female politician.

The double bind interrogated

In the story *Mai Mujuru vanopedza zvidzidzo zvavo payunivhesiti* (translation: Mrs Mujuru completes her university studies; *Kwayedza*, 25 December 2005), the location of the double bind in the story ostensibly celebrating Mujuru's academic success seems peculiar, as the private notions of motherhood and wifehood are apparently given pre-eminence in a public event where Mujuru's status as a leading public figure is underscored by the presence of her colleagues in party and government. A possible explanation of this discursive strategy is the politicization of the title *Mai* and the noun *Amai*, such as it is used (virtually exclusively) in *Kwayedza* in relation to First Lady Grace Mugabe, to mean mother of the nation. This would therefore mean that, in the stories, the motherhood/wifehood and political success binary are used to develop two levels of double-bind dilemma. The surface level dilemma comprises the paradox of blending the values of motherhood with those of politics to construct the subject. The deeper level dilemma consists in using motherhood/wifehood to ostensibly elevate a female politician to the level of 'mother of the nation'. This result in a blend of characteristics of first lady discourse and politics as *Mai* shifts from its use in general Shona to denote the private sphere of motherhood/wifehood to a political use in ZANU PF discourse practice to denote a certain (if officially unacknowledged) rank in that social group.

Thus, the subject is 'doubly' set up to fail, particularly at the deeper and less obvious level where she has no control of one of the sides in the double bind since she is not married to the president of the country. The double-bind discourse strategy can be deployed longitudinally over a period as a newspaper builds up a certain construct of a group of female politicians. To illustrate this strategy, two stories about two prominent ZANU PF female politicians published in *The Financial Gazette* in the same year around the same period (the period leading up to the 2008 general elections) are examined concurrently. These politicians are Edna Madzongwe and Joice Mujuru. Both are ZANU PF stalwarts, veterans of Zimbabwe's liberation war, and both have been politically active throughout all the years of Zimbabwe's independence. At the time the stories examined here were written in 2008, Edna Madzongwe was Senate President while Joice Mujuru was vice president of both ZANU PF and Zimbabwe. Coincidentally, they both ascended to those positions in 2005.

Sinner/saint double bind

The story published in the *Financial Gazette* of 5–11 January 2005 discusses the saint or sinner double bind titled 'Mujuru's gospel of non-violence gives hope', with the noun 'gospel' immediately evoking Jesus Christ, the gentle Messiah who preached love and non-violence. She is therefore deliberately cast as a messianic figure from the very title of the story. Her supreme altruism and integrity are also highlighted in the statement within the story, which reads: 'When the scandal involving the war victims fund surfaced, Mujuru was the only person to surrender the inflated amount of money she had been allocated.' Indeed, the article constructs her in terms of difference from the rest of ZANU PF politicians, such as Madzongwe. The caption beneath a portrait of a very feminine Mujuru highlighting soft plump features on a calm and serene face reads: 'Vice President Joice Mujuru ... a different kettle of fish.' She is thus cast as a rare dove among rapacious vultures, a saint lost among sinners, an example for female politicians of all political persuasions. Given its prominence, the picture cues the reader to construct Mujuru in terms of her cleanliness and moral rectitude.

The *Financial Gazette* story of 5–11 January 2005 Reporter Mavis Makuni, herself a woman, who sets herself in her portraiture of Mujuru is to naturalize the notion of the inherence of non-violence in female politicians. To validate this claim, she cites British military practice: a short while after the invasion of Iraq by Britain and America in 2003, an overseas newspaper published a story cited in the *Financial Gazette* story of 5–11 January 2005 concerning a debate that had been raging within the British military establishment. The debate centred on whether or not women soldiers should be deployed to the frontlines of battle. The question was asked whether women had the emotional inclination, an ability to shoot another human being from point blank range. In the end, it was decided that women were not suited for such a gruelling task. Far from conveying the impression that women were perceived as weaklings, this decision represented recognition of the compassionate nature of women. This was acknowledgement that women are more uneasy about using violence as a tool in conflict resolution.

The female freak double bind

This examination of two *Financial Gazette* stories about two different female ZANU PF politicians has revealed strategies used to construct the woman/ female freak double bind as well as its possible rhetorical effects. Thus, at first glance, nothing in the story about Edna Madzongwe suggests that anything but her apparently corrupt use of power is in question. There is not even a single trace of gendered discourse, such as notions of sex, marriage or motherhood in the story. In 2005, not long after she was appointed vice president of Zimbabwe and the ruling ZANU PF party, the *The Standard* weekly ran two stories about Joice Mujuru, one in its 'Standard Business' section and the other in the 'Local News' section. Both stories focus on Mujuru's work with Zimbabwe's struggling 'parastatal' companies, a responsibility given to her by the President Robert Mugabe. The two stories examined here are titled 'Mujuru cracks whip' *The Standard* 7–13 February 2005 and 'Mujuru berates Air Zim bosses over Dubai Trip' *The Standard* 28 October to 4 November 2005 respectively. The story titled 'Mujuru cracks whip' is located in the 'Standard Business section' of the newspaper, suggesting that it is concerned with financial or commercial matters or any other aspects of business. The venue of the meeting, however, raises eyebrows: the meeting takes place at the Reserve Bank of Zimbabwe and not at the Vice President's offices or at any other venue in Harare. That the meeting takes place at the Reserve Bank of Zimbabwe warrants some scrutiny as it draws attention to one of the participants in the meeting, Reserved Bank Governor, Gideon Gono and the role, if any, he is to play in the work given the vice president.

The vice president's task is summarized in the story's first paragraph: 'Government began a promised clean-up of state enterprises last week by threatening to sack non-performing heads at an eight-hour meeting chaired by Vice President Joice Mujuru.' Mujuru is therefore government's chosen enforcer of its decision to demand results from the executives running Zimbabwe's perennially underachieving parastatals. However, locating the meeting at the Reserve Bank gives the role of host of this powerful meeting and exercise to Gideon Gono. Taking that role away from Mujuru diminishes her stature while incorporating that detail into the second paragraph of the story gives it a prominence that suggests desire to quickly draw attention to the Reserve Bank governor. That discursive strategy is confirmed in the suggestion in that paragraph's first sentence that Mujuru and Gono were co-speakers: At that meeting – held on Tuesday at the Reserve Bank – Mujuru and Central Bank Governor Gideon Gono announced a raft of performance targets that the parastatal heads will be expected to meet in the next few months. The double bind here in which Mujuru, being a woman, could only be seen as benefitting from a SADC quota on the representation of women, and yet benefitting from that quota set her up to fail as it implied that she lacked the necessary qualities for the job. By constructing her as the epitome of the ZANU PF 'feminine' politician, the independent press was setting Mujuru up to fail.

The Standard's construction of her in the story examined shows that one way of naturalizing the impression that she will inevitably fail is to portray her as needing Gono to share the microphone with her from the very outset of the story. The reader is likely to take as the beginning of her speech in the meeting and which is also her very first gesture in her very important task of stopping the rot in the parastatals. Thus, it painted the picture of a poor housewife thrust into the deep end of the political administration pool, a pool where Gono and the rest of the participants, the vast majority of them males, will be thought of by the reader as being more at ease than Mujuru. The story is concerned with a meeting that Mujuru had with Reserve Bank Governor, Gideon Gono, and a coterie of officials described as 'top management of over 16 parastatals, their board members and senior government officials under whose ministries parastatals fall'. Such a gathering, in terms of both sheer numbers and stature of participants, reflects the power vested in and the responsibility placed on Mujuru's shoulders by means of her task to directly oversee state enterprises. That a female politician has been placed in charge of the business side of the state suggests that she is highly trusted by the president and his cabinet as a whole. The question, however, remains as to the 'whip' she is said to be cracking in the title. It turns out that Gono is portrayed as having his hands more firmly on that 'whip' than Mujuru. The first discursive clue to that reversal of the balance of power between the two protagonists is the distribution of actions and sheer textual space to either of them. After blending the two into one voice in the story's second paragraph, the first of the two to be cited separately by the story is Gono. His voice occupies virtually the entire second column. It is followed by that of Mujuru, which is accorded only one short paragraph. Mujuru is thus muted and demoted to a place after Gono while Gono is not only given the megaphone but thrust to centre stage. While Gono and Mujuru are each quoted as making one announcement, the story explains Gono's announcement in detail while that of Mujuru is merely stated. Quotations of Gono are categorical: 'Gono has announced'; 'Gono has tied strict performance targets to the funding'; 'The RBZ's new plan was announced'. This builds an impression of self-assurance, surefootedness and leadership, so that Gono is seen as capable and trustworthy. The second story *The Standard* 7–13 February 2005 examined here is written to look like an illustration of the expected failure of Mujuru. Its title clarions Mujuru's frustration: 'Mujuru berates Air Zim bosses over Dubai trip'. Her anger is the very first word of the story: 'Angered by the ill-fated Dubai trip, Vice President Joice Mujuru last week read the riot act to Air Zimbabwe bosses at a stormy meeting held at her Munhumutapa offices'. The story portrays her as a woman using more of her emotions than anything else. Given that anger is a sign of defeat and frustration, highlighting it could be indicative of an intention to suggest to the reader that Mujuru is out of her depth in the business world, the one world where cool temperaments thrive better than tempestuous ones. Indeed, loss of control is suggested by the description of Mujuru's meeting with Air Zimbabwe officials as 'stormy'. Mujuru's frustration is underscored in the story by the frequency of futile meetings she has already had with Air Zimbabwe officials – three meetings in seven months.

The woman/freak double bind discovered in the *Financial Gazette*'s coverage of Mujuru is now complete in *The Standard*. Mujuru displays both the feminine and freakish aspects of her in the two stories examined here. The freak is the one who resorts to violence, wielding a whip, proffering all manner of threats and is prone to ill-advised displays of anger. Interestingly, this story cites the one titled 'Mujuru cracks whip': 'In February Mujuru [...] summoned top management to a meeting at the Reserve Bank of Zimbabwe (RBZ), where she warned that non-performers would be sacked.' This throwback to the earlier story reminds the reader of how Mujuru played second fiddle to Gono in that story. Recall of the whip and threat to dismiss non-performers contrasts with Mujuru's frustration to painfully highlight her inability to act on her threats. This confirms that the whip she cracked in the first earlier story was indeed more firmly in Gono's hands than hers. The suggestion is thus made that her femininity softens her while her attempts at being strong and aggressive are but the vain ranting of a frustrated woman.

Conclusion

The data examined here suggests that the media still represents female politicians in terms of double binds. The polarization peculiarity of the Zimbabwean media did not have an effect on how Joice Mujuru was represented by the selected newspapers as both private and public media portrayed women in a way that marginalizes and disadvantages them. In addition, Joice Mujuru's experience and age did not change or alter the way the media views her. Being the only female politician who was consistently in Mugabe's Cabinet of Ministers since independence until her fallout with Mugabe in 2013 indicates a long span in Zimbabwean politics. Some of the significant conclusions point to the embeddedness of patriarchy in the

Zimbabwean society as even other female politicians and journalists felt that she was inadequate and inexperienced particularly for the post of vice president. The research also concluded that whether a female politician was represented as a mother, wife or through double-bind dilemmas, regardless of the ideology of the selected papers, the objective of the concerned newspaper would be to frame the female politician as inherently incapacitated or unfit for political office. Judging from the discursive choices made by its articles on female politicians, it is evident that there is preference by the *Kwayedza* newspaper to confine female politicians to the domestic sphere. *Kwayedza* newspaper also frequently used the double-bind dilemma to frame Joice Mujuru. As a politician, she is represented either as a good mother who cannot be good politician or as a good politician who is an unfit mother. The stereotypes served to remind the reader that politics is a tough job for women and the place of a woman is the home. An example that has been highlighted in the analysis is that even though Joice Mujuru was the most senior female politician in ZANU PF and in government and arguably the most successful of all female politicians in ZANU PF, *Kwayedza* newspaper still viewed her more as a mother and wife instead of the vice president of both ZANU PF and Zimbabwe. This double-bind position was often used by the *Kwayedza* particularly in instances where they want to make female politicians feel guilty about being career or professional women. The evidence from findings point to Joice Mujuru as a female politician being represented around family first before she is acknowledged for any other role in her life. Thus, the media treats the male and female genders as professionally separate and different.

This research suggests that the reason for these biases and stereotypes is that *Kwayedza* newspaper prefers to maintain the traditional gender roles of women. This finding is attributable to the fact that *Kwayedza* published in Shona, which makes it susceptible to Shona traditional culture, which tends to locate women more in the private than the public spaces. For instance, Shona traditional culture, like virtually every other African culture, values the traditional role of motherhood (Familusi 2012). This is contrary to the Western worldview informing public debate on the place and role of women in Zimbabwean society. Elsewhere the *Financial Gazette* does not dwell on the motherhood double bind though the stereotype is always indirectly imposed on them. The comparative analysis of *Financial Gazette* stories about two different female ZANU PF politicians of which one of them is Joice Mujuru has revealed strategies used to construct the woman/female freak double bind as well as its possible rhetorical effects. The analysis has suggested a negative goal to develop a certain construct of the female politician. The construct revolves around the simplistic notion that female politicians are either 'true' women who display certain stereotypical feminine traits such as motherhood and non-violence or female freaks who are in fact men in women's bodies. Both types are bound to be disliked by the reader, thus reducing the chances of success of female politicians in an election year. The *Financial Gazette* and *The Standard* newspapers also use subtle suggestions through selected textual and linguistic strategies to build the impression that female politicians are inherently incapable and unfit as politicians.

Such strategies are highly sophisticated and subtle and may be denied by the newspaper and the ordinary reader who they influence even more effectively because of their very subtleness. In some *Financial Gazette* and *The Standard* stories on female politicians discourse representation is used as a subtle means to incorporate elements of the discourses of marriage and motherhood.

Note

1   http://www.iol.co.za/news/africa/mugabe-s-deputy-aims-for-top-spot-1.1609319#.U_oZk6NMj_

References

Atkeson, L. R. (2003): 'Not All Cues Are Created Equal: The Conditional Impact of Female Candidates on Political Engagement', *The Journal of Politics*, Vol. 4 (November), 1040–61.

Bateson, G. (1972): *Steps to an Ecology of Mind: A Theory of Play and Fantasy*. Chicago: The University of Chicago Press, pp. 177–93.

Bateson, G., Jackson, D., Haley, J. and Weakland, J. (1956): 'Toward a Theory of Schizophrenia', *Behavioural Science*, Vol. 1, 251–4.

Bhabha, H. K. (1994): *The Location of Culture*. London: Routledge.

Bhebhe, S. (2016): 'Zimbabwean Women in Social Media Spaces: A Critical Analysis of the Potential and Challenges Facing Women in Social Media based Democratic Struggles'. from http://alexmagaisa.com/2016/08/24/zimbabwean-women-in-social-media-spaces-a-critical-analysis-of-the-potential-and-challenges-facing-women-in-social-media-based-democratic-struggles. Accessed 20 May 2015.

Braden, M. (1996): *Female Politicians and the Media*. Lexington: University of Kentucky Press.

Brooks, D. E. and Herbert, L. P. (2006): *Gender, Race, and Media Representation*. Handbook of Gender and Communication, p. 16, 297–317.

Brooks, J. D. (2010): *Assessing the Double Bind: Public Reactions to Displays of Toughness by Male and Female Candidates*. Retrieved from http://themonkeycage.org/wp-content/uploads/2011/06/Deb-J-Brooks-Double-Bind-APSA-DC-2010-2.pdf. Accessed 23 July 2013.

Carter, C. (2011): 'Sex/Gender and the Media: From Sex Roles to Social Construction and Beyond', in K. Ross (ed.) *The Handbook of Gender, Sex and Media*. Oxford: Wiley Blackwell.

Druckman, J. N. (2001): 'The Implications of Framing Effects for Citizen Competence', *Political Behavior*, Vol. 23 (September), 225–56.

Dube, R. (2013). '*Parliamentary Performance and Gender*', http://archive.kubatana.net/docs/demgg/rau_gender_analysis_7th_parliament_1311.pdf. Accessed 12 May 2015.

Durkin, K. (1985a): 'Television and Sex-Role Acquisition: 1', Content. *British Journal of Social Psychology*, Vol. 24, 101–13.

Eagly, A. H. (2007): '"Female Leadership Advantage and Disadvantage: Resolving the Contradictions', *Psychology of Women Quarterly*, Vol. 31, No. 1, 1–12.

Eagly, A. H., Makhijani, M. G. and Klonsky, B. G. (1992): 'Gender and the Evaluation of Leaders: A Meta-analysis', *Psychological Bulletin*, Vol. 111, No. 3, –22.

Eagly, A. H. and Carli, L. L. (2007): 'Through the Labyrinth: Women as Leaders', *Presentation at Harvard Kennedy School*, Vol. 2, No. 5, 09.

Eagly, A. H. and Johnson, B. T. (1990): 'Gender and Leadership Style: A Meta-analysis', *Psychological Bulletin*, Vol. 108, 233–56.

Eagly, A. H. and Karau, S. J. (2002): 'Role Congruity Theory of Prejudice toward Female Leaders', *Psychological Review*, Vol. 109, 573–98.

Eagly, A. H., Johannesen-Schmidt, M. C. and Van Engen, M. (2003): 'Transformational, Transactional, and Laissez-faire Leadership Styles: A Meta-analysis Comparing Women and Men', *Psychological Bulletin*, Vol. 95, 569–91.

Eagly, A. H. and Johannesen-Schmidt, M. C. (2001): 'The Leadership Styles of Women and Men', *Journal of Social Issues*, Vol. 57, No. 4, 781–97.

Eagly, A. H. (2009): 'The His and Hers of Prosocial Behaviour: An Examination of the Social Psychology of Gender', *American Psychologist*, Vol. 64, 644–58.

Eagly, A. H., Wood, W. and Diekman, A. (2000): 'Social Role Theory of Sex Differences and Similarities: A Current Appraisal', in T. Eckes and H. M. Trautner (eds) *The Developmental Social Psychology of Gender*. Mahwah, NJ: Lawrence Erlbaum Associates Publishers, pp. 123–74.

Falk, E. (2008): *Women for President: Media Bias in Eight Campaigns*. Chicago: University of Illinois Press.

Familusi, O. O. (2012): 'African Culture and the status of women: The Yoruba Example', *Journal of Pan African Studies*, Vol. 5, No. 1, 299–313.

Fowler, L. L. and Lawless, J. L. (2009): 'Looking for Sex in All the Wrong Places: Press Coverage and the Electoral Fortunes of Gubernatorial Candidates', *Perspectives on Politics*, Vol. 7 (September), 519–36.

Fridkin, K. K. (1994): 'The Distorted Mirror: Press Coverage of Women Candidates for State-wide Office', in Karen O'Connor, Sarah E. Brewer and Michael Philip Fisher (eds) *Gendering American Politics: Perspectives from the Literature*. New York: Pearson Longman, pp. 203–18.

Garcia-Blanco, I. and Wahl-Jorgensen, K. (2012): 'The Discursive Construction of Women Politicians in the European Press', *Feminist Media Studies*, Vol. 12, No. 3, 421–41.

Glick, P., and Fiske, S. T. (2001): 'Ambivalent Sexism', in M. P. Zanna (ed.) *Advances in Experimental Social Psychology*, Vol. 33. Academic Press, pp. 115–88.

Holt, L. F. (2012): 'Hillary and Barack: Will Atypical Candidates Lead to Atypical Coverage?', *Howard Journal of Communications*, Vol. 23, 272–87.

Irvin, M. (2013): 'Women in TV Broadcast News: Reporters and Sources in Hard News Stories. *The Elon, Journal of Undergraduate Research in Communications*, Vol. 4, No. (1).

Johnstone, D. D. and Swanson, D. H. (2003): 'Undermining Mothers: A Content Analysis of the Representation of Mothers in Magazines', *Mass Communication & Society*, Vol. 6, No. 3, 243–65.

Kahn, K. F. (1992): 'Does Being Male Hel? An Investigation of the Effects of Candidate Gender and Campaign Coverage on Evaluations of U.S. Senate Candidates', *The Journal of Politics*, Vol. 2 (May), 497–517.

Kahn, K. F. (1994): 'The Distorted Mirror: Press Coverage of Women Candidates for State-wide Office', in Karen O'Connor, Sarah E. Brewer and Michael Philip Fisher (eds) *Gendering American Politics: Perspectives from the Literature*. New York: Pearson Longman, pp. 203–18.

Lovenduski, J. (2002): 'Feminizing Politics', *Women: A Cultural Review*, Vol. 13, No. 2, 207–20.

Malcom, S., Hall, P., and Brown, J. (1976): *The Double Bind: The Price of Being a Minority Woman in Science*. Washington, DC: American Association for the Advancement of Science.

Markstedt, H. (2007): *Political Handbags: The Representation of Women Politicians: A Case Study of the Websites and Newspaper Coverage of the Women Candidates in the Labour Party Deputy Leadership Election*. Masters Dissertation. London: London School of Economics and Political Science.

Mashingaidze, T. (2003): 'Review: For better or worse? Women and ZANLA In Zimbabwe's Liberation Struggle'. https://www.ajol.info/index.php/ajcr/article/view/136415.

Mawarire, J. (2009): 'Rethinking Gender Mainstreaming in the Media: Lessons from Zimbabwe Media Coverage of the First Six Months of the Government of National Unity'. http://www.genderlinks.org.za/attachment.php%3Faa_id%3D12172. Accessed 12 April 2014.

Mayer, T. (1999): *Sexing the Nation: Gender Ironies of Nationalism*. London: Routledge, pp. 1–25

Meeks, L. (2012): 'Is She 'Man Enough'? Women Candidates, Executive Political Offices, and News Coverage', *Journal of Communication*, Vol. 62, 175–93.

Morna, C. L. (2002): 'Promoting Gender Equality in and through the Media. A Southern Africa Case Study'. *United Nations Divisions for the Advancement of Women, DAW*. http://www.un.org/womenwatch/daw/egm/media2002/reports/EP5Morna.PDF.

Moscovici, S. (2000): *Social Representations. Explorations in Social Psychology*. Cambridge: Polity Press.

Okwemba, A. (2013): *Women in Political News Study*. Nairobi: Africa Woman and Child Feature Service.

Pantti, M. (2006): *Literary Review for the Project Gender, Politics and Media: Challenging Stereotypes, Promoting Diversity, Strengthening Equality, and Portraying Politics*. http://www.wunrn.com/news/2006/12_25_05/123005_europe_gender.htm. Accessed 15 July 2013.

Parichi, M. (2017): The Representation of Female Politicians in Zimbabwean print media: 2000-2008. A Ph.D thesis presented at UNISA.

Parpart, J. L. (2011): 'Gender, Patriarchy and development in Africa: The Zimbabwean Case', in V. M. Moghadam (ed.) *Patriarchy and Development: Women's Positions at the End of the Twentieth Century*.

Podsakoff, P. M., S. B MacKenzie, J. B. Paine, and D. G. Bachrach (2000): 'Organizational Citizenship Behaviors', *A Critical Review of the Theoretical and Empirical Literature and Suggestions for Future Research Journal of Management*, Vol. 26, No. 3, 513–63

Ross, K. (2002): *Women, Politics, Media: Uneasy Relations in Comparative Perspective*. Cresskill, NJ: Hampton Press.

Ryan, K. (2013): 'The Media's War on Women: Gendered Coverage of Female Candidates. All Politics is Local', conference paper at Walsh University in Canton, Ohio.

Sools, A. M., Van Engen, M. L. and Baerveldt, C. C. (2007): 'Gendered Career-making Practices: On 'doing ambition' or How Managers Discursively Position themselves in a Multinational Corporation', *Journal Of Occupational & Organizational Psychology*, Vol. 80, No. 3, 413–35.

Primary sources

Kwayedza newspaper article, 13–21 August.

Kwayedza newspaper article, Mbudzi 7–13 November 2008, p. 9

Kwayedza newspaper article, 4–10 December, p. 9.

Kwayedza newspaper article, 22–28 August, p. 8.

Kwayedza newspaper article, kukadzi 4–10 February, p. 6.

Kwayedza newspaper article, 14–20 January 2005.

Financial Gazette newspaper, 27 August–2 September 2010.

Financial Gazette, 1–7 June 2000.

Financial Gazette, 13–19 January 2005.
Financial Gazette, 25–31 July 2002.
Financial Gazette, 22–28 May 2002.
Financial Gazette, 5–11 January 2005.
Financial Gazette, 1–7 June 2000.
The Standard, 12–18 February 2005.
The Standard, 23–29 July 2000.
The Standard, 13–19 February 2005.
The Standard, 30–6 April 2005.
The Standard, 07–13 February 2005.
Daily News, 21 October 2014.
New Zimbabwe.com (accessed 11 December 2009).
Herald 29 January 2015

3

Candidate training programmes in Africa – A waste of resources or pedagogies of the oppressed? Experiences from Letsema training workshops in Botswana (2013–19)

Sethunya Tshepho Mosime and Maude Dikobe

Introduction: Questioning candidate training programmes in Africa

Candidate training workshops and programmes for women done in partnership with local and international organization have become a big phenomenon across the world, including Africa. Botswana has not been left out. Although one of Africa's strongest democracy, Botswana is one of the lowest in the representation of women in political office, going against the trend where Africa is one of the leading continents in the numbers of women in political office. After over three decades of training workshops for women in politics, albeit sporadic, intermittent and uncoordinated, it appears they have failed to help increase number of women contesting for and winning political seats. The numbers of women in parliament have in fact dwindled between 1999 and 2019, despite these training initiatives. This has led some critics, especially from the United States, to dismiss these candidate training workshops. They argue that they do not make sense in many contexts outside the United States, where there is no opportunity for candidates to enter the elections through self-nomination. In most countries where these training workshops are rolled out, it is political party structures that nominate candidates, and they remain patriarchal and male-dominated, closing out women, no matter how well trained.

According to this school of thought, no amount of spending on these workshops will make any difference in terms of increasing the number of women in political seats, because trainings are said to miss the mark by asking the wrong question: of why women do not step forward, rather than *why parties do not choose women.* Jennifer Piscopo (2018) among others dismisses candidate training programmes because she argues that they do not address the institutional, organizational and structural barriers that limit women's access to elected offices.

To reflect on whether training workshops for women in politics have been an exercise in futility, in this chapter, the authors share experiences from a candidate training initiative for Botswana women done by Letsema between 2013 and 2019. Together with several others, the authors co-founded the Letsema Resource Support for Botswana Women in Politics. The Letsema experience shows that, as critics of candidate training workshops correctly observe, it is not true that women do not stand for political office because they lack confidence and therefore all they need is 'empowerment'. It became evident during the Letsema training workshops that in fact there was more to learn from local women in politics. As much as it is extremely important to have more women take up political office, there is a danger in measuring women's political participation only in terms of numbers of women occupying political seats. Women occupy political party spaces for more than the promise of a seat; they use the space to build their political-social capital and to enhance their other *strategic life choices.*

Women and political participation in Botswana

In 1995, when Botswana women activists came back from the Beijing Platform for Action conference, the mood was upbeat, with a clear sense that women in Botswana would become a force to reckon with. They came back determined to achieve the objectives of the Beijing Platform of Action; to build a critical mass of women leaders, executives and managers in strategic decision-making positions, governments would have to commit to at least 30 per cent of the parliamentary seats being reserved for women. This became the basis for the demand by gender activists through the Southern African Development Community (SADC) Protocol of Gender and Development. The Protocol stipulated that by 2015, women with the use of the Affirmative Action clause hold at least 50 per cent of all decision-making positions in the public and private sectors where necessary. The Botswana government refused to sign the Protocol and only conceded to signing the revised Protocol of 2016 which was less prescriptive.

Low numbers of women in political office coupled with dwindling donor support for women's organizations as Botswana had become a middle income country led to the emergence of a narrative that Botswana women did not support each other and in fact had a 'pull her down' syndrome or that the radical feminism movement of the 1990s had past its sell-by date. The media particularly celebrated the eminent 'death' of feminism and popularized the notion of a post-feminist era. A local Botswana newspaper, *The Sunday Standard*, declared in 2014 that the women's movement in Botswana was 'greying and shrinking' (*Sunday Standard 2014*).

Because there are no special quotas for women in Botswana, the number of women in parliament has only been increased through special election by former presidents, especially Festus Mogae (1998–2008). While this affirmative action was a welcome development, it did not do justice to women's representation, as the highest number of women brought into politics as specially elected has only been two out of the four provided for by the Constitution.

Lessons from other African countries with constitutional quotas for women have proved that, simply allocating women some seats does not necessarily address the institutional, organizational and structural barriers that limit women's access, not just to elected offices, but also to political voice. Why then do women remain very actively in party politics that at first glance have nothing for them? This was the main lesson that Letsema training workshops revealed about Botswana women in politics – that using the party space, they took advantage of every available opportunity, including candidate training workshops.

A critique of women's 'empowerment' approaches

The term empowerment has been used widely in the research on women and politics. Like everywhere across the Third World, empowerment of women has become a buzzword, specifically following the World Population Conference in Cairo in 1994, and the United Nations Conference on Women in Beijing in 1995. It raised expectations that it would result in the development of appropriate policy and practice aimed at women's empowerment and gender equality (Rowlands 1998). It was popularized by the United Nations Development Programme (UNDP) annual publication, the Human Development Report, and progress towards it came to be measured using the Gender Empowerment Measure (GEM). From that point, agendas towards empowerment of women soared to the top of the development agenda, philanthropic efforts of big businesses, and came to be energetically promoted by myriad of civil society organizations (Cornwall and Anyidoho 2010). According to Cornwall and Anyidoho (2010), it seemed as if everyone could find something in the term that resonated with the world as they would like to see it.

However, it would soon become apparent that the 'power' had been removed from the centre of the concept, and as Cornwall and Anyidoho

(2010) put it, all that was left was *em-ment,* empowerment with the power taken out, which in the end does not help the women realize their abilities or potential, but disenfranchise them instead. By the mid-2000s, there was a growing discontent about the notion, best expressed by Batliwala (2007) who contends that of all the buzzwords that have entered the development lexicon in the past thirty years, *empowerment* is probably the most widely used and abused. While the one side of the critique of women's empowerment focuses on Western development actors and feminists from the West, the other focused on the failure on the part of African states to devote budgets and audits to their gender-equality rhetoric.

For postmodern feminists, the problem with the notion was that it depended on grand narratives such as the idea of the 'nation' as a unified entity. Postmodern feminists called for a more nuanced appreciation of the fact that women's experiences can be better articulated by paying attention to context, history and diverse identities (Shohat 1997). The legal and regulatory measures of empowerment were found to perpetuate privilege for women in higher educational and income levels because of its emphasis on: (i) the proportion of seats held by women in national parliaments; (ii) the percentage of women in economic decision-making positions, including administrative and managerial positions, as well as professional and technical occupations; and (iii) the female share of income (Beteta 2006).

From a post-colonial critique of Western feminism, the notion of 'empowerment' was found so problematic that it needed to either be deepened (Giles 2006) or abandoned. In the attempt to 'deepen' empowerment, participatory practices came to be seen as the panacea for reversing the 'top down' approaches of many development initiatives. By the mid-2000s, there was an emerging worry of 'participation as the new tyranny' (Giles 2006). Those that found it necessary to abandon it suggested it had become something of a 'white women's burden', describing what they saw as careerism on the part of white women feminists and enhancing of the power of the pro-Western economic elite in the Third World at the expense of the poor (Jawad and Ali 2011).

Shelley Budgeon (2011) among others welcomed the promise of the third wave of feminism to react to the failure of structural approaches to feminism by claiming 'allowing' women to develop their relationship to feminism in ways that are more relevant to the contradictions which characterize their lives. Led by post-colonial feminist thinkers, the 'third wave' of feminism emphasized the need to decolonize feminism in post-colonial societies and approach questions of gender equality not as a universal struggle that affects all women the same way, and also take into account the intersection between gender inequality, race and class. As such, women are affected by inequalities in very specific ways that lend them in different struggles and outcomes in the journey towards gender equality. While opening space for more nuanced definitions of feminisms, this trend was not without its limitations and contradictions. Despite all its attempts to provide analytical frameworks that put women's agency at the centre of feminist critique, third wave feminism maintained the *status quo* where feminism remained a largely academic and educated middle classes undertaking, without much traction in popular discourse. In Africa, feminists remained antagonized using 'culture' and 'religion', even as African feminists like Ifi Amadiume (1987) and Oyeronke Oyewumi (1997), among others, provided compelling evidence that gender binaries taken for granted in Western societies are not necessarily a traditional African point of reference and that the juxtaposition of men against women is part of the colonial legacy.

Admittedly, the backlash against third wave of feminism was inevitable following its undeniable success in effecting legal reforms and increasing women's spaces for democratic participation. Governments became less responsive to gender-equality demands. By 2013, Ann Stewart was asking if African women should give up on the state, because what could seem like very basic demands by African women from the state was often met with great public controversy and resistance. She further gave examples of four women from four different African countries, including Unity Dow from Botswana, on how they met resistance from the state asking for as little as permission to bury a husband, to sell land, extending one's citizenship to children as their mother, and protection from family patriarchs that demanded compensation from partners of grown daughters choosing to get pregnant (Stewart 1996).

Letsema approach to candidate training: Training workshops as pedagogies of the oppressed

Letsema to date has provided training for more than 300 women in Botswana's various political parties, including political candidates over the last five years. The objective of Letsema was to pull together available human and financial resources to train women from all the different parties who are contesting for political office, or any party structures, even if they have not yet pronounced an aspiration to run for office at some point in their lives. The insert in Figure 3.1 was part of Letsema's call to sensitize and call upon Botswana to vote for women candidates who were running for positions as parliamentarians for the 2019 elections. The heading of the insert says, '*Tlhopha Mosadi, Palamente le khansele di thata ka basadi ba tsone.*' Translated into English, it means 'vote for a woman, because parliaments and local government councils are stronger with women representation'.

Figure 3.1 '*Tlhopha Mosadi*'.

Rather naively, the founders of Letsema had initially taken the same instrumentalist approach to training of women in politics, expecting their efforts to cause an increase in the number of female candidates in the 2019 general elections. The concern about the efficacy of workshops in bringing about desired change was also expressed during some of the Letsema training workshops. The argument is often that women politicians in Botswana have undergone numerous training workshops over the years yet are still lagging behind in occupying positions of power. Five years of working with grassroots women in politics was to completely transform the thinking around efficacy of these workshops that women saw their role as more than occupying particular offices, but also about occupying the wider political spaces as citizens.

During the five years of engagement with women, it became necessary to reappraise the initial thinking that Letsema would 'empower' women and gear them up for political office. It became to approach women's empowerment in the manner that has long been proposed by Naila Kabeer, that empowerment must be understood as the ability to make *strategic life choices* through an interplay among access to resources, ability to exercise agency and with very clear achievements or outcomes even in the face of opposition, dissent and resistance from others (Kabeer 1999). Letsema extended women's access to other women that would otherwise simply be perceived as opponents.

Lessons from the training workshops showed that women joined and stayed in political parties more than just to contest for political leadership. Wherever possible, they use the space to meet their own strategic life choices and to expand their alliances and networks in ways that empower them to better access resources and maximize achievements within a very patriarchal space. Some of the participants at the training workshops shared that as some of the beneficiaries of Letsema training workshops they were able to approach their party politics through an intersectional framework that enabled them to change party affiliation when necessary, employing the use of social media groups and networks to mobilize any resources they need and share with the wider political community. Another participant from a farming background shared how she simultaneously takes up party politics and sustains her agricultural project because she has come to master the art of accessing government grants and even helps youth in her area to write proposals to acquire land and accesses other schemes offered by the government. As an entrepreneur, and an aspiring politician, she also understands the power of constantly upgrading her business while sharing knowledge and cultivating strategic networks on different fronts. While we cannot claim that the training workshops make the women who they are, the workshops definitely reveal why they stay in party politics. The workshops provided a platform for the participants to expand their discursive communities and communities of action, as they connect across parties and move beyond partisan politics.

Granted that women's participation in training workshops did not directly translate into increased numbers of women in parliament. The question then is: what can we learn through these training workshops in terms of why women stay very active in party politics when they know it is pointless unless the electoral laws of their countries are changed so that self-nomination or quotas are introduced? In this book chapter, we propose the need to reconsider or revisit how we conceptualize a 'political' candidate and look beyond seats so that we are able to understand women's participation in politics as more than just becoming 'candidates'. In this way, rather than dismissing training programmes for women in politics simply on the technicality that they may not run and win as candidates, we see political education not only as a tool to help women to enter the political space for candidacy. More importantly, these have expanded the otherwise limited platforms for women to share experiences, expand their networks and occupy an intersectional space where belonging to political parties simultaneously unlocked opportunities for women.

Lil M. Kim has warned against the danger of placing emphasis on one variable when in fact issues are more intersecting and complex in her paper titled 'I Was [So] Busy Fighting Racism That I Didn't Even Know I Was Being Oppressed as a Woman!' (Kim 2001). Although her comment calls for an intersectional approach to gender and race among women of colour in the United States, the approach can be used to gain an insight into the multi-layered oppression experienced by women in other cultures. To focus on one outcome such as the number of women occupying political seats can only render an incomplete understanding of the realities of women's participation in party politics. The same intersectionality is required for a deeper understanding of what else political party participation represents and makes possible for women beyond numbers as a space for agentic negotiation of access to party decision-making processes, resources, lobbying, easier access to social grant-making processes, access to land and small stock farming, business opportunities, and sometimes even direct monetary support by the politician they lend their support, especially in times of bereavements. We thus need to look into pedagogies of women, who, in spite of efforts by their patriarchal political parties to oppress them, have continued to occupy the political party space and unlock some value, no matter how seemingly small.

The Letsema methodologies: Song, social media, professional networks and a feminist participatory action approach

Letsema training workshops combine song, storytelling, social media and professional expertise. For financial and human resource mobilization, we utilize our professional networks who often share their expertise for free. Premised on Feminist Participatory Action Research (PFAR), we take a decidedly feminist approach. Caitlin Cahill et al. (2010) have called Participatory Action Research a 'Feminist Praxis of Critical Hope' for its potential to bring actors together in solidarity and negotiation through working with rather than for our participant (Cahill et al. 2010). We use a hybrid of typical political training content and local methodologies. Participants are exposed to a wide range of experts, activists and practitioners who cover topics ranging from campaign strategies, team building, social and traditional media strategy, using social media as a campaign tool, the *Elevator Speech* to assist them make their message clearer, profiling and branding themselves, profiling and knowing their constituencies, personal and social etiquette as well as designing one's action plan.

Feminist Participatory Action Research (PFAR) requires not only a strong message about the importance of equal representation of genders in politics, but also highly values participants' own ways of knowing and doing. Central to our engagement with participants is the feminist slogan that *the personal is political*, first popularized by Carol Hanisch in the 1970s who argued that many personal experiences (particularly those of women) can be traced to one's location within a system of power relations. Hanisch insisted that 'women are messed over, not messed up! We need to change the objective conditions, not adjust to them' (Hanisch 1969). It is thus crucial that the participants at Letsema trainings position themselves within the Botswana political culture as both a resource and a constraint, but first as women and agents of change.

Typically, our training workshops start with song and end with song. In Africa, song is very central to political expression and action. Women singing in political parties is a highly contested practice within feminist discourses. It has come to be highly criticized as one of the ways in which political 'gender roles' have come to be inscribed in African politics, where women are seen as praise singers for male politicians while their own access to political decision making is constrained (Gilman 2001). However, it has also been recognized that song remains a uniquely powerful mode of expression for African women (Hogan 2019). Through song, a mood is created of a common struggle and common purpose.

> 'Mma Mmati, mpelegele ngwana yo kea lema …
> Ke lema kele nosi!
> Wa mpona ke a lema,
> Ke lema kele nosi!'

The lyrics above are from a folksong that has organically become the signature song for Letsema workshops. It is a plaintive song of a woman carrying a baby on her back while ploughing seeds using a hoe with no help. She cries out to a sister, *mma mmati*, to come to her aid and help her with the child. Letsema in Setswana means the ploughing season, during which farmers usually organize themselves into teams and rotate around each other's fields, working together to increase their productivity. Letsema is thus embedded in a solidarity philosophy of care of women lifting each other up as women. We sing many other songs throughout the training workshops as the content changes. On the Letsema Facebook page, Women in Politics Botswana, one such captivating moment was captured during one of the trainings, where one woman broke into a song and others joined her (Women in Politics: Botswana 2016).

One of the earliest problems identified by women in the initial workshops was their lack of visibility, despite the fact that they had a lot to say and share – a lack of equal platforms to be heard and share in their different political parties still left a lot to be desired. Yet, one of the most profound experiences that the Letsema methodology has unearthed is that many women in Botswana's politics are unsung sheroes, often dismissed solely on the roles they play at major political party events. While in actual fact little is known of their daily community-building efforts of widening access to education, health and available albeit limited economic opportunities and government programmes. For this reason, sharing the women's stories using social media contributes towards making women leaders both visible and audible. With their permission, but without flouting their political party's campaign regulations, we have helped put some on the country's political map through Facebook.

In terms of resource mobilization for the training workshops, professional networking has become a key strategy for Letsema, all the time using our professional and social networks to pull together both soft skills and financial help where necessary. Our training workshops with the University of Delaware Mandela Washington Fellow and with Friedrich Ebert Stiftung are such examples.

Feminist Participatory Action Research also insists on cultivating safe spaces where participants can 'take a break' from the often exclusionary and oppressive socio-political environments. However, it is widely accepted that 'a safe space is never completely safe' bringing together political opponents into one space required an intentional cultivation of our workshops as safe spaces, in the manner described by the Roestone collective 'as a site for negotiating difference and challenging oppression' (The Roestone Collective 2014). At the beginning of the workshops, a substantial amount to time was allocated to 'getting to know each other', through the use of an icebreaker around the slogan Letsema adopted, *'First I am a Woman ...',* before they proceed to introduce themselves along political party lines. As the participants come from different classes, age groups and educational backgrounds, we minimized this problem by training in both Setswana and English.

Letsema growing from a US-funded political training consultancy to a home-grown strategic local and international resource mobilization and sharing network

In October 2013, Sethunya Mosime, co-author of this chapter and co-founder of Letsema, was approached by the US-based National Democratic Institute (NDI) Program Manager for southern Africa to serve as a fifteen-day short-term consultant on their new women's political participation programme targeted at Botswana women in politics. NDI was already at that time working in more than sixty countries, 'creating programs that are specifically tailored to women'. NDI's experience in Botswana reached as far back as 1989, when the Institute observed parliamentary elections and made recommendations to the election commission and political parties on ways to increase voter participation. NDI was also part of a regional programme from 2006 to 2010, where it assessed barriers to women's participation in political parties of Botswana. The consultant had to be engaged as soon as possible as the 2013 programme was ending in November of the same year, and this was already mid-October. The consultant would work closely with Botswana-based civil society organizations and leaders focused on gender to recruit members for an executive board to lead a coalition focused on supporting an increase in the number of women elected into office in Botswana. NDI committed to providing any technical assistance as identified by civil society and women in politics in areas that were more generic such as campaign budgeting, developing a fundraising strategy, sharing experiences and preparing a pre-election work plan. The consultant was also to collaborate with political parties to ensure civil society representation at multi-sectoral summit, locally known as *pitso* to build support for greater women's political participation. Inasmuch as the TORs would resemble that of many other similar training workshops across the world, the fact that local partners had more input on content and the choice of resource persons discounted the dismissal of these training workshops as mere copy and paste of content that is irrelevant to local contexts, as sceptics claim. This approach encouraged participation and ownership of the programme by the participants and could become part of existing effective political trainings that adopt bottom-up approach in order to empower women in politics to use the skills acquired not only in politics but in other areas as well. The lead consultant was also at liberty to work with local experts and activists to draw a locally responsive training programme. She set about putting together a working group including at the time, the Chairperson of the University of Botswana Gender Policy and Programmes Policy (GPPC), a representative from the oldest women's rights organization, Emang Basadi, the Director of the Gender Affairs Department and the Director of the NDI South Africa office. A local political analyst and a young economist who was to later become the younger Minister of Trade and Industry were also brought in to help with logistics, branding and contact with political party structures. Although initially 'American' donor funded, the project did not receive any more funding beyond the fifteen-day consultancy period, stretched over a five-month period. Soon after the initial consultation funded by the NDI, the initiative fell on the local working group to fundraise and make strategic alliances with different other local and international partners. What follows are the encounters between Letsema and Botswana women in politics, and the process of cutting off its umbilical cord from its American kick-start.

Using experiences and stories of women and politics as the foundation of Letsema's mission statement

Right from the beginning, NDI had supported all efforts to grow an organic local support for Botswana women in politics. The process was to be inclusive and consultative of Botswana-based civil society organizations, female leaders of corporate organizations and women's rights organizations. The first Breakfast Consultation was held on the 4 February 2014 with Botswana Business Community and Civil Society Organisations to start up the dialogue on how to build a coalition that would support and help increase the number of women elected into political office in Botswana. It attracted industry leaders in an array of fields from business, banking, academia, finance, women's rights groups, journalist and the NGO community.

At this first meeting, we ensured that the way forward would be informed by and responsive to local needs. Right from the start, the local team customized the TORs to the local context, and so, while the financial and technical support was provided by a US-based organization, the needs assessment for training were shaped by local partners, especially women. The specific history and context of women and politics was to become the basis of the training. The second consultation meeting, held on 24 February 2014, drew from local expertise and activists. For example, the then director of the Botswana Council of Non-Governmental Organisations (BOCONGO) guided the nascent women in politics support coalition on possible strategic alliances within the NGO community. One of the leading gender activists provided insights from the regional Southern African Development Community's SADC Gender Barometer Emang Basadi Women's Association, the women's human rights organization formally established in 1986 shared lessons learnt in their over thirty years of existence as one of the pioneering women's movement groups in the country, also representing the defunct All Parties Women's Caucus. The authors of this chapter provided the background research on gender and politics in Botswana and proposed possible models for the formation of the women in politics fund. This was to ensure that the technical support provided by NDI responded to actual or tangible needs on the ground identified by local women and movement builders.

In March 2014, NDI brought in Ambassador Meryl Frank from the United States and Xolisa Sibeko, director of the NDI South Africa office, to provide technical training support workshop on 'Strengthening Women Leaders in Botswana'. Ambassador Frank was former mayor of Highland Park and at the time serving as ambassador to the United Nations Commission on the Status of Women. She was also to guide with strategic planning and to hold workshops with different stakeholders in the political party landscape in Botswana. Some of the topics covered included how to define mission, goals and objectives; establishing and promoting a group identity; using regional and international gender equality standards to strengthen image; models for campaign funding and support for women candidates.

Storytelling is a big part of information sharing in many African cultures and even within politics, sharing stories has proved to be invaluable towards shaping the kind of support women in politics would need. To contextualize the content and make it relevant to Botswana, the American trainer had to listen to stories of local struggles and lessons women in Botswana had learnt from their previous efforts, as a collective and within their various political parties. One story that was fascinating was around the existence of a Botswana Women's Political Caucus. Some of the women that have been in its structures claimed it still existed while many others declared it long dead. Formed in the mid-1990s, the last election of the committee of the Caucus had been in 2010. Although the elected candidates seemed to be a fair representation of all the parties, by 2014 when Letsema met with women from the different parties, though some of the women still identified themselves as members of the Caucus, the majority agreed that it had ceased to exist. The reasons advanced for its collapse were that there was a perception that the ruling Botswana Democratic Party (BDP) wanted to control the Caucus rather than seeing it as a forum for equal partners.

Interestingly, at the 2010 Caucus elections, the then newly elected President Moggie Mbaakanyi had echoed the very same concerns that emerged at this March 2014 workshop; that poverty and a lack of resources were the main challenge faced by women in politics; and the fact that the male-dominated parties were not committed to the empowerment of women through political funding. Some of the political parties only had women's quota systems only on paper and not in practice. She had wanted to use her role to push for amendment of the electoral laws to do away with the *first-past-the-post* system and introduce quotas for women (Mmegionline 2010). As argued, putting in quotas without change of constitution was a nonstarter.

One interesting story shared by a veteran woman politician, Mrs Binkie Kerileng was of thirty years of her efforts trying to push for more women in labour unions and the two political parties she had been a member of, showing just how slow change was. She had been a long-time member of the ruling BDP and now the treasurer of the then three-year-old splinter party from the BDP – the Botswana Movement for Democracy (BMD). At both parties, she has always been at the forefront of advocating for inclusion of women in key positions of leadership since the party's formation. She was very instrumental in ensuring that five Central Committee membership positions were reserved exclusively for women. At the time of this training workshop, they had seven women in a Central Committee of twenty-two in the BMD. She believed they could do better than that. Sharing her experiences, Kerileng revealed that her fight for women's participation started in the labour movement and continued in politics. She was somewhat disappointed that there were no satisfactory results after some thirty years of her being at the centre of this fight. At one point Kerileng had served at local government level as local government Councillor and was of the opinion that women make better councillors than men because they tend to know their communities better. She built enduring relationships with her constituents to the extent that they still address her as 'Councillor' long after she left that position.

With this history as a backdrop of the new effort to create a coalition that would provide support for all women across the party lines, the meeting proceeded to constructing the mission statement. The local women brainstormed several ideas of what should be reflected in the organization's mission statement. Words and phrases such as sustainable, active participation, empowerment, change, equality, development, advocacy, security, opportunity, life-long, intergenerational, justice and facility were suggested. Among the issues that were raised in the process of constructing the mission statement was the intergenerational factor. In a participatory and open dialogue, Ambassador Frank was also able to share her own experiences regarding ageism in politics in the United States, where women who are past child-bearing age were often dismissed as too old, and yet many had much to offer having spent their lives building networks and now having time at their disposal to share this wealth of knowledge. This resonated with some of the older women and they shared their own experiences of ageism, and opened the meeting to the realization that women often experienced similar challenges across economic and geographical locations. The gathering arrived at a final mission statement after several configurations. What resulted was the following phrase: '_____ is a non-partisan organisation dedicated to empowerment of women in politics by facilitating effective leadership with necessary resources and information.'

With the mission statement agreed, the group set the goals for the coalition, once again tailoring them to local needs. The participants engaged at length on what should shape the goals. *Resources* were unanimously agreed to be key; however, it was made categorically clear that support with resources was not only limited to money. In-kind resources were also included. These could include expertise, printing or internet access and providing a platform for dialogue. Expertise or technical assistance could include, but not limited to, research, policy briefing, campaign management and etiquette. Financial resources were also to be provided where available and needed.

More than just increasing the numbers of women in local government and parliamentary seats, women demanded *effective leadership*. Participants at the workshop were of the view that once elected to political office, women should not rest on their laurels and risk not getting re-elected but ought to adhere to principles of effective leadership. Therefore, the organization could assist clients by equipping them with necessary skills to uphold the standards of delivery (follow through), commitment, accountability responsiveness and helping them to move an agenda forward as incumbents. It was resolved that the coalition would target women of all ages to ensure it was *intergenerational* across local and national political contests, party affiliates and the non-aligned. The coalition would not only support women that had won elections but would also pay attention to potential candidates and potential supporters. *Information* production, sharing and archiving was also seen as priority, to ensure that women in politics had easy access to all the necessary information on global trends and major local issues, policy and research, rules, regulations and laws government the political environment in which they operate. It was agreed that, in order to better support women vying for political leadership at local and national level, that we focus on the following; creating a database for women who were active in politics; provision of public education on women in politics; mobilizing resources necessary for political campaigns; and to improve women's visibility in politics and promoting effective leadership, accountability and responsiveness. At the end of the workshop, Letsema was adopted as the local name for the coalition to provide resource support for Botswana women in politics. Letsema directly translates to the ploughing season, but it also extends to the common practice among local subsistence farmers to come together as a team and take turns to work on each other's farms. This was found to contain the central idea of sharing resources, especially skills and experiences.

Once the roadmap for the coalition was drawn in consultation with both partisan and non-partisan stakeholders, the next logical step was to bring the leadership of the political parties on board. Initial discussions were held with leaders of Botswana Democratic Party (BDP), Botswana Movement for Democracy (BMD), Botswana National Front (BNF) and Botswana Congress Party (BCP) to secure buy-in for participation in the programme. In terms of training women candidates, Letsema coordinated an interactive strategy session on campaign skills-building, including fundraising, for women preparing to run as candidates in 2014 from the targeted political parties. A *Pitso* or summit was also organized to bring together women candidates and civil society representatives to engage political, social and business leaders. The aim was to build a sustainable coalition, with a governing board, to support women candidates and hopefully see an increase in the number of women in elected office in Botswana.

Cutting the umbilical cord: Letsema forging strategic partnerships beyond the NDI

For the next five years, Letsema Resource Support for Women in Politics, although not an officially registered organization, came to be one of the leading inclusive training projects for women within party politics, often bringing them together with other women and men outside party politics – from the academy to sex workers, women in agriculture and corporate institutions. By the seventy-second session of the Committee on the Elimination of Discrimination against Women (CEDAW) on 18 February–8 March 2019, the Botswana government acknowledged the tremendous work of Letsema in their replies to the list of issues for consideration under Article 18 of the Convention. In the fourth periodic report of Botswana, on the questions of women's 'participation in political and public life', the reply from Botswana was that:

Letsema on the other hand offers training of women in politics, in partnership with development partners such as the British High Commission in Botswana; Westminster Foundation for Democracy and the Botswana Resource Support for Women in Politics. The Organisation supports women that are either in or wish to enter politics across all parties by providing the following: Expertise and technical assistance; In-kind services such as printing, campaign photography or video; Vouchers for services or goods; Fora and venues to improve women's visibility and public exposure; Data-base of information of interest to women in politics; Public education on women's role in politics; and Advocacy on policy to enhance women's political participation. (Replies of Botswana to the list of issues to the Committee on the Elimination of Discrimination against Women, Seventy-second session, 18 February–8 March 2019)

Letsema and Democracy and Human Rights Grant (DHR): Making 2014 women parliamentary candidates visible

As the second quarter of 2014 began, and the October elections drawing closer, Letsema had an important mission statement but no seed money. We immediately needed to fund raise and we applied for US$900 from the US Democracy and Human Rights Grant (DHR) in March 2014. Small as the amount was, we achieved a lot. We trained and profiled a small number of female candidates across all parties as they prepared for the 2014 Botswana General Election. Central to this initiative was that we work closely with the party leadership across all parties. The training included campaign finance budgeting, use of social media and traditional media, handling media interviews and personal branding. For the last two weeks before the general elections, Letsema with the support of the editor of one of the local newspapers ran a poster with all the parliamentary female candidates across the political parties. For many of them, it was a first time that their picture appears on print media. The only woman from the opposition who won a parliamentary seat, the late Same Bathobakae, MP for Tlokweng constituency, credited the Letsema training and media support for her success.

In addition, the women appreciated the psychosocial support that Letsema organized after the elections for those that had lost elections. Mrs Ntombie Setshwaelo, a veteran women's rights champion, but also a counsellor, spoke to them about the trauma of losing an election. They highly appreciated that their pain was validated and acknowledged, something they had not had the chance to have within their different political parties. They also appreciated the kingship of suffering as they reflected on the gender inequalities they experience in their respective parties. Most of them came out of the 2014 general elections feeling betrayed, even by their own campaign teams. Votes went to those that paid voters to take snapshots of their ballot papers as proof that they voted for them.

Most importantly, the women appreciated Letsema as a concept – the idea of sharing experiences and ideas without seeking 'funding' or having to be formally registered. This resonated with their own *motshelo* rotating credit system, where mostly women, but increasingly men, put together money towards projects of each member, one at a time. The realization that much of the skills they needed were already available within their communities, and that they were also a resource, shifted the discourse from waiting for a big benefactor to sharing and caring as critical skills in politics. This innate agency was one of the forces that brought the women together even after the training was over.

Training inclusive of collective self-care: Letsema in partnership with the Westminster Foundation for Democracy (WFD)

The traction Letsema has been able to create with the support of NDI and the DHR grant had sparked a lot of interest in Letsema among local women and development partners outside party politics. Although Kenewendo left Letsema, she had put out word about the work Letsema was doing and another important networking partnership was born, between Letsema and the Westminster Foundation for Democracy (WFD) through Nomsa Thema, then consular officer but also gender activist working for the British High Commission in Botswana. Thema invited Letsema to some of their own training workshop, and the conversation ushered in yet another collaboration. She raised funding from WFD and in 2016 we designed a training programme informed by our field experience and with a completely local team of experts and activists 'donating' their soft skills. This time we intended to get a few women from each of the fifty-seven constituencies in Botswana who had some role in the party, even if it was at ward level. Letsema provided training free of charge and the funds from WFD were mainly used to provide transport, food and accommodation. We replicated six two-day training workshops spread over four months, reaching a total of about 150 women across the country.

Collective self-care was at the centre of this particular initiative. Not only did we raise enough funds to pay for venues and resources, but we also ensured that the weekend stay was for the women a comfortable retreat away from their taxing daily struggles trying to make ends meet and also advancing their party agendas. For many women that attended the training, it was the first time that they shared a room with their political opponents. Rather than coming out as shy, reserved and lacking confidence, which is often said to be the reason women are 'scared' of political office, the women came across as self-assured, confident and very experienced in politics. All of them had been part of a losing or winning campaign team. They bore the scars from the battles for political power that they wore proudly. They were confident that none of the members of parliament would have made it without strong women in their campaign teams. While they acknowledged the patriarchal constraints they faced in their daily lives at their home and within parties, women in politics had negotiated some leg room to participate in all party activities, and there was no turning back until the whole body was in.

One of them, then thirty-six years old, Virginia Ganetsang of the BDP representing Mahalapye East shared her goal as becoming a councillor and parliament representative for her constituency someday. She also dreamt of improving the lives of women and youth through jobs creation. She looks up to the first President of the Republic, Sir Seretse Khama, and the first-ever female member of parliament in Botswana, Dr Chiepe, who became an MP from 1974 to the late 1990s. Another participant, Amantle Moeti, then twenty-nine and in BMD was representing Gaborone Bonnington North. Moeti said that the training she received from Letsema motivated her to run for a position yet to be revealed. Moeti was later to quit the UDC and she and other members started a new party, the Alliance for Progressive, and contested for a parliamentary seat. She was passionate about tackling issues of teenage pregnancies, drug abuse and prostitution in her community. Then fifty-seven years old, Thedila Mpotokwane of the BDP representing Jwaneng joined politics specifically to help empower single and young parents with parenting skills. Some of the participants were as young as twenty-three years old Lesedi Aobakwe Keagoletse of the Botswana National Front, who was representing Molepolole North. Keagoletse felt it was her duty to be a positive representative of both youth people and women in politics. Even if in the opposition, many of the younger women looked up to women that had made it in the ruling party such as Dr Chiepe for being the first woman government minister. She was also inspired by Dr Margaret Nasha, then speaker of the National Assembly, for being a go-getter and speaking up her mind on issues she felt mattered even when it was taboo to do so. Overall, their goal was to keep growing in influence in their different political parties by 2019.

Letsema in partnership with University of Delaware Mandela Washington Fellow Lame Olebile – your political net worth is your professional networks

Early in 2017, Lame Olebile, an alumnus of a University of Botswana Young Women's Leadership project, approached Letsema, with the spirit of 'sharing is caring'. Olebile was a 2016 University of Delaware Mandela Washington Fellow, and as part of the fellowship benefit, she applied for and received a reciprocal exchange award to host training in Botswana. During the fellowship, she has met Latisha 'Tish' Bracy, campaign manager for the general election for US Representative, Lisa Blunt Rochester, who was elected in 2016 as the first-ever female and African American Representative from Delaware. Olebile got inspired by how women in the Coalition of 100 Black Women were organizing to get their issues on the agenda, which Tish was a part of. In May 2017, Tish came to Botswana, invited through the partnership among the Botswana YALI Network, Letsema, and the University of Botswana Young Women's Leadership Project, to offer a two-day training workshop aimed at empowering young women between the ages of nineteen and thirty-five pursuing political office. It was titled 'Campaign 101'. The training focused on young women in politics, which included those in student representative councils. The highlight for the young women was that Minister Kenewendo attended the training. Many of the young women 'knew' each other from exchanging hostile Facebook posts from the safety of their party corners, but had never met face to face as fellow women. This on its own was quite transformative in the way that it allowed the participants to see each other as having a common purpose, and realizing that first they are women and face similar problems in politics, which is predominantly a male preserve.

Letsema in partnership with Friedrich Ebert Stiftung (FES)

From working with Friedrich Ebert Stiftung (FES) on labour unions as the then president of the University of Botswana Academic and Senior Support Staff Union, Mosime was introduced to a political feminist projected that was being incepted by the FES Maputo office. She was invited into the African Feminist Idea Laboratory and Feminist Reflection and Action Working Groups. The lab included feminist academics, social activists and progressive women in trade unions and other spaces, and the central idea was to shift the discourse from liberal notions of feminism to a radical idea of women`s agencies realizing alternatives to patriarchy. Letsema became the platform through which local thinking about our own feminist politics could be explored. Before heading out to the capital city of Mozambique, Maputo in November 2017, Letsema convened a small group of women from Botswana's different political parties, academics and the sex workers association of Botswana. The objective was to understand what feminism means for women across different political parties and other spaces of marginalization of women. The question was, 'what is the "faith" that can bring us together as women from different experiences to work together towards gender equality in Botswana and to forge a clearly feminist path for the gender equality movement?' It was argued that despite its shortcomings, the feminist movement in Botswana had made gains that ought to be recognized, protected and improved upon.

Whether the 'faith' that brings women in politics together is radical enough or complicit to the liberal framework is a debate for another day, but a consensus was built around a sisterhood that understands the game of power, the institutions upon which power resides whence decisions are made. These included both modern institutions such as parliament and traditional institutions such as the *Kgotla*. It was agreed that women needed to take time to invest in themselves to attain 'self- mastery'. Resulting from the conversation with the invited sex workers from Sisonke Association of Sex Workers, inclusion became an important feature of this sisterhood. Inclusiveness was explained as avoidance of 'othering' and realizing that 'womanness' is not all about femaleness, that there is 'no one woman' hence intersectionality had to be recognized. It was also agreed that the sisterhood must stay vigilant of co-optation by those with power. Because the question of quotas had not been supported by their political parties, the women agreed that building a 'critical minority' of women in positions of power, for instance, a critical minority in parliament, which could strengthen advocacy for women. They also wanted to debunk the misconception that women in politics had to behave like men, and that it was important to bringing younger women on board and invest in them (notes from the meeting provided by Pusetso Morapedi – FES programme officer).

In May 2018, the second African Feminist Idea Laboratory was held in Kampala, Uganda. It focused on critically thinking about socially and gender-just economic models. This was in recognition that many countries in the continent had adopted models of economic development mostly based on extractivism, understood not just as extractive activities of the commodity industry, but in the broader sense of a predatory economic model, which exploits all kind of 'raw materials' (minerals, oil, land, work, bodies, food, etc.) to convert them into cash regardless of the consequences. Coming from Kampala, Mosime convened a Letsema workshop for women in the intersection between politics, unionism and agriculture in order to better understand what extractivism meant in Botswana and for Botswana women in politics.

A very interesting dynamic became apparent as to the other reasons that women stay in political parties even if they are not rewarded with political positions. The women that this workshop confirmed the differential difficulties that women faced in agriculture compared to men. However, their being in politics put them at a greater advantage of unlocking the few but definitely emerging opportunities, especially in urban farming that did not require large tracts of land. Just like men, women understood that the political party space was also useful for building networks and partnerships with local and international 'investors', for personal gains, especially in an increasingly neoliberal post-colonial Africa. Women recognize this shift, and some of the participants in our training workshops have accordingly used the political space to position themselves for business opportunities.

Letsema followed stories of eight women simultaneously in politics and agriculture and they told a very rich story of using party networks and associates to learn the skilful art of accessing government grants and subsidies. One of them was Botshelo Kgathiswe. She grew up in a peri-urban town of Molepolole, 50 km out of Gaborone. She was not able to go beyond a junior level certificate (form 3), but worked in local retailers before becoming active in party politics. Having a cousin in politics led to her attending political meetings, further birthing a love in political movements. She was first in the ruling BDP as a branch secretary in her community and was further nominated as a councillor in her town, Molepolole. After her five-year tenure, she moved to the BMD, contested for elections in 2014 and lost. She is currently the national organizing secretary of the Alliance for Progressives (AP) and is contesting for a parliamentary seat in her home town.

Two years later, Botshelo applied for the Women's Economic Empowerment Program under the Ministry of Labour and Home Affairs. She collaborated with another woman in her area and created a proposal for livestock farming (primarily goats). After they received funding, she needed access to land. With knowledge that land access can be granted by the land board if you are government funded, and a letter proving funding is presented, she received a 3-hectare commercial lot in the outskirts of Molepolole.

Shortly into her business, a jackal killed sixteen of her goats, needing her to move close to the farm as the government grant she received did not cover salaries for workers. In the time that she has been farming, she has taken advantage of available short courses at the Botswana University of Agriculture and Natural Resources (BUAN). She not only learnt how to increase security of her livestock, but additionally learnt about the intricacies of health care of different livestock.

What's most inspiring about Botshelo is her passion for women empowerment and collaboration, particularly in political movements and societal unity. Botshelo counsels and helps mobilize resources for different women living in Molepolole who are experiencing different challenges. For example, a family had their house burn down. Through social media groups and networks, she helped mobilize resources and further aided in counselling to help them rebuild their lives. She had also organized a leisure group which has South African and Botswana women where people speak on business issues and engage in knowledge sharing. Additionally, she has helped seven youth in her area to write proposals and taught them basic accounting skills. These youth are in milling, livestock farming and even tailor making.

Letsema *le thata ka beng*: Challenges and inspirations from the Letsema workshops

Funding remains a challenge for Letsema to be able to roll out the project, especially to reach women in parts of the country further away from the capital city of Gaborone. Funding is also a challenge for women to conduct their campaigns or even travel to attend the limited available training opportunities. However, with very limited funding, the feedback we always got from participants was that the Letsema workshops were a resounding success. It became common practice for the participants to erupt into impromptu song and storytelling as they became comfortable that the workshops are a safe space. One of the most difficult challenges at the first meetings was to get the women from the different political parties to work together as there was lack of trust among the participants. This did not come as a surprise because traditionally networking and training have been done along party lines and mainly benefitted women residing in Gaborone. Letsema training was different because it included women from rural areas. The sessions often turned from a tense mutual suspicion among the participants to enthusiastic engagement and mutual respect. From their testimonies, it became apparent that political party structures remained patriarchal and operate on systems of patronage that favoured men. For many, the Letsema workshops helped wake them up to the possibility that they too could become political leaders. Some had run and lost elections, and they shared with others the persistence of violence (threats, physical and verbal abuse) that they had to deal with during their campaigns. Overall, women were very grateful for the trainings and said the workshops raised awareness of a common struggle and purpose and gave them a sense of belonging to a community of like-minded women. Networks were built, business ideas exchanged. In the end, there was also a reckoning with the Setswana idiom that Letsema *le thata ka beng ba lone* – a successful work party at any farm depends most on the farmer's own input, if the farmer slacks off, the team coming to help will also slack off. Women were very much aware that, within the very patriarchal political party space, they could advance their strategic life goals through intentional use of the resources that they already have to help themselves and others.

Conclusion

The Letsema experience confirms the party bias against women, but goes beyond to explain why women still find this biased space attractive and lucrative as they seize the political space to advance their other personal aspirations. We thus propose the need to reconsider how we conceptualize a 'political' candidate and look beyond seats so that we are able to understand how 'candidate' training takes different meanings and uses apart from the original limiting intentions of the Western sponsors. We approach empowerment from the perspective of Naila Kabeer, as the ability of women to question, analyse and act on the structures of patriarchal constraint in their lives, not necessarily in the ways that make immediate change, but initiate longer-term processes of change in the structures of patriarchy (Kabeer 1999). Beyond *questioning* patriarchy, which Kabeer insists on, as do many feminists who focus on structural oppression, this chapter extended women's political agency to what Obioma Nnaemeka (Nnaemeka 1995) calls a 'feminism of negotiations – nego-feminism'. This is to allow us to avoid what Amina Mama, in Lewis (2001), has described as 'deductive generalisation', which we find to inform of the sceptics of the candidate training trend and their 'analytical distance'. We seek to replace it with what Amina Mama calls the 'rigorous critique of intersecting power relations that stems from involvement in gendered African processes' (Lewis 2001). Sobering about the Botswana situation is that as the number of seats occupied by women declines, women stay politically active and also use the party space to forge alliances and networks that meet their own strategic life choices like taking advantage of available government funding programmes and meeting the more mundane everyday life needs such as food for their families and getting airtime as they continue to negotiate their multi-situated positionalities.

References

Amadiume, I. (1987): *Male Daughters, Female Husbands: Gender and Sex in an African Society*. London: Zed Books.

Batliwala, S. (2007): 'Taking the Power out of Empowerment – Experiential Account', *Development in Practice*, Vol. 17, No. 4/5, 557–65.

Beteta, H. C. (2006, July): 'What Is Missing in Measures of Women's Empowerment?', *Journal of Human Development*, Vol. 7, No. 2, 221–41. Doi: 10.1080/14649880600768553.

Budgeon, S. (2011): *Women's Leadership and Third Wave Feminism*. Sage Publications.

Cahill, C., Cerecer, D. A. and Bradley, M. (2010): '"Dreaming of ...": Reflections on Participatory Action Research as a Feminist Praxis of Critical Hope', *Affilia: Journal of Women and Social Work*, Vol. 25, No. 4, 406–16.

Cornwall and Anyidoho (2010): 'Introduction: Women's Empowerment Contestations', *Development*, Vol. 53. Issue, 144–9.

Giles, M. (2006): 'Beyond Participation: Strategies for Deeper Empowerment', in B. a. Cooke (ed.) *Participation: The New Tyranny?* London: Zed Books, pp. 153–67.

Gilman, L. (2001): 'Purchasing Praise: Women, Dancing, and Patronage in Malawi Party Politics', *Africa Today, Musical Performance in Africa* (Winter, 2001), 43–64.

Hanisch, C. (1969): *Women of the World Unite*, Writings of Carol Hanisch. Retrieved from http://www.carolhanisch.org/CHwritings/PIP.html

Hogan, B. (2019): 'Gendered Modes of Resistance: Power and Women's Songs in West Africa', *Ethnomusicology Review*, 1–12. Retrieved from https://ethnomusicologyreview. ucla.edu/printpdf/journal/volume/13/piece/498. Accessed 11 May 2019.

Jawad, S. and Ali, F. (2011): 'The White Woman's Burden: From Colonial Civilisation to Third World Development', *Third World Quarterly*, Vol. 32, No. 2, 349–65. Doi: 10.1080/01436597.2011.560473.

Kabeer, N. (1999): 'The Conditions and Consequences of Choice: Reflections on the Measurement of Women's Empowerment', United Nations Research Institute for Social Development.

Kim, L. M. (2001): 'I was [So] Busy Fighting Racism That I Didnt Even Know I Was Being Oppressed as a Woman!": Challenges, Changes and Empowerment in Teaching About Women of Color', *NWSA Journal*, Vol. 13, No. 2, 98–111.

Lewis, D. (2001): 'African Feminisms', *Agenda*, Vol. 16, No. 50, 4–10.

Mmegionline (2010, October): 'Mbaakanyi Leads New Women's Caucus' (C. Baputaki, Compiler), Gaborone, Botswana. Retrieved from https://www.mmegi.bw/index. php?sid=1&aid=5839&dir=2010/October/Friday22//. Accessed 25 April 2019.

Nnaemeka, O. (1995): 'Feminism, Rebellious Women, and Cultural Boundaries: Rereading Flora Nwapa and Her Compatriots', *Research in African Literatures*, Vol. 26, No. 2, 80–113.

Oyewumi, O. (1997): *The Invention of Women: Making an African Sense of Western Gender Discourses*. Minneapolis: University of Minnesota Press.

Piscopo, J. M. (2018): 'The Limits of Leaning in: Ambition, Recruitment, and Candidate Training in Comparative Perspective', *Politics, Groups, and Identities*. https://doi.org/10. 1080/21565503.2018.1532917.

The Roestone Collective (2014): 'Safe Space: Towards a Reconceptualization', *Antipode*, Vol. 46, No. 5, 1346–65.

Rowlands, J. (1998): 'A Word of the Times, but What Does It Mean? Empowerment in the Discourse and Practice of Development', in H. Afshar (eds) Women and Empowerment. Women's Studies at York. Palgrave Macmillan, London. https://doi. org/10.1007/978-1-349-26265-6_2.

Shohat, E. (1997): 'Framing Post-Third-Worldist Culture: Gender and Nation in Middle Eastern/North African Film and Video', Retrieved from CUNY-Graduate Center, https://legacy.chass.ncsu.edu/jouvert/v1i1/SHOHAT.HTM

Stewart, A. (1996): 'Should Women Give Up on the State? An African Experience', in S. Rai and G. Lieveslye (eds) *Women in the State: International Perspectives*. London: Taylor & Francis.

Sunday Standard (2 March 2014): 'Grey and Shrinking – the State of Botswana's Feminist Movement', Retrieved from www.sundaystandard.info, http://www.sundaystandard. info/grey-and-shrinking-%E2%80%93-state-botswana%E2%80%99s-feminist-movement

Women in Politics: Botswana (18 September 2016): 'Women in Politics: Botswana', Retrieved from Facebook, https://www.facebook.com/120040618454902/ videos/123600621432235/

4

Party primary candidate nomination institutions, informality and women's candidature in Malawi's parliamentary elections

Asiyati Lorraine Chiweza

Introduction

While several studies have discussed how candidate selection procedures within political parties affect women's chances of winning a party nomination (Bjarnegård 2016; Caul 1999; Norris and Lovenduski 1995), few studies have focused on poor, newly democratized African countries. In Malawi, as in many other emerging democracies, there is an inconsistency in the rules used in primaries and minimal transparency in the process. Since Malawi adopted democratization in 1994, presidential and parliamentary elections have been conducted every five years. By 2019, six rounds of parliamentary elections had been held and the number of women elected into the national assembly has remained stubbornly under the regional average, with the exception of the 2009 elections when women won 22 per cent of the seats. Since democratization, the low numbers of women elected to political positions have received recognition in Malawian debates and advocacy concerning gender inclusivity. Despite various efforts by various stakeholders to address the gender deficits in political representation, the continued low numbers of women in the elected bodies and growth of independent candidates suggest the presence of entrenched systemic issues and practices in Malawi that significantly disadvantage women so much that they are unable to register significant numerical visibility in the National Assembly. In the run-up to the 2019 elections, the 50-50 Management Agency, an organization responsible for running a campaign to increase the representation of women in elected bodies to 50 per cent, noted that one of the key challenges still hindering women's entry into parliament relates to the informality surrounding party candidate nomination processes, popularly known as party primaries. During the primary elections that took place between August 2018 and February 2019, the agency recorded over thirty complaints from women that related to irregularities in management of primary elections of various political parties. In its post-election report, the agency argued that party primary elections across all political parties displayed systematic efforts towards barring women from actively participating in leadership positions, and most of the political parties did not take the necessary steps to ensure that their primaries were conducted in a free and fair manner; hence, many women lost the primaries. Yet others who lost decided to stand as independent candidates. As a result, out of the 309 women who contested as parliamentary candidates, 117 contested as independent candidates. Even when both male and female contestants are combined, 1,331 candidates qualified to compete for the 193 parliamentary seats in Malawi Assembly. Of these candidates, 501 did not belong to a party and competed as independents – 84 more independent candidates from the previous 2014 election. Indeed since democratization, the number of female independent candidates has been increasing steadily reflecting the hostile environment for female aspirants within the political parties (Chingaipe 2015) and dissatisfaction with primary elections as a result of inability of parties to establish and to implement a set of rules regulating the nomination process (Patel and Mpesi 2009). Yet there have been few studies conducted on gendered analysis of party primary candidate selection processes (Patel and

Mpesi 2009). This chapter builds on the work that was carried out by Chiweza and Sainala in 2009 on the institutions governing United Democratic Front (UDF) primary election in 2004. The chapter draws from the 2014 and 2019 elections and analyses the institutions governing primary elections of two of Malawi's major parties, the Democratic People's Party (DPP) and Malawi Congress Party (MCP). It illustrates how informality is a key feature of institutions regulating party primaries of the main political parties in Malawi and how this continues to affect women's entry into parliament. The chapter starts with a theoretical discussion, and then examines the women representation context, and the data and methods guiding the study. It then provides an overview of the country's formal institutions governing primary nomination of parliamentary candidates, followed with a discussion of the various party rules institutions and how this plays out in practice and finishes with concluding reflections. The chapter offers an important contribution to institutional factors that affect women's descriptive representation in parliament in Malawi, particularly how party nomination processes influence and shape the fortunes of women that stand as candidates during general electoral processes. In particular, the chapter provides qualitative data of how unwritten and vague candidate nomination rules and norms allow particular powerful actors and undemocratic practices to thrive and influence the outcome of party nomination processes.

Party primary selection institutions and processes

Within the scholarship on gender and politics, an emerging literature discusses how certain features of candidate selection, mainly the degree of centralization and/or inclusiveness, affect the likelihood of women being selected (Hinojosa 2012). Candidate primary selection processes are the intra-party institutional mechanisms by which parties select their candidates in advance of general elections (Barnea and Rahat 2007). Caul (1999) argues that in a highly centralized party, leaders have the control to create openings for women – when they want to do so. In parties with exclusive selection procedures prospective candidates seek to please party leaders and this makes those seeking a candidacy behave in a party-centred manner, emphasizing their loyalty to their party. Under such circumstances, a record of party loyalty may be sufficient to convince the party leader to adopt you as a candidate. In other contexts, national party leaders may also have an incentive to diversify their ballot lists, and to make the party overall more attractive to different societal groups. Party leaders might also want to answer to demands for gender balance in political recruitment presented by international agents, the government or women's activists, and might be interested to nominate more women to reach a certain threshold. Local party leaders, on the other hand, might be interested in other kinds of qualifications, like identifying the one most able to bring back developments to the region: to who a candidate owes one's nomination is thus an important question if one wants to understand how party primary institutions affect the entry of women candidates into parliamentary arenas.

The concern is, however, that in the absence of interventions that force party leaders to select women, party leaders prefer to recruit men (e.g. Butler and Preece 2016). Evidence suggests that not only do male party leaders prefer, but they also more actively support and promote the nomination of male candidates (Carroll and Sanbonmatsu 2013; Dittmar 2015; Verge and Kenny 2016). Some studies argue that decentralized and more inclusive selection procedures might benefit women, because it opens up the process and allow newcomers to enter the party primaries. In other cases, there might be a disjunction between what the rule on paper is and what is actually practised on the ground. In a comparative study of Thailand and Scotland, Bjarnegård and Kenny (2016) find that, despite candidate selection being formally centralized in both cases, it is informally decentralized and localized and marked by clientelism and patronage. In this informal recruitment system, key local party actors in positions of power (mainly men) were able to use informality to keep outsiders (mainly women) out of their networks. Bjarnegård and Kenny's (2016) study illustrates that candidate emergence is likely to be a multifaceted process even in cases where the formal rules appear relatively straightforward. In their ideal typical and extreme forms, both inclusive/decentralized and exclusive/centralized systems may benefit women, but as political parties are voluntary organizations with weak formal rules, the rules that apply in practice might change from election to election and differ not just between, but also within parties. In the context of many African countries, it has been argued that some advantages with centralized-inclusive candidate selection procedures might not even apply due to the widespread use of majoritarian electoral systems. For instance, Itzkovitch-Malka and Hazan (2017) have shown that party loyalty, as an effect of exclusive candidate selection system, is contingent on having a proportional representation (PR) electoral system. In majoritarian systems with exclusive candidate selection methods, the party-based incentives are coupled with the personally focused incentives of the electoral system. Consequently, 'legislators are faced with conflicting incentives, which may pull in opposite directions' (Itzkovitch-Malka and Hazan 2017: 458). Hence, while the use of primaries to increase women's chances of winning a nomination, as suggested by Hinojosa (2012: 155), may work in the context of Latin America where proportional representation is the most common electoral system, the same is not the case in the context of SMD election systems. Malawi uses a simple majoritarian electoral system ('first-past-the-post', FPTP system), with only one candidate declared winner of each constituency. In this system, the winner only has to pool a simple (and not necessarily an absolute) majority of votes.

Conceptual framework and methodology

The study on which this chapter is based focused on the experiences of selected women who went through the candidate nomination process of the DPP and the MCP in the 2014 and 2019 elections. Since the first multiparty elections in 1994, three to four parties have dominated each election in Malawi. This includes the DPP, UDF and the MCP.[1] All these parties have been able to win a significant share of seats in the National Assembly until recently when the UDF representation in parliament has been dwindling. The 2009 analysis of primary election rules (Chiweza and Sainala) focused on the UDF as the party that won the first Malawi democratic elections in 1994, after thirty years of highly authoritarian one-party rule. The party also won the next two presidential elections that took place in 1999 and 2004. The present analysis focuses on two parties that have gained parliamentary strengths over the years. The DPP is one party that has been successful in all presidential elections since it was established in the mid-2000s and has a stronghold in some parts of the Southern region. The MCP founded in 1959 is known to be most institutionalized party in Malawian politics that has a huge following in the central region of Malawi. Out of the thirty-two successful women in the 2014 elections, sixteen were independents and seven from DPP, five from MCP and four from UDF. In the 2019 elections out of the forty-four women that won, seventeen were from DPP, fourteen were independent, eleven from MCP, one from UDF and one from United Transformation Movement (UTM).

An institutional approach to politics acknowledges that institutions affect the outcome of any social interaction and gender relations. The approach pays attention to the role of institutions in structuring the dynamics of political life. Examining candidate nomination processes on the basis of the institutional rules, practices, actors, their authority, and control structures helps us to understand who does what, who gains, who loses (which men and which women). Institutions in this chapter are defined as 'rules and procedures (of how things get done) both formal and informal that structure political, economic and social interaction by constraining and enabling actors behaviour' (Helmke and Levitsky 2004: 727). A distinction is made between formal and informal institutions. Formal institutions are created, communicated and enforced inside officially sanctioned channels while informal institutions are socially shared rules, usually unwritten that are created, communicated and enforced outside of officially sanctioned channels (Helmke and Levitsky 2004: 727). Helmke and Levitsky argue that informal rules emerge when formal institutions do not yield results that satisfy the actors or when actors pursue goals that are not publicly acceptable, either because they are unlikely to stand the test of public scrutiny or because they will attract international condemnation.

A further categorization of institutions is provided by Krook (2010: 711) in which a distinction is made between systemic institutions, normative and practical institutions. Systemic institutions are formal features of political systems, which encompass the laws and organizations that officially structure political life. These include electoral and party systems. Among these, the electoral system has been identified as one of the most important factors explaining cross-national variations in women's representation. Normative institutions relate to principles or norms of equality and representation. Practical institutions include formal credentials set down in the law such as age, citizenship, party membership, term limits; and informal criteria such as ticket-balancing, skills, experience, prominence, party activism, family ties, money; as well as method of ballot composition such as centralized or decentralized, group rights to nominate or veto candidates during party primaries, secret or open ballots etc. (Krook 2010). In the case of political recruitment, practical institutions relate to the procedures and criteria that parties employ to select their candidates including the formal and informal practices of elites. They can thus be viewed as institutions that shape perceptions as to who is a 'qualified' or 'desirable' candidate, a set of beliefs that can be gendered to varying degrees. While we acknowledge that both systemic and normative institutions do play a part in influencing representation of women in parliament, our interest in this chapter is on examining practical institutions of DPP and MCP and how they influence the success of women candidates to move from being party aspirants to being nominated or rejected as party candidates during their primary election processes.

In line with this framework, the study investigated the lived experiences of selected cases of individual women who went through the primary election process in constituencies under the DPP and MCP ticket and did not succeed in getting party nominations, thus learning from the failed cases. The focus was on the nature of the rules that the party used for nominating the parliamentary candidates, how they were applied and the key actors who were involved in each case. In order to gain an understanding of the rules that were followed by the party, how they were applied and the actors involved, open extended interviews were conducted with the selected women who went through the primary election process to enable them to narrate their experiences of the primary election in terms of the role of the political party vis-à-vis the rules, resources, activities and people that were involved. Data was also collected from sixty-five key informant interviews with party leaders at area, branch, district, region, and national executive level. Although the primary focus of the study was on women's experiences, key informant interviews with male and female party leaders were deemed essential because these actors were uniquely positioned to provide in-depth information on the selection process.

Data analysis involved a combination of content analysis and process tracing. In order to glean a set of rules from the qualitative narratives, content analysis was done on the data from key female aspiring candidates and informant interviews with party leaders. This entailed a continuous process of compressing words, sentences and their contexts portrayed by respondents into categories or group of words with a similar meaning or connotation (Stemler 2001). In addition, the occurrence of particular rules was assessed from each respondent's textual data. Content analysis was followed by process tracing which involved going through the narratives of all the respondents and making an individual woman's case analysis in order to understand how the rules were applied and the causal processes.

Formal institutions governing party primary nomination of parliamentary candidates in Malawi

Malawi is a multiparty democracy that follows a FPTP electoral system. MPs are elected by a simple plurality of votes in single-seat constituencies[2]. Candidates can either run on a party ticket or stand as independents, but most candidates prefer to stand on a party ticket. The experience from the four electoral cycles since democratization has shown that those that are elected on an independent ticket tend to join the ruling party after they get into parliament because the political leaders have created a dynamic that government MPs are the only ones who can 'bring development' to an area. However, in order to run under the party banner, candidates must first win the party nomination of the local constituency, which organizes and oversees nomination races.

The Constitution of the Republic of Malawi (1994), The Malawi Electoral Commission Act, The Political Parties Registration Act, the Parliamentary and Presidential Elections Act, the Local Government Act and the Communications Act form the relevant institutions that regulate political parties. However, what has been noted is that these institutions contain some elements affecting political parties because the acts address functions that political parties perform. A key formal institution that is important here is the Constitution of the Republic of Malawi, which was established in 1995. The Malawian Constitution specifies conditions for individuals applying for registration as candidates, but does not say anything about the nomination process in parties *per se*. Parties are free to choose their own nomination method (Svåsand 2014). Section 51 of the Malawian Constitution outlines the eligibility criteria for those who wish to contest the elections as one who should be a citizen of Malawi at nomination; should have attained twenty-one years of age to contest in local government and parliamentary elections, and thirty-five years for presidential elections; and should be able to speak and read English well enough to actively participate in parliament.

Additionally, no person is eligible to participate in presidential, parliamentary and local elections if the person owes allegiance to a foreign country; is adjudged or otherwise declared to be mentally incompetent; has, within the last seven years, been convicted by a competent court of a crime; has, within the last seven years, been convicted by a competent court of any violation of any law relating to election of the president or election of members of parliament, belongs to, and is serving in, the Defence Forces of Malawi or the Malawi Police Force; holds, or acts, in any public office or appointment, except where the Constitution provides that a person shall not be disqualified from standing for election; and has been adjudged or otherwise declared bankruptcy. These are the formal rules that the Malawi Electoral Commission enforces and regularly reminds all political parties to adhere.

Beyond these formal rules stipulating eligibility of parliamentary candidates, parties are free to choose their own nomination method and rules for conducting the nominations (Svåsand 2014: 12). Political parties can choose to establish formal, explicit rules for selecting their candidates for the legislature and members of internal decision-making bodies. This means that the nomination of parliamentary candidates is supposed to be guided primarily by the parties' own statutes and the way those statutes are applied in practice. Many African parties are heavily dependent on the party leader and typically 'lack a structure that can penetrate the national territory, have inadequate communication links between the central leadership and lower party units, dormant organisation between elections, and few, if any, organisational resources' (Rakner et al. 2007: 1114). Parties have few or no resources with which to support themselves (Manning 2005: 721) and are often heavily dependent on the leader for its finances (Svåsand 2014: 278). Consequently, the party leader sometimes appears as the party 'owner' and as the owner; he or she is rarely constrained by the formal rules of the party organization, if there are any formal rules at all.

However, by 2019 none of the main parties in parliament, the UDF, the MCP, and DPP including the People's Party (PP) had in their Constitution a clear procedure for nomination of parliamentary candidates. In addition, none of the parties possessed a written official set of internal explicit rules on candidate selection, which are standardized and implemented by party officials. This reflects the limited degree of institutionalization of Malawian political parties. In highly institutionalized processes, candidate registration is defined by internal party rules that are detailed, explicit, standardized and implemented by party officials and authorized in party documents (Lovenduski and Norris 1993). So, what happens in practice during the primary nomination of candidates?

DPP and MCP party institutions governing primary nomination of candidates

Using the 2014 and 2019 elections (as was the case with the 2004 UDF electoral experience), the study found that in the party primaries, local party members in the constituencies get to choose among their local candidates and there were no real differences between the two parties. One of the major explanations is that the main party that emerged after democratization, UDF, had its roots in MCP, the only and oldest party during the one party state. Englund (2002) attests to this and argued that the fact that many leading politicians in the 'new' Malawi also held prominent positions in Banda's one-party state seemingly helps to explain continuities in political behaviour. Similarly, DPP emerged as a breakaway of UDF so most of their practical rules of procedure are not different. In both parties voting in the primaries is based on constituency structures, which are the area committees. Each area committee has three sections: the Youth wing, the Women's wing and what is called the Mother body (or main area executive). Delegates (selectorates) are drawn from the area committees in a constituency. The number of delegates in primaries varies from party to party. In the case of the DPP, for example, fifteen (with five from each of the three wings) members from each committee form the selectorate. These ones are allowed to vote on the day of the primary elections. The MCP area committees contribute nine delegates to the primaries with three from each of the wings.

In both DPP and MCP, party rules regarding the conduct of the actual candidate nomination processes were transmitted orally from the national executive party leaders to other relevant party leaders at the regional, district, constituency and other lower levels. This was done through party meetings with the leaders. In both DPP and MCP aspiring women candidates did not have a clear written set of rules in advance to enable them understand how the process works and develop strategies of how to take advantage of them. They were able to pick the rudimentary of primary elections along the way from the constituency party leaders. Other women got a sense of these rules through their interaction with constituency party members and friends who had been in the party for a considerable period. However, all the women candidates interviewed intimated that some kind of a form (document) existed whose contents were read out on the day when aspirants expressed an interest to stand as candidates on a party ticket. Each of the women interviewed was not able to precisely indicate the full contents of this form/document,[3] but were able to mention about this document being read out to them and being asked to sign that they will not contest as independents if they lost the primary elections. As one party aspirant indicated:

> There was a document which was read during a meeting in Liwonde when I went to register as a candidate. It was also read before voting. The document explained what we should do during primary campaign period, that there should be no violence, and that an aspirant who loses primaries should not

stand as an independent candidate. We were told to sign the document after we had paid a registration fee. I was a new comer in the party such that I did not know most of the rules regarding primary elections.

(extract from an interview with a female DPP aspirant, 2019)

In effect, the parties do not really provide documentation that offers comprehensive information about the procedures of the primary nomination process. Rather political parties ask candidates to sign a code of conduct which states that if they lose primaries, they cannot stand as independents and this is against the basic principles of human rights enshrined in Sections 20, 24 and 30 of the Malawi Constitution (50-50 Management Agency 2019). Thus, the knowledge of the primary nomination rules of procedure that the women and other candidates possessed was mainly based on what the party constituency or other members had relayed to them. Incumbent candidates and others who had gone through the primary nomination processes before possessed experiential knowledge. In the sections that follow, I provide a synthesis of the most commonly narrated rules by both male and female candidates and other party members. They are in four categories. The first category relates to procedural issues on the conduct of the primary nomination process. The second category of rules deals with expectations on candidates and voter nomination. The third category of rules relates to norms and expectations on resources required for party nomination and the final category of rules articulates the key actors and their roles in the process of party primary elections. These rules were orally narrated by the women candidates and corroborated by other party members from the national, regional, district and constituency level.

Category 1: Procedural rules guiding the conduct of primary elections

A synthesis of their interviewee narratives revealed that the rules in this category revolved around responsibility for organizing the primaries, scheduling of the primaries, campaign period, who could serve as a presiding officer, voting method and counting of votes. The oral rules stipulate that primaries are organized by party leaders at regional level. The team comprises

Director of Elections, people from National Executive, regional governor and constituency members. The requirement is that the governance team at regional and district level is not allowed to organize and conduct primary elections in their own district but rather they go to organize and conduct primaries in other districts. The primaries are supposed to take place at a location to be advised by the constituency committee and presiding officer. Voting is supposed to be done through a lining-up system where contestants are blindfolded or covered with a cloth and the voters would line up behind the candidates. Votes for each candidate are supposed to be counted by the presiding officer with the help of other party members, chosen by the party elections presiding team. Campaigning or discussing candidates on the day of voting is not allowed. Results of the vote are supposed to be announced publicly at the end of the process by the organizing team but are also subject to approval by the National Executive Committee.

Category 2: Rules and expectations on candidate and voter selection

The second set of rules that women candidates and party members explained dealt with who qualifies to stand as a candidate and the question of who could be a delegate (selectorate) who can take part in voting during the actual primaries. On candidate qualification, four rules stand out as areas where there was some consensus among the women and party actors: that the candidates needed to be well known in the constituency; they are supposed to be sons and daughters of the soil; they are supposed to be well behaved according to the local traditions and customs and have to demonstrate that they are development conscious and they have to demonstrate that they are genuine party members. On who is eligible to vote what is clear through the narratives is that the process of primary nominations is one that is highly localized, where party members at the constituency level represent the key selectorates (delegates). The rules require that they should be party members from the branch areas of the party within a constituency. They also have to be recognized party members selected from the women, youth and executive wings of the party. The constituency committee led by the constituency governor was the entity responsible for screening and accepting candidates to contest during the primaries, hosting primary elections and providing security on the actual nomination day. However, what was less clear is how these delegates or constituency selectors would be identified and verified. This is a challenge given the lack of clear mechanisms for registering and verifying political party members in Malawi as there are no party cards and formal records of party members.

Category 3: Norms and expectations on resources required for party nomination

The third category of rules most commonly cited related to expectations on resources and activities required for successful nomination. The norms are very explicit on no support from the party during the primary elections. All primary campaign costs such as transport, fuel, food and cash for campaign helpers are supposed to borne by the aspiring candidate herself. In the case of DPP and MCP, the aspirants (both male and female) were also supposed to pay a sum of MK 50,000 (about US$80) upon registration to help meet the costs of running the primary elections. During primary elections the party does not provide material support to any aspirant; it remains neutral until primary elections are over. Candidates are also expected to visit the areas that make up the constituency for campaign purposes. Campaign volunteers can visit some areas for the candidate if the candidate is unable to visit all areas. Generally, the electoral experience in Malawi since 1994 has seen a similar bidding-up process in the value of financial investment needed to win an election both at the primary and actual parliamentary levels. Victories are contingent on the ability of candidates to distribute large numbers of small gifts to citizens such as sugar, cloth and soap to constituents both as an upfront resource transfer and as a visible sign that the member of parliament (MP) has the potential to deliver after being elected. These purely private demands are extremely important, as it is not uncommon for MPs to spend as much on primaries as elections.[4] Competition drives up the investment needed to win and sets the bar higher for subsequent elections. The combination of these factors means that it is increasingly expensive and difficult for women to win parliamentary seats especially for those that may not have the financial muscle to sustain the expectations (Muriaas 2009; O'Neil et al. 2016). The lack of financial resources is frequently held to constitute a barrier for women's entry into politics everywhere, but especially in developing countries where women's socio-economic status is disproportionately low relative to that of men (Bauer 2010). In a pre-elections statement released by the Technical Working Group on Political Empowerment of women of the Ministry of Gender, Children, Community and Social Welfare, on 16 May 2019, they raise the problem of commercialization of politics in Malawi. They stated:

> We bemoan the many economic hardships most women candidates have been subjected to due to highly monetised politics in Malawi. It has become almost impossible to run a political campaign in Malawi, without spending huge *amounts* of money in order to garner support. This political culture has made voters prone to voter bribery as they become enticed by handouts from the political elites. The persistence of 'money-politics' is unfortunate considering the many economic inequalities that exist in our society between men and women.

Several authors have argued that one way of achieving gender balance is to limit primary spending (Hinojosa 2012: 158) and / or provide gendered cost relief to women candidates and aspirants (Muriaas et al. 2019). In Malawi, a cost relief under the banner of the 50-50 campaign was provided to female aspirants and/or nominees to boost their electoral campaigns and ultimately to increase the number of women in politics in the 2009, 2014 and 2019 elections. Under this campaign women were given cash, campaign material and airtime to make them better equipped to run for seats in the national parliament. Assessing the impact of the 2009 and 2014 campaigns, Wang et al. (2019) found that the impact was varied because the actual strategies used in the 50-50 campaign differed in the sense that in 2009 support was extended to aspirants during the primary process, while in 2014 support was only provided to candidates. Wang et al. (2019) also noted that handouts are a key campaign strategy, and although many aspirants and candidates do not like this, they feel compelled to uphold this practice in order to stand a chance in the elections. A criticism of targeted gendered funding in the Malawian context is thus that it does not address this problematic mechanism – the tradition of candidates' use of handouts to win votes that favours the well-resourced (mostly male) candidates. They conclude that due to the high costs involved in standing for primary elections, providing cost relief to aspirants appears to be of greater consequence in terms of motivating more women to enter politics than providing support to female candidates only later in the electoral process.

Category 4: Rules on key actors and their roles

The final category of rules most commonly cited provides guidance on key actors and their roles in the nomination process. Although the primary electoral process takes place at the local level and the ground preparations are done by the constituency committee, the presiding officer, who is usually a representative of the regional and national level party structure, takes charge of the whole process in any given constituency. He or she is a key actor in determining the outcome of a primary election process. Where there is a desire to manipulate the process, this presiding officer becomes the target of bribery and corruption by other higher-level party actors. The rules show that the constituency governor is also a key person whose support is crucial in ensuring that aspiring candidates are welcomed into the party. The constituency committee as a group of people are responsible for hosting primary elections and accepting candidates to contest in the primaries. Local traditional authorities have liberty to propose a candidate but party leaders have the final say on who should represent the party. The rules also allow that campaign volunteers who are normally youths from the party can assist a candidate of their own choice. Generally absent from these rules are transparent mechanisms for dispute resolution, in case there are queries on the process. Also not explicit are mechanisms or rules for process oversight, accountability of key facilitating actors and periodic review of the primary nomination procedures. Consequently, nomination issues frequently end up in the courts (Svåsand 2014: 11). In each election there are numerous instances where defeated aspirants in the nomination process either take the party to court or decide to run as independents (Musuva 2009).

The application of the rules in practice: Lessons from selected women aspirants

An examination of the six cases of women who were unsuccessful in the party primaries of both MCP and DPP in 2014 and 2019 discussed below reflect the dissonance between the orally handed down rules and the practice on the ground. The evidence from all the cases studied shows that aspiring candidates did not have access to the entire set of rules until closer to the time of the actual primary elections and some candidates did not have any information at all. Even then, it was constituency leaders who bore the task of explaining these rules to the candidates. The 50-50 Agency also noted that during the 2019 elections information on primaries such as access to candidate forms, venue, guidelines, delegates and zones was kept as a secret and a privilege of selected few (Chavula 2019). As a result, it was difficult for new members to understand how the process works, what will be expected of them and to hold the political parties accountable.

In practice, the rules that have been discussed in the previous section are not seriously adhered to and a lot of informality exists. Due to unwritten nature of the rules, candidates and party leaders particularly presiding officers and regional actors and to some extent district and constituency leaders were able to bring other practices that did not in some cases seem to be in tandem with the orally articulated rules. Through these practices, the parties were behaving strategically, selecting their preferred party loyalists who were mostly male candidates. The study noted that there were three possible avenues of informality and manipulation that stood out: selection and identification of delegates (selectors), scheduling of time and dates for the primaries, and non-adherence to campaign rules and the results approval process.

Informality around selection and identification of delegates (selectors)

The importance of clearly identifying delegates and ensuring that all aspirants know them from the early stages of the process cannot be overemphasized in promoting a level playing field and fairness in the electoral process. Delegates (selectorates) are an important entity of the whole primary elections. As one female MCP aspirant expressed:

> The aspiring candidate is expected to work closely with branch committee members who form the delegates/selectorates (actual voters) during primary elections. These people are supposed to hear the candidate's manifesto during the party primary campaign process. They are also the same people that help in canvassing support for the candidate amongst other party members. The aspiring candidate is supposed to explain to the committee what is in her manifesto.
>
> (extract from an interview with a female MCP aspirant in Lilongwe, 2019)

Lack of clarity in the definition of legitimate delegates to vote in the primary elections and lack of clear mechanisms for identifying and certifying delegates (selectorates) allowed party leaders who wanted to manipulate the process to bring in new delegates on the day of voting to favour their preferred candidates. This was evident in the case of Ms A and B. Ms A (*MCP Candidate, 2014*) was competing with three other candidates: two male candidates and one female candidate. Ms A was a first-time aspirant competing against long-serving MCP party loyalists. Party primary elections in this constituency were held three times and they were characterized by chaos, violence and irregularities. Chaos and violence have indeed been a feature of the 2019 MCP primary elections as a manifestation of dissatisfaction with the processes. In many constituencies, this led to the postponement or cancellation of scheduled primaries. In the case of Ms A, the first-time primary elections were called by the organizing team, her male contenders deliberately disturbed the whole event by bringing unknown delegates from the market and other places. This confused the identification of delegates, chaos ensued, and the regional actors and presiding officer cancelled the event. This happened several times. The 50-50 Agency also noted in their analysis of the 2019 elections that there is no standardization when it comes to dealing with the names of delegates and zones, little clarity on who is the custodian of this information and limited agreement on who the delegates (selectorates) are (50-50 Management Agency 2019). A case in point is that of Ms B, a 2019 *DPP* female candidate. Ms B was competing against four male DPP aspirants. The constituency party governor in collaboration with the presiding officer decided to come up with new delegate areas in the constituency to favour their male-preferred candidate. This allowed other delegates beyond those 'officially' known by all other aspirants to join and boost the votes for their preferred male candidate. Conflict ensued and tear gas was used to disperse people. Despite these discrepancies, the party presiding officers who are often members of the same party still continued with the process. Counting was not effectively done and the presiding officer declared the party's favoured male candidate as the winner. These experiences point to a general lack of transparency and accountability in many parties' primary election processes but also vested underhand interests by party leaders and organizers to manipulate the process.

Informality related to the scheduling of time, date and venue for the primary elections

Lack of prior disclosure of information on venues and scheduled times for the elections and sudden unilateral changes of venue was another informal practice that was employed by party leaders to manipulate the process and favour particular candidates, mostly men and other influential long-serving members of the party. The example of Ms C (*MCP 2014 Candidate, 2014*) illustrates this point. Ms C was competing against four male aspirants and one female aspirant. The constituency party leaders used to give Ms C and other aspirants possible dates for party primaries, but when the aspirants turn up on the announced dates and venues they were surprised that the organizers were nowhere to be seen. The reality was that the MCP party leaders at the national executive level had taken a decision that primaries in the said constituency were not going to be held because they wanted to protect the seat of long-serving senior member of the party who was the incumbent MP. However, they did not divulge this information to Ms C and the other four aspirants until a few days before the end of the party primary elections period as the voice of Ms C illustrates:

> We were spending thinking that we were going to have MCP primaries which did not happen. The party used to give us dates, okay we'll do it on this day, we go there nobody comes. We even walked with chiefs to the MCP headquarters but nobody responded to our query. Eventually at the last minute, they said no primaries will be held and we became independent candidates. So when you are independent that means you have to stand on your two feet, you have to do everything alone. So we continued campaigning, spending money, lots of money and time came for the elections. We had to have our own monitors in all the places where the polling was being done and you don't just get someone without paying them. You have to pay, you have to transport them, you have to feed them, and you have to meet all their needs. This was really hard for me.
>
> (extract from an interview with a female MCP aspirant in Lilongwe, 2014)

As a result, the withholding of critical information about the date of the primary elections did not allow Ms C and other aspirants to strategize on their next course of action. Consequently, Ms C stood as an independent candidate not by choice but because of the circumstances that ensued. This contributed to the escalation of the aspirants' campaign costs because Ms C had already spent a lot of money preparing for the MCP primaries that never took place. The change to independent status necessitated increased expenditures; as a result, she could not compete favourably during the general election. Another case in point that illustrates the deliberate withholding of information is a story of a 2019 female aspirant who narrated how on the eve of a primary election she kept visiting the house of the constituency chairperson starting from morning and only to get the information about the venue of the primaries at 10:00 p.m. in the evening when the wife of the constituency chairperson called her (Chavula 2019). Chavula notes that the information about the venue changed in the early morning hours of the next day. Consequently, she had no resources to hire a vehicle to transport her supporters to the new venue and this gave her male contenders an advantage.

Informality around the results approval process and non-adherence to campaign rules

The third arena of informality related to lack of adherence to campaign rules and manipulation of the results approval process. For example, Ms D (a 2014 DPP candidate) won the primary elections but had her nomination approval manipulated. Ms D decided to run as a parliamentary candidate on a DPP ticket at the request of chiefs and area members of the party from her area because they were not happy with the development performance record of the incumbent MP, although he was a party loyalist. She was competing against other five DPP male aspirants. Primary elections were conducted three times because the constituency governor and the area members of the party were not happy with the manner in which the presiding officer and regional team conducted the primaries. The regional team appeared to favour the male party loyalist against the female candidate that most selectorates/delegates preferred. Although the presiding officer declared Ms D as the winner during the third run of the primaries, things changed when they went to receive nomination certificates from the President of the DPP. Ms D's name was not called out. Instead, it was the name of the failed male candidate (party loyalist) which was called out. The regional governor of the party did this substitution. Chavula (2019) notes that with regard to manipulating the final nomination list, the dynamics are different from each of the dominant parties in Malawi. In other dominant parties, it is a clique around the presidency that is responsible for this machination. In other parties, it is the party's secretary general's office, and yet in others, it is the director of elections and the entire primary election administration team of the party.

The key point is that because of the informal nature of the primary electoral processes, the rules as articulated do not seem to be followed and procedures are easily flouted; yet, there does not seem to be a clear mechanism for sanctioning wrongdoing. There were examples of campaigning of some candidates beyond the period stipulated by the party to the disadvantage of some of the candidates in question and also alleged partisanship by some officials involved in the administration of the elections. Two key examples are worth mentioning here: examples of Ms E (MCP, 2019 Candidate) and Ms F

(DPP, 2019 Candidate, 2019). Ms E was competing against a male and female candidate. On the day of primary elections, the presiding officer openly favoured the male candidate by indicating to the delegates in his opening speech that they were supposed to vote for a male candidate. The supporters of the male winning candidate came in party colours, were very intimidating and were visibly urging other delegates to line up behind the male aspirant. No action was taken to stop these malpractices. The male candidate had a lot of resources and he was handing out money to the delegates and other party leaders even on the day of primary elections. The worst part of it all is that votes were never counted, and the male candidate preferred by the presiding team was declared winner. When a formal complaint was lodged at the district and later at the regional level, no action was taken. Similarly, Ms F, another DPP candidate, was campaigning against three male and two female aspirants. One male candidate had the full support of the constituency governor and presiding officer. Therefore, although campaign is not allowed on the polling day, the preferred male candidate gave drinks and money to all the selectorates on the day of voting. The night before primary elections, he also gave money and party cloth to all delegates participating in the DPP 2019 primary elections.

In summary, the cases and examples discussed herein illustrate how a weakly institutionalized party nomination process, with rules that are not explicitly documented, without a clear enforcement and grievance handling mechanism can easily be prone to patronage and favouritism. In many cases, despite the observed irregularities, elections proceeded to be held without such issues being resolved. Lack of effective institutional grievance handling and oversight procedures promote behaviours such as violence, which are aimed at intimidating and instilling fear in contending candidates, particularly women candidates.

Conclusion

Despite the fact that Malawi is considered to have a progressive Constitution and has ratified several international and regional gender-related instruments that seek to enhance the status of women, the unsupportive party environment and lack of clearly written primary election rules and specific legislative provisions on quotas is a barrier to the increased number of women standing as candidates in elective positions.

This chapter has demonstrated that the practical institutions for candidate nomination that DPP and MCP party members were articulating as '*formal rules*' are difficult to be classified as formal institutions as in Helmke and Levitsky's categorization of formal and informal institutions. In the context of these parties, the term '*formal*' institution appears to cover more ground to include practices and norms that were not written down but were passed on orally from the top political leadership to the local district and branch level. These were considered by the party members and candidates as '*formal rules*'; yet, none of the candidates or party leaders interviewed were able to provide a written outline of these rules. The rules, though not written in any party documents, are communicated orally and enforced inside officially sanctioned channels – from the National Executive Committee down the party hierarchy to the regional leaders, constituency leaders and branch members through party meetings.

Thus while internal political party electoral systems and procedures, especially for primary elections, can play a major role in promoting the election of women to positions of power, the chapter has shown that a major problem common to all parties is related to lack of adherence to the rules regarding the identification of the selectorates and the number of area committees acceptable in each constituency. In practice, presiding officers (who are mostly male) utilized these loopholes to connive with other constituency party actors to favour their preferred male candidates. These male-preferred candidates are mostly party loyalists with extensive networks in the party and connections even at the regional and headquarters level. The party candidate selection experiences discussed in this chapter resonate with Seeberg et al. (2018), who found that 80 per cent of the African parties studied either have no clear rules for candidate selection or, more often, have rules that they regularly disregard, as elites push for their favoured candidates. What this means is that gendered electoral funding schemes that overlook the political dynamics of party primary elections that mainly involve influential local-level selectorates and handouts are likely to have less impact in improving the fortunes of women to stand as parliamentary candidates.

There is a need for political parties to make the process more predictable by introducing clear, transparent and written primary election institutions. This requires a fundamental transformation of party structures, rules and institutional cultures to make them more encouraging to women candidates. Such a culture must be internalized by party members, who should feel a sense of ownership of the process rather than see candidate nomination process in narrow terms as the agenda and responsibility of the women members of the party to learn the party's complex internal politicking and the ropes of the trade.

Notes

1   There have been other parties such as PP and UTM that have emerged out of disagreements in DPP that have also been active in particular years, for example, 2014 for PP and 2019 for UTM.
2   This section largely draws from Chiweza and Sainala (forthcoming) because there has not been any change in the formal institutions since 2004.
3   Upon further probing, it was discovered that the so-called document was essentially a code of conduct for primary elections.
4   Although government passed a law to ban handouts, its effect in deterring handouts in practice remains to be seen.

References

50-50 Campaign Management Agency (2019): *Independents and Party Primaries*, unpublished policy brief. Lilongwe.

Asiyati, L. Chiweza and Sainala Kalebe, A. (forthcoming): 'Party primary candidate nomination processes and women's descriptive representation in Malawi parliament: Insights from the United Democratic Front Party'. *Malawi Journal of Social Science.*

Barnea, S. and Rahat, G. (2007): 'Reforming Candidate Selection Methods: A Three-Level Approach', *Party Politics*, Vol. 13, No. 3, 375–94.

Bauer, G. (2010): 'Cows Will Lead the Herd into a Precipice: Where Are the Women MPs in Botswana?', *Botswana Notes and Records*, Vol. 42, 56–70.

Bjarnegård, E. and Kenny, M. (2016): 'Comparing Candidate Selection: A Feminist Institutionalist Approach', *Government and Opposition*, Vol. 51, No. 3, 370–92. Doi: 10.1017/gov.2016.4.

Butler, M. and Preece, J. (2016): 'Recruitment and Perceptions of Gender Bias in Party Leader Support', *Political Research Quarterly*, Vol. 69, No. 4, 842–50.

Carroll, S. J. and Sanbonmatsu, K. (2013): *More Women Can Run: Gender and Pathways to the State Legislatures*. New York: Oxford University Press.

Caul, M. (1999): 'Women's Representation in Parliament: The Role of Political Parties', *Party Politics*, Vol. 5, No. 1, 79–98. https://doi.org/10.1177/1354068899005001005.

Chavula, V. (2019): *Challenging Informality as a Patriarchal Dividend*. A Policy Brief. Independent Management Agency: Lilongwe, 2019.

Chingaipe, H. (2015): 'Analysis of the Contribution of First-Past-The-Post Electoral System to the Low Numbers of Women in the National Assembly and Local Authorities in Malawi and Options for Addressing the Gender Deficit', chapter prepared for UN Malawi.

Dittmar, K. (2015): 'Encouragement Is Not Enough: Addressing Social and Structural Barriers to Female Candidate Recruitment', *Politics and Gender*, Vol. 11, No. 4: 759–65.

Englund, H. (2002): 'Introduction: The Culture of Chameleons', in H. Englund (ed.) *A Democracy of Chameleons: Politics and Culture in new Malawi*. Blantyre: CLAIM, pp. 11–24.

Helmke, G. and Levitsky, S. (2004): 'Informal Institutions and Comparative Politics: A Research Agenda', *Perspectives on Politics*, Vol. 2, No. 4, 725–40.

Hinojosa, M. (2012): *Selecting Women, Electing Women: Political Representation and Candidate Selection in Latin America*. Philadelphia, PA: Temple University Press.

Itzkovitch-Malka, R. and Hazan, R. Y. (2017): 'Unpacking Party Unity: The Combined Effects of Electoral Systems and Candidate Selection Methods on Legislative Attitudes and Behavioural Norms', *Political Studies*, Vol. 65, No. 2, 452–74. https://doi.org/10.1177/0032321716634094.

Krook, M. L. (2010): 'Beyond Supply and Demand: A Feminist-Institutionalist Theory of Candidate Selection', *Political Research Quarterly*, Vol. 63, No. 4, 707–20.

Lovenduski, J. and Norris, P. (1993): 'If Only More Candidates Came Forward: Supply-side Explanations of Candidate Selection in Britain', *British Journal of Political Science*, Vol. 23, No. 3, 373–408.

Manning (2005): 'Assessing African Party Systems after the Third Wave', *Party Politics*, Vol. 11, No. 6, 707–27.

Muriaas, R. L. (2009): 'Reintroducing a Local-Level Multiparty System in Uganda: Why Be in Opposition?' *Government and Opposition*, Vol. 44, No. 1, 91–112.

Muriaas, R. L., Wang, V. and Murray, R. (2019): 'Introduction: Introducing the Concept of Gendered Electoral Financing', in R. L. Muriaas, V. Wang and R. Murray (eds) *Gendered Electoral Financing: Money, Power, and Representation in Comparative Perspective*. Oxford, UK: Routledge Studies, pp. 1–24.

Musuva, C. (2009): 'Malawi: Political Violence, Intra-Party and Inter-Party Conflict', in K. Denis and S. Booysen (eds) *Compendium of Elections in Southern Africa 1989–2009: 20 Years of Multiparty Democracy*. Johannesburg: EISA, pp. 235–7.

Norris, P. and Lovenduski, J. (1995): *Political Recruitment: Gender, Race and Class in the British Parliament*. Cambridge: Cambridge University Press.

O'Neil, Kanyongolo, Wales and Mkandawire (2016): Women and Power: Representation and Influence in Malawi's Parliament. London: ODI Report.

Patel, N. and Mpesi, A. (2009): 'Between Choice and Imposition: The Politics of Nominations', in O. Martin and E. Kanyongolo (eds) *Democracy in Progress: Malawi's 2009 Parliamentary and Presidential Elections*. Kachere Books No. 48.

Patel, N. and Mpesi, A. (2009): 'Malawi General Elections 2009: The Politics of Nomination', chapter presented at the Malawi's 2009 Parliamentary and Presidential Elections: Democracy in Progress, Election Evaluation Conference, Lilongwe 23–26 June 2009.

Rakner, L., Svåsand, L. and Khembo, N. (2007): 'Fissions and Fusions, Foes and Friends: Party System Restructuring in Malawi in the 2004 General Election', *Comparative Political*, Vol. 40, No. 9, 1112–37.

Seeberg, M, Wahman, M. & Skaaning, S. (2018) Candidate nomination, intra-party democracy, and election violence in Africa, Democratization, 25:6, 959–977.

Stemler (2001): *An Introduction to Content Analysis*. ERIC Digest. www.eric.ed.gov.

Svåsand, L. (2014): 'The Regulation of Political Parties and Party Functions in Malawi: Incentive Structure and the Selective Application of the Rules', *International Political Science Review*, Vol. 35, No. 3, 275–90.

Verge, T. and Kenny, M. (2016): 'Opening Up the Black Box: Gender and Candidate Selection in a New Era', *Government and Opposition*, Vol. 51, July 2016, 351–69.

Wang, V., Muriaas, R., Kayuni, H. M., Chiweza, A. and Soyiyo, S. (2019):'Relieving Women's Costs of Standing for Election: Malawi's 50/50 Campaigns'. in R. L. Muriaas, V. Wang and R. Murray (eds) *Gendered Electoral Financing: Money, Power, and Representation in Comparative Perspective*. Oxford, UK: Routledge Studies, pp. 113–32.

5

'Inspiring a revolution': Women's central role in Tanzanian institutions, independence and beyond

Catherine Cymone Fourshey and Marla L. Jaksch

Introduction

Critical readings of institutionalism reveal a disturbing, yet common pattern – a pattern in which women and their contributions – if they make it into the picture at all – are distorted and pushed to the margins. In-depth analyses of women's political engagement in Africa continue to be limited and underdeveloped (Mulligan 1999; Yoon 2013, 2011). Major scholarly works rarely address the gendered nature of political processes and political institutions; rather, they are androcentrically presented as normatively male. This persists despite a growing and rich feminist literature on women in the fields of history, sociology, development and politics. For the most part the scholarship examines aspects of women's oppression and victimhood but rarely the consistent examples of women's achievements and societal contributions.

This is evident in the Tanzanian context (Hodgson 2001, 2005, 2017; Mbilinyi 2015; Ndziku 1994; Nsekela 1984; Shetler 2015; Tripp 2009; Tripp and Kang 2008; Tripp et al. 2006). The silence on women as political actors in Africa broadly, and Tanzania specifically, is inconsistent with what we know about individuals who served as leaders in precolonial times both politically as chiefs and socially as spiritual and cultural leaders (Achebe 2005; Berger 1976; Hanson 2002; Musisi 1996; Schoenbrun 1998; Willis 1981; Wright 1990). We also know that women did not stop ascending to positions and titles of authority – at least at the local level – in colonial times, though they were not always respected or acknowledged by colonial rulers as rightful decision makers. In the nationalist era, there were indeed women who led efforts in developing and sustaining the anti-colonial struggles in Tanganyika and Zanzibar. There is scant recognition of women's engagements in politics in Tanzania's larger society; the most well-known source on women's political lives in Tanzania is a single book length work on Bibi Titi Mohamed (1925–2000) by historian Susan Geiger (1997), a few journal articles, and a few reports from government offices and non-governmental organization (NGO). Geiger's twenty-three-year-old work is essential as it placed Mohamed's central role, in the independence struggle and the project to conceptualize the Tanzanian Nation, in the context of other contemporary women who were also activists, agents of political ideas and mobilizers of people in the movement.

The aim of this chapter is to explore a theoretical argument focused on an African feminist institutionalism particular to Tanzania in East Africa. Specifically, we make visible the connections between political representation in leaders and ideas and the role of symbolic items women often employ for political messages like cloth, songs and sites of memory. It is our contention that the common focus on recognized, elected leaders and/or women's participation in voting politics in Tanzania mirrors patterns in other countries. We suggest an expansive approach that takes into account embodied and symbolic language and praxis in political arenas. We focus on one particular case study, through which we might better understand how nationalist projects have unfolded over time and consistently erased women of all ages and social classes. Of interest is how this erasure has continued and expanded well into the contemporary moment. A dichotomous pattern persists. We point to ways one might recupperate political history and the contributions women have made actively, publicly and behind the scenes, even if not in elected positions.

We mediate by asking why there is a persistent erasure as well as how this might be remedied. The starting point of our intermediation is to deliberate on how the historical reality of women's active but 'unofficial' political and bio-cultural participation in Tanzanian politics and how to bring it into conversation with work being done currently to encourage increased political representation and official participation of women. Through what mechanisms might this dialogue take shape to increase opportunities? Furthermore, how might feminist institutionalism, as a critical framework for understanding power inequalities and for increasing women's participation, be informed by African feminist theory and advocacy?

Drawing connections from the past to current struggles regarding women's full participation in and impact on Tanzanian political institutions, we argue for a broader view of feminist institutionalism than is currently offered. By this, we mean to expand focus to consider more kinds of activity and performances of politics than the normative ascendance to named political positions and titles. Centring African feminist theoretical perspectives and drawing upon gendered historical accounts and including the symbolic in rendering women's contributions visible, we provide an example of expansive **African feminist institutionalism**. Attention to and inclusion of African feminist theorizing and advocacy allows for an expansion of current work in institutionalism, especially feminist institutionalism(s). Moreover, we argue that African feminisms, as intersectional and interdisciplinary praxis, have much to offer in expanding consideration of what counts as an institution and demands a turn beyond a singular focus on gender – particularly as imagined in the west.

Exploring the emergence of feminist institutionalism, we make a case for the value of African feminist critiques and approaches to institutions, specifically in the complex nationalist political context of Tanzania. Current feminist institutionalist work is interested in the 'rules of the game' in political institutions; how institutions create more gender-just conditions is critical in terms of policy and actions and in the makeup of the elected representatives. Greater attention must be paid to how nationalist institutions resist and/or obstruct positive gendered change (Bauer 2008; Ibrahim 2004; Mosha and Johnson 2004; Tomale 2020). We link contemporary feminist institutionalist work to the historical praxis of feminist leadership in Bibi Titi Mohamed (1926–2000). In her mid-twenties during the 1950s, Mohamed became a well-known activist for the cause of Tanzanian independence and national building in concert with the Tanganyikan African National Union (TANU). Her voice as a popular singer and compelling speaker made her both a powerful advocate for nationalist messages and mobilizer of Britain's Tanganyikan colonial subjects.

We, the authors of this piece, spend a great deal of time personally and professionally engaged with issues Africans, particularly Tanzanians, raise as critical to daily life. As scholars based in North America, specifically the United States where the nation at its founding moment excluded those who were not land-owning northern European descended (white) men, we are deeply committed to making sense of Tanganyika as it claimed its independence and unfolded as a nation-state to become Tanzania. From the inception, men and women in the political space conceived institutions with gender equality at the centre from their founding. To what extent did they achieve their stated goals? We start with the case of Bibi Titi Mohamed as a means of deconstructing the male-centric heroic narrative and to make way for additional work on the full spectrum of descant and negated voices particularly of Tanzanian women over the last seven decades. In the case of Mohamed her negation is both specific to how she was used, disabused, imprisoned and cast aside, yet also generalizable to the experiences of women's precarious positions in the contexts of post-colonial Tanzania, patriarchy locally and globally, and neo-colonial institutions broadly. Despite principles that centred equality and inclusion or supposed gender-neutrality in Tanzanian founding documents, political, social and economic institutions are almost entirely male-dominated at the leadership level.

We then return to explore the contemporary landscape for women in politics. To do so we turn to the development of gender-reserved spaces (110 special seats) in parliament, touching upon the successes and failures of the recent 2015 election politics in Tanzania. We conclude our chapter by linking the importance of historical and symbolic work in the African context to feminist institutionalism to develop potential ways to bring about impactful gendered change.

'Inspiring a revolution': The case of Bibi Titi Mohammed

Tanzania marked its fiftieth anniversary of liberation from colonial rule 2011–12. Various conferences, speeches, workshops and celebrations commemorated those involved in the liberation struggle and reflected on continuing struggles for equality and autonomy in this country and world region. A closer look at the commemorative events and materials in Tanzania reveals distorted depictions and narrow imaginings of what stories are worth telling. Whose experiences and contributions are noted in official records matters. There is a 'pattern of forgetting' women's roles in favour of a uniform representation of the liberation movement. This not only erases women's political agency in Tanzania and across the African continent (Coombes 2003: 7)' but also leaves audiences ignorant of large parts of the process of nationalist struggle. Furthermore, excluding women leaves half the population outside processes of anti-colonial struggle, nation building, and leadership.

Focusing on the life and work of Bibi Titi Mohammed provides an opportunity to consider the complex nature of women's stories and representations in ways that have an impact on not only the telling of history but also women's ability to sustain a meaningful political life and agency (Mohanty et al. 1991). While Mohamed was the author of important legal policies and major directions taken by TANU, she is most commonly mentioned in scholarship almost exclusively in regards to her flaws and transgressions. She and other ignored politically active women of her era are otherwise mostly ignored.

Berger (2003) argues that there exists an enduring normalizing masculinist and patriarchal tendency in Western historiographies that focuses almost exclusively on the experiences of men. When they appear, women are depicted as victims or marginal figures with no subjectivity or agency. Geiger (1997) also challenges dominant Western feminist frameworks about women and nationalism by providing a rich contextualization of Bibi Titi Mohamed's leadership in TANU. She raises many questions and contradictions and writes that the dominant narrative does nothing, however, to explain how

> Bibi Titi Mohammed, a 30-year old lead singer in the popular ngoma (musical) group, 'Bomba', became an actual rather than fictive TANU leader, and why thousands of women became nationalist activists as a result of her political acumen and enthusiastic work.
>
> (Geiger 1997: 11)

Through interviews, oral histories and testimonies of women involved in the liberation struggle, it is evident that women remember this time very differently than men. For example, Geiger notes that the women she spoke to offered a very different picture in their construction of the present and the reconstructions of their past political involvement. Their narratives show that in the 1950s, 'ordinary' (illiterate frequently self-identified Swahili, Muslim) women created and performed Tanganyikan nationalism or 'culture of politics' (1997: 15).

Bibi Titi Mohamed became the leader of the women's section of TANU and initially the sole woman in President Julius Nyerere's post-independence government and inner circle. Bibi Titi has been quoted as saying that being a part of a singing group led her to politics and allowed her to successfully recruit members to TANU. She stated,

> Nobody knew anything about independence or what it was. People were afraid …. But we approached them slowly and tactfully, explaining what it meant, and where we were going, and the meaning of what we were doing. And they accepted. But my position was helped by these people of the organisations.
>
> (Bibi Titi Mohamed in Geiger 1997: 50–1)

Bibi Titi Mohamed is an important and complicated figure in Tanzanian liberation history. Since Geiger published her work on TANU women in 1997, little attention was paid to Mohamed (or the thousands of women who worked with her) until liberation commemorations were held across Tanzania 2011-12. This oversight is partly due to the notion that Mohamed's story disrupts dominant nationalist history in Tanzania. Specifically, life history narratives of women activists in TANU disrupt the view that liberation happened in progressive stages to develop a nationalist consciousness of African socialism that borrowed heavily from Western forms and ideals (Geiger 1996). Eight years after these public commemorations, Mohamed has once again fallen to the sidelines of this political history.

On 8 July 1955, holding her first political meeting of the Women's Section of TANU Mohamed legendarily convinced 400 women to join the organization. By October of the same year, Mohamed became well-known for having enrolled 5,000 women members. TANU's Organizing Secretary, Oscar Kambona, signalled her contributions when he wrote to London that although only 'semi-literate', Mohamed was 'inspiring a revolution in the role of women in African society' (Kambona as quoted in Geiger 1997: 11). Geiger argued that the understandings she assembled from her interviews with TANU women did not easily fit with existing explanations of nationalism – in part because it denied the contributions of ordinary, Swahili women with minimal schooling. Chronicling the success of Mohamed through TANU required admission that she and other women profoundly shaped the party's values and thus made it a relevant and viable political movement for women and men. This realization suggests the problematic of, dominant and recurring narrative depicting a small cohort of men as the 'proto-nationalists whose anti-colonial actions set the stage' for later Western-oriented political work of nationalists in Tanzania (Geiger 1996: 465; Lal 2010: 6, 2102: 219). Women's stories confirm that their lived experiences (which reflected trans-ethnic ties and affiliations) did not merely react to TANU's political rhetoric; these women actively 'shaped, informed, and spread a nationalist consciousness for which TANU was the vehicle' (Geiger 1996: 465).

Mohamed and her fellow activists' political work did not end with the struggle for independence but was instrumental in the continuation of women's political culture of nationalism in post-independence years' through efforts like the spearheading of the formation of the All Africa Women's Conference in Dar es Salaam in June 1962. Mohamed even held a short-lived position in parliament and within TANU leadership until she resigned due to conflicts over ownership of property prohibited in the Arusha Declaration. Her ideas also conflicted with ideas espoused by TANU's male leadership. In November of 1962, President Nyerere declared that all women's organizations should be dissolved and merged into one national women's organization, *Umoja wa Wanawake wa Tanzania* (UWT). The move seemed to be an effort to diminish power but Mohamed led UWT until she resigned in June 1967. Tensions and conflict persist and in 1969, Mohamed was arrested and detained on charges of treason. Mohamed and four others were tried, found guilty and sentenced to life in prison for attempting to overthrow the government and kill Nyerere. She served two years and two months in prison before she was released. President Nyerere pardoned her in 1972. Mohamed paid a great personal price fro asserting her ideas.

Belied by erasures of African women in scholarship and public displays, many women were deeply involved in sustained national liberation struggles and nation-building efforts. Kim Miller's (2011) work on women and commemorative practices in post-apartheid South Africa asks how historical truth is possible without an account of women's experiences. The life history of Bibi Titi Mohamed illustrates how nationalist history is diminished without all stories Bibi Titi Mohamed. Her involvement in the Tanganyikan, African National Union (TANU) shaped the party and was essential to the success of the liberation struggle. It is important to visibilize women's identities as political actors historically to contemporary times. Many of the women involved in the establishment of TANU were Muslim had little formal schooling; thus they were constrained by emerging institutional practice. Yet, these women were able to negotiate these restrictions and, in a very short period, recruit thousands of members. Considering women's spaces and spheres of influence in scholarship challenge the patterns of forgetting and makes visible a more comprehensive trail to freedom' through the living rooms, kitchens, marketplaces and alleyways to stadiums and halls that served as political education and recruitment sites. These spaces contain stories that extend beyond the passive setting for historical action to profoundly shape the popular political organization that TANU became. Attention to space along with intersectional approaches to retelling women's stories that challenge normative depictions of African women visibilizes people and audibilizes voices of contest and difference. This approach renders more complex contradictory textual, oral and visual representations of liberation. In doing so, we contribute to a wider debate regarding African feminisms, nationalism and transnational struggles.

Feminist scholars Alexander and Mohanty (2010), McFadden (2005, 2018) and Mama (2001: 2010) agree that to fully understand the meaning of struggle, it is vital to know how a broad spectrum of society's – particularly women's – knowledge shaped the movements in which they held active leadership roles. We must be committed to moving on from celebration to deep analyses and drawing connections between the precolonial conditions that produced a figure such as Mohamed to the post-colonial conditions that have allowed for her erasure, as well as those that followed her (Lal 2010). In the African context, we see the convergence of patriarchy, Western forms of sexism and misogyny mapped onto colonial practices that have played out in various ways in the post-colonial context through factors such as structural adjustment programmes (SAPs), the rise of international development schemes and neoliberalization of local economies.

Paradoxically, Mohamed's case not only demonstrates women's potential for political office, and the ability to ecite mass movements, but also highlights what happens when gender and masculinist politics collide. Tanzania has a long history of women in leadership. Additionally, founding documents proclaimed a gender-just society, yet, historical and theoretical underpinnings succumbed to nationalist paradigms. The feminist lens through which Mohamed saw, interpreted, and lived in the world and emerges in the tensions with founding documents, policy and values represented in the discussions and accusations made by the early political leadership. Mohamed negotiated her political criminilization and marginalization, which manifested as insidious sexism, patriarchy, religious constraints and sanctions, among other things. by carving out a space in the UWT and outside the party as a figure in the business community. Mohamed is often held up as an exception to the rule and a cautionary tale; mainstream retellings render her political successes invisible. Mohamed's approach to politics and the world can be read as an example of nego-feminism (described in depth below) and part of the long-term feminist institutionalism project.

Chandra Mohanty et al. (1991) analyses the silence, resistance and/or ambivalence regarding women's involvement in two-thirds of the world's liberation struggles and argues that Western feminists (and others) have been tempted to think of colonialism as a mostly material practice that involves political, economic and social systems of overt domination. She draws attention to forms of discursive colonialism less explicit, but no less significant, than the scholarship and expressive culture that reproduces unequal relations of power. Her post-colonial feminist framework deploys intersectional identity to construct the category of 'women' in 'a variety of political contexts that often exist simultaneously and overlaid on top of one another' (Mohanty et al. 1991: 65). This approach is critical for its links between women and among groups of women of various economic, social, political, ethnic and religious statuses; without falling into false generalizations it acknowledges the contradictions as well as commonalities in women's experiences.

Mohanty's approach is valuable, when considered along with scholars who contend, gender in Africa is an ambiguous category when we look back over the historical landscape. The reasons are multiple, but two of those reasons are the power lineages held and the fact that physical bodies were not necessarily a logical means of deciding who could make decisions, hold power or wield authority (Oyěwùmí 1997). Societies certainly recognized biological distinctions expressed in people's bodies, yet physical differences of male and female were not the basis of granting power and authority or doling out responsibility; rather, it was more likely to be what Abosede George (2018) calls status of 'juniority' or 'seniority' that determined one's societal influence and authority.

Over the last three decades, Amina Mama has questioned the legitimacy and relevance of European men's imaginings of African women. Certainly these constructions have played out in African and African descendant women's lives (1989, 1995). In particular, Mama has examined how the Western academic establishment has historically constructed the black female subject in ways that perpetuate patriarchy and uphold white privilege. Analysing African women's subjectivity through the lens of raced and gendered oppression, Mama rightly challenges the victim construction of women. Instead, she contends African women have self-defined dynamic and creative subjectivities (1995: 145). Mama asks, 'What does it mean to say that subjectivity is gendered? Are all positions that women or men for that matter take up gendered; that is to say, specifically 'feminine' or 'masculine'? Or are femininity and masculinity aspects of subjectivity that are not always manifest? (1995: 147–8). Since at least the 1990s African feminists have continued to challenge whether gender is really the best way to categorize and identify humans, especially when done along rigid and binary lines.

Nigerian scholar Obioma Nnaemeka's (2004) articulation of 'nego-feminism' provides a useful theoretical framework. Work in African feminisms highlights deep engagement with pre-colonial histories, and Nnameka suggests that contemporary African feminists continue the art and legacy of negotiation as a primary political strategy. We contend nego-feminism is useful in analyzing eastern African women's sites of knowledge and authority production. Nego-Feminism also speaks against some of the problematics of Western feminism that Nkiru Nzegwu captures in a term she coined sisterarchy, whereby Western feminists reinscribe domination over African women. In contrast to imperialistic tendencies of western feminism, Nnemeaka contends:

First nego-feminism is the feminism of negotiation; second nego-feminism stands for 'no ego' feminism. In the foundation of shared values in many African cultures are the principles of negotiation, give and take, compromise and balance. African feminism[s] challenges through negotiations and compromise. It knows when, where, and how to detonate patriarchal land mines; it also knows when, where, and how to go around patriarchal landmines'.

(Obioma Nnaemeka's 2004: 377)

In essence, the argument is that there is a form of African practice and theory that does not perpetuate oppression through ego and hierarchies. Nego-feminism also hopes to detach personal gain and pride from the overall goal of achieving equity for women – thus "no ego"' (Nnaemeka 2004: 377–8). African feminist scholar Sinmi Akin-Aina sees nego-feminism 'as a guide for dealing with the feminist struggles that occur on the continent; it considers the implications of patriarchal traditions and customs and aims to dismantle and negotiate around these'.

Attention to African feminist theories and practices is critical in understanding women's current and past engagement in politics as actors, build institutions, not just how they are limited and shaped by existing institutions. To date, Historical Institutionalism (HI) does not fully engage African women's history through a feminist lens precisely because it centers nationalist patriarchal narative. In the next section, we briefly explore African women's leadership historically in order to argue for a Feminist Institutionalism (FI) that is interdisciplinary – incorporating feminist historiography into the process rather than existing as silos of literature.

Pre-colonial and anti-colonial women's leadership

Although twentieth century national politics were dominated by men, Mohamed grew up in a community that afforded women identities, roles and positions in which they were socially, politically and economically influential. Many women had privilege, and exercised authority and responsibility in decision making at various stages in their lives within their social, familial, political and economic networks. Yet centuries of both internally generated inventions and transformations in values and beliefs, often along with influences from Islam and Christianity as well as colonial-style capitalism and neoliberalism, have collectively solidified the hold patriarchy has in most corners of the continent. The rise and entrenchment of patriarchal forms are both anathema to the multidimensional forms, processes and choices regarding authority, position and responsibilities that many in Africa find valid and efficacious. In the decades since independence, African countries have failed to remedy much of the erosion to women's social, political and economic positions that colonial rule set in motion or accelerated.

As an intervention into studies of leadership and nationalist struggle, we contend the legacy of Tanzanian women's agency in ending colonial rule and forwarding pan-African political struggles was central and drew on centuries of women's political engagement. It is critical to also place women in the context of East Africa's historical legacy – prior to the nation state – women were socially, politically and economically influential. Even with, centuries of internally generated inventions and transformations in values and beliefs nationalist politics had unprecedented impacts that collectively led to erasure of women in official recognition. Considering the historical and continued roles women play, conventional masculinist historical frameworks are inadequate for capturing the complicated and complex nature of women's contributions to the struggle and reasons for their continuous marginalization in this history.

Despite levels of authority women have held locally and regionally in Tanzania's mainland Geiger (1997) suggests at least two reasons for women's exclusion from the history of the liberation struggle and leadership in Tanzania. Firstly, she explains that the marginalization of African women in history tends to reflect an all too familiar androcentric bias in recorded history. This process of erasure is accomplished through successive accounts in primary (produced by colonial officials/travellers) and secondary (produced by Western and African scholars) records that echo the silence of the previous one. Secondly, Geiger proposes that the erasure of women has been more thorough in accounts of Tanzanian nationalism written in English than in those texts written by Tanzanian scholars and activists produced in Swahili. Given the dominance of English publications by scholars outside Tanzania, these omissions become unquestioned historical facts that have remained stubbornly fixed for decades. In the following sections, we consider the concept of representation and how it connects to feminist institutionlism.

Representation and feminist institutionalism

Feminist institutionalism emerges from critiques and through expansions of institutionalism and new institutionalisms. New institutionalism (NI) has focused on the centrality of institutions as key variables in political analyses for more than three decades (Mackay and Waylen 2009, 2010). The singular focus on the significance of institutions emerges from the recognition that we inhabit a world that was, and continues to be, increasingly dominated by national and supra-national economic, social and political institutions. NI provides scholars with useful alternative frameworks to analyse 'political dynamics and outcomes that shape everyday life' (Mackay et al. 2010: 573) and as such emphasizes the co-constitutive nature of politics, the role of political actors, and the role of norms, rules and policies which limit or facilitate agency for political actors.

In the case of Tanzania's nation-building efforts over the last six decades, NI serves as a critical approach to understanding women's political representation or lack thereof and in most cases their marginalization. Despite early rhetoric about socialism and gender equity and equality as the Tanzanian nation was being imagined and formed, nationalist institutions have clearly become gendered male. Though the construction of political space is gendered male, women have worked their way into parliament and have long been at the forefront of some of the most important political and civic organizations like Tanzania Networking Programme (TGNP), that have shaped the nation. Women have fought for women's rights alongside their struggles for the rights of all Tanzanians. The significance of women's contributions has been tokenized and marginalized due to their exclusion from political representation over the last sixty years. A narrow understanding of what constitutes a political actors and actions persists. Knowledge of gendered history disrupts the established masculinist presentations of history and liberation struggle. Disrupting the ideologies that privilege men as the only (and main) actors in the political processes, however, have not necessarily meant that the legacy of women's efforts to end colonial rule and the significance of Tanzanian women in pan-African political struggles. In fact, it is our contention that conventional pan-African historical frameworks are masculinist and inadequate for capturing the complicated and complex nature of women's contributions to nation building. This is a primary reason for their continued marginalization in history and politics. The life of Bibi Titi Mohamed, a self-described Tanzanian activist, illustrates how her involvement in various political activities shaped and was essential to the success of the liberation struggle in Tanzania. However, it will take more than celebrating her story or representing her as the singular figure – and therefore the exception to the rule – to upend the well-worn patterns of recent history. Our focus on Bibi Titi Mohamed is intended to encourage studies of her contemporaries and those who came after her by highlighting gaps in scholarship. The connections made between masculinist nation-building projects, erasure of women's contributions and anti-colonial mobilization and women's marginalization into twenty-first-century politics and the instituting of special reserved female parliament seats should be assessed as a complex mix of rupture and continuity with precolonial practice.

Similar to male figures, Bibi Titi Mohamed spoke at rallies, gave speeches and contributed many ideas in the shaping of policies from the 1950s to 1960s. However, records of her many actions and words are not preserved in state records to the extent and in the way nationalist voices and actions of her male contemporaries have been. Male voices and actions are not just documented but also presented in multiple archives and displayed in museums. The erasure of women is made clearer by the fact that Mohamed – though herself largely glossed over or ignored – has become the symbol of all women. She is the singular woman best remembered from the nationalist project. African feminist institutionalism would call for looking beyond the colonial and nationalist paradigms that highlighted forms of speech and action that privilege male figures who had greater formal education relative to women. Likewise, expanding beyond the contributions of well-known individuals like Bibi Titi Mohamed and Julius Nyerere would reconfigure institutionalism beyond 'leaders' to include the many voices and actions of the everyday individuals who brought independence and the nation into being. We contend this ought to be done by examining ephemera and durable items of material culture significant to Tanzanians and particularly to women. Songs, recipes and culturally significant cloth like the *khanga* are a few important forms that would allow researchers new insights into independence. African Feminist Institutionalism advocates for just such analyses that move beyond the official icons, speeches, laws and policies passed in cabinets and parliaments first exclusively male and more recently majority male, to consider locally generated forms of communication and action. Mohamed, a Muslim woman from a typical lower-class neighbourhood in Dar es Salaam, was adept as speaking to the masses as she understood their economic struggles and social-political values. Her political effectiveness is evidenced by the fact that at age twenty-nine she was named chair of the UWT, which was TANU's branch for women. By the later 1960s, Mohamed was pushed out of TANU as a result of her strong advocacy for women and the rights of women to own rental properties to sustain themselves financially. She took several other positions at odds with the male leadership. Ultimately Mohamed was accused of a conspiracy against President Julius Kambarage Nyerere and imprisoned for several years. After her release Mohamed remained sidelined from the political arena. In some ways, her case relates to many other women in different locations across the continent and the globe.

In the following section we argue for the inclusion of the symbolic in feminist institutionalism. By considering the ideas and efforts of women in producing, transmitting and commemorating women's work. Women as political actors, and the hand they have had had in shaping institutions are well articulated in cultural symbols.

Feminist symbolic institutionalism

Symbols are important. They signal what a society values and respects (Bourdieu and Thompson 1991). Choices that those in power make, about memorialization in museum displays, monuments, locative nomenclature and public shrines that serve as sites of commemoration to past deeds and contributions of individuals, can be as important as appointments and positions of authority in signaling who can and should have decision-making opportunities in a society. Museum images of men actively making speeches and women static carrying babies on the sidelines is a strong signal. While these are public sphere spaces that grieve and celebrate the past, they are an inner reflection of the state and also have private and personal meaning for individuals (Nieves 2008, 2009). A nation whose face reflects only one facet of society – elder men who have been given the opportunity to serve as statesmen for example – leaves no opportunity for others to imagine their own possibilities and contributions (Miller 2009, 2011). This is a nationalism that is exclusionary, narrow in its imagining because it allows the public sphere to overshadow both the private sphere and the behind-the-scenes sphere. Women like Bibi Titi Mohamed, Mwami Theresa Ntare, Fatuma Karume and the millions of other anonymous rural and urban women, who contributed to the nation building so critical to Nyerere and his cohort at the moment of precarious transition, were rarely, if ever, working entirely in the domestic sphere colonialism constructed and tried to box them into. Rather the women of Tanzania were typically out in the public, on the front lines, but often to remain behind-the-scenes and only rarely allowed to claim their rightfully earned positions in the official structures of the nationalist government. Ironically, women are central in oral histories across Tanzania

Figure 5.1 *Bibi Titi Mohamed Road, Dar es Salaam, Tanzania Photo Credit: Marla Jaksch.*

symbols reflect not only the easily visible action, rhetoric, and thinking behind independence struggles and nation building, but also the less easily seen but equally important work of women. Even symbols the state has placed on the built environment and landscape in Tanzania hardly recognize women individually or collectively to the extent they do men.

One of the early acts undertaken by the new Republic of Tanzania's government to create unity and to celebrate liberation after independence was to rename many of the major roads in the city of Dar es Salaam in honour of significant heroes of African liberation history. A major road was named for Mohamed in recognition of her role as a TANU leader (Figure 5.1). This recognition of Mohamed is interesting given the reluctance to acknowledge individual women as leaders in the liberation struggle and due to the few memorials that exist in Tanzania commemorating liberation history (Bold et al. 2002). After Mohamed was imprisoned, the road was renamed *Umoja wa Wanawake wa Tanzania* (Union of Women of Tanzania) but was eventually changed back again in the mid-1980s to Bibi Titi Mohamed during the thirty-year independence celebrations. While the work of Bibi Titi Mohamed illustrates women's involvements both at the forefront and in the margins of various political activities. They shaped and were essential to the success of the liberation struggle in Tanzania, yet recognition was hard to come by and grudgingly granted.

Another significant example of feminist symbolic institutionalism that is critical to conversations regarding women as actors in the political process is that of the *khanga*. We foreground the *khanga* as a critical example of a Tanzanian women's knowledge and symbolic institutionalism that demonstrates women's political actions, especially in raising awareness. Khanga are both billboards broadcasting and archives chronicling information legacy building, and as a form of nego-feminism. By men on occassion in private, in most of East Africa, *khanga* is an art form that is typically viewed as a cheap women's cloth that is ubiquitous and mundane. As such, it is hardly considered as a meaningful site of knowledge production, resistance and authority. *Khangas*, originating in coastal areas, are rectangles of pure cotton cloth, printed colourful designs with a central motif called *mji* (central portion), a *pindo* (border) along all four sides, and a *jina* (name or message) along the bottom which are worn, designed and exchanged by ordinary women across East Africa. *Khangas* uniformly measure five feet long by three feet high and always come in identical pairs imprinted with a wide variety of designs. They are typically worn to protect clothing from being ruined and dirtied as women travel on public transport work, or complete household tasks. Portions are used as head wraps, scarves and babies slings. A *khanga* is the perfect item to bundle a large load of goods into. In more contemporary times they have often been sewn and transformed into fashionable items and it can be wrapped to form a cushion rested on the head to buffer and stabilize a load of goods.

Khanga may be named after the colourful guinea fowl called a *khanga* in eastern Africa. The cloth can be tied on the head in the shape very similar to this bird. While khanga began as a small handkerchief-sized cloth that those with little disposable income could acquire to display some fashionability and as they accumulated and sewed pieces together to display some economic upward mobility. In time, it became a fashion staple that carried political and personal significance (Ryan 2017).

Though khanga were a commodity, over time the cloth began to carry political weight that Elisabeth Linnebuhr (1992) points out British colonial representatives tried to control because khangas contained messages that could be deployed to mobilize people. Khangas were messages visual, verbal and proverbial. Their meanings were always multiple, though they also reflect literal transparent messages that express simple statements, the opaque meanings in the messages are particularly intriguing. When deftly employed these denseley packed phrases can serve as a powerful social commentary. The *khanga* has become a powerful tool both for women to carve out subjectivity and to demonstrate authority as an individual and within a community. Resistance can be encoded in personal choices like clothing that may be displayed in either the private or public sphere. While the private and public can have very different impacts and ramifications, Stephanie Newell contends, popular culture including clothing can be used to shape and exhibit political and social resistance and self-defined authority.

In terms of serving as inventories and archives of social and political thought the *khanga* has been used to communicate disruptive messages. Emerging from everyday cultural production of women and girls they are powerful forms of subaltern connection and global networking. Swai describes khangas as functioning as a form of 'radical aesthetics of double-coding' which occurs when a saying has at least two meanings (Swai 2010). Double coding is a strategy that *khanga* authors strategically leverage to publicize their message when direct speech is not possible or desirable. In this case, the double coding functions as a way to subvert patriarchal norms and conventions on speech and space. Saida Yahya-Othman (1997) argues that khangas are not only deeply symbolic of womanhood, they represent a uniquely female form of communication. It is important to note that Yahya-Othman does not make this argument from a biologically essentialized position. Rather, the author points to modes of communication that women have carved out for themselves in circumstances where men have captured control over official political discourse and decision making in a post-colonial patriarchal system. Men typically own the modes of producing the cloth, serve as the distributors of it, and own the local shops selling it. While women are rarely connected to controlling the cloth before it is sold, they are the primary purchasers and recipients of khanga. The importance of the khanga is its role as a as a form of subaltern language; women shape the meanings of the written, visual and bodily language of the cloth. Women have made use of khangas as an additional strategy that allows them to make strong statements about their concerns while at the same time avoiding direct conflict, which might arise from their individual actions. Nigerian feminist Obioma Nnameaka (2004) notes that women can turn cultural norms against patriarchy. *Khanga* functions as a clear example of this type of feminist approach in action. Language on *khanga* are at once incisive and cryptic. Women can express thoughts and feelings publicly through this popular culture medium, because they masterfully deploy indirectness. In a patriarchal postcolonial society, those assigned the gender female at birth often employ *khanga* to work both within and against the constraints placed upon them. *Khanga* sayings are a politeness strategy that women adopt to express their feelings and resistance simultaneously (Yahya-Othman 1995).

Zanzibari feminist scholar Amina A. Issa situates the *khanga* as a political intervention, in which women were central figures in the liberation struggle. Zanzibari women deployed *khanga* as a 'weapon of political struggles'. In this context *khanga* served as a foundational vehicle to verbalize and vizibilize women's consciousness about the struggle for independence (2016).

Umoja wa Wanawake wa Tanzania – Tunaweza (Women's Union/Party of Tanzania — We Can!). Along with the familiar and politically charged words, images and colours conjure up histories of liberation struggles and revolutions. The *khanga* pictured below, printed in the colours of the nationalist ruling party Chama cha Mapinduzi (CCM), references the women's wing of the party – the UWT. Formed in 1962 with its head office in Dar es Salaam Bibi Titi Mohammed served as first chair. Since its founding, the UWT has played major roles in shaping Tanzania, but it is the the organization launched *khanga* in the liberation struggle that we foreground. Mohamed, in the 1960s went as far as referring to the *khanga* as an important 'nationalist tool of empowerment and self-expression' (Geiger 1997: 180).

However, years later women deployed *khanga* the nation of unfulfuled promises made to women during the liberation struggle. The promises made

Figure 5.2 Khanga *representing the work of Umoja wa Wannawake wa Tanzania – Tunaweza – 'Tanzanian Women's Union – We Can Do it!' Photo credit: Marla L. Jaksch.*

Figure 5.3 *Commemorative* khanga *for the life of Bibi Titi Mohamed reads* Daima Tutakuenzi *'Always (forever), we do these things for you (in your memory)'. Credit Marla L. Jaksch.*

to women in political slogans were enshrined in the Republic of Tanzania constitution. Thus they needed to be enacted. The use of text, colour and imagery, on khanga highlight how independence era women leveraged their interests and how feminist concerns post-independence have drawn on those strategies. In this way, these khangas are historical records, archiving political promises and thought, and tools women use to educate, remind and build solidarity, making them a strategy to hold to account those who had forgotten or refused to centre women's rights in contemporary political, social and advocacy work.

Women in politics in Tanzania today

The argument is that the greater numerical representation of women in parliaments will lead to improved articulation of so-called 'women's issues' and positive legislative changes for women. However, what does it mean to argue this to be the case without understanding the history of women's political participation and connecting their struggles against exclusion to the legacy of women before them?

In 1985, a quota system was introduced in Tanzania to increase the number of women in parliament – becoming a pioneer of reserved seat quotas. In 2015, women represented in parliament increased to 34 per cent and by 2020 it stands at 42 per cent.[1] This percentage is a greater proportion compared to women members of parliament (MPs) in Southern African Development Community (SADC) countries. This number is also beyond the target established by both the SADC community and the 1995 Beijing Platform for Action goal of 30 per cent female representation in elected parliamentary membership (Gender Links 2015; Sadie 2005; Strachan 2015).

Women in Tanzania have certainly made inroads in national politics, joining the ranks of parliament. One might conclude that with women in seats of power and decision making that so-called 'women's issues' and legislative changes that might bring benefits for women would be articulated and realized. Without an understanding of women's political participation historically and without context for the struggles, it is hard to create a meaningful narrative of what women can achieve politically. Likewise, without stories of previous generations of women leaders who forged a path into political representation, women have no models to inspire them of possibilities.

Recently, there have been calls for the special seats for women to be abolished because the quota system has reified women's marginalization. women hold 100 per cent of special seats and make up 42 per cent of parliament, which creates some semblance of equity in numbers. However, women only hold 13 per cent of constituent seats and that represents 21 per cent of women in parliament. Despite the problematic nature of the need for special seats to balance out constituent seats, of which men hold 87 per cent (193 of the 223 constituent seats). Recent NGO reports highlight calls for an increase in the quota for women to be raised to 50 per cent of seats, without a call for those being constituent seats. Women rarely occupy leadership positions in national political parties. Currently political parties 'make provisions' for women's issues being represented in parliament in their constitutions and manifestos; however, there is often little mention of women's roles in shaping political parties. In local governance, studies show that women landowners tend to have more power through their marital relationships – leading to an increase in women's level of political participation. However, currently at the local level evidence suggests political participation has little impact on policy change, especially policies directly effecting women and girls.

Special seats

In Tanzania allocation of special seats is assigned based upon the number of votes a party wins in the parliamentary elections (Seppänen and Virtanen 2008). Parties then have their own internal systems for allocating these special seats. Many argue that the selection methods party officials employ are opaque and have the potential for corruption, including sexual corruption (Seppänen and Virtanen 2008) which undermines the integrity of female candidates. The process of selecting female representatives for special seats complicates women MPs' accountability to female constituencies, as their loyalty remains with the party (Seppänen and Virtanen 2008). More positively, Yoon (2011) argues that the increase in the number of women in parliament has gradually changed negative attitudes towards women in politics. Some legislation on so-called 'women's issues' has passed and there are reports of improved interactions between male and female MPs.

Yoon (2008, 2011) also notes that there are calls from certain quarters to abolish the special seats citing that special seats were never meant to be permanent, but rather a temporary measure until women's political participation could be normalized. It was imagined that women would enter the political process in the same ways as their male counterparts. An additional argument for abolition of special seats has to do with term limits. Critics argue that many women have held their seats for more than two terms and therefore special seats reduce opportunities for other women to gain experience. CCM, the leading party, is now forcing maximum two-year term limits on their allocation of special seats (Yoon 2013: 146–7).

Feminists have noted that special seats do not always work to women's advantage; in addition to the critiques listed above, special seat MPs are viewed as inferior. This has led to women's desire to compete for constituency seats; three special seat MPs won constituency seats in the 2010 election. Seppänen and Virtanen (2008) critique the special seats system as having 'eroded the competitive power in the basic democratic system' (121). Some have argued that the need for and critique of special seats along with the levels of graft should be seen as an erosion of the basic democratic system (Bauer 2008). Feminist scholars such as Tripp and Kang have argued that quotas serve as a system of 'fast-tracking' allowing for significant growth of female representation in legislatures across sub-Saharan Africa (Tripp and Kang 2008; Tripp et al. 2006). Others assert that the introduction of gender quotas has resulted in the widest reaching electoral reforms in the world over the last two or so decades (Wang and Yoon 2018).

Clearly there is little agreement about the value of special seats, there is, however, consensus in the literature on the lack of gender equity within the political parties. Tanzania electoral and political systems have marginalized women in intra-party and inter-party competitions (Babeiya 2011: 94). No political party has achieved gender parity at the decision-making level (Tenthani et al. 2014: 6). This originates in male dominance in national imaginings down to the way the political parties are organized and function as 'old boy' networks to the common educational and military backgrounds priviledged. This is compounded since social, cultural and religious norms (often rooted in colonialism) are the basis of national politics. Women often lack political networks honored and therefore lack required experience and financial resources. There is also a profound lack of support for female party members from party leadership, despite some improved gender relations (2014: 121). What might improve women's political participation, political agency and numerical representation from here? In the next section, we briefly explore the potential of the establishment of an African feminist institutionalism and what it might mean for women's rights and participation in the political process and institutional building.

Towards African feminist institutionalism(s)

It is our view that Western feminism undergirds much of emergent feminist institutionalism literature. Western feminism has been critiqued sometime for its racial and other biases. This has led to the accusation that most forms of mainstream Western feminism are actually 'white feminism'. Feminist scholar Jessie Daniels (2016) describes white feminism as a form of liberal feminism whose goal is to attain white women the same levels of compensation, representation and power in the public sphere as white men. It advances social change focused solely on gender while disregarding other oppressions. As such, white feminism is rooted in colonial, orientalist, and racist institutions. According to Meyda Yegenoglu (1998), it is through cultural representation 'of the west to itself, by way of a detour through the other' (1) that a sovereign subject status for the West is secured. It is important to note that contemporary African feminisms have emerged from work within the development sphere via what Amina Mama (2004) critically names 'developmental feminism', which is the result of the relationship between feminism and the development industry and is characterized by 'entryism': 'getting women into existing institutions and into development rather than transforming them' (121). This reifies marginalization.

Can attention to and inclusion of African feminist theorizing, symbolic work and advocacy allow for a transformation of the current formation of feminist institutionalism and to institutions? In order to be accurate, African feminism must be spoken of in pluralities. In a recent special issue on African feminisms in the journal *Meridians*, Alicia Decker and Gabeba Baderoon (2018) state that based on a survey of recent interdisciplinary work in research, policy and advocacy,

> African feminisms are not only diverse in their various forms but are also in vibrant and sometimes tense relation to one another around topics such as sexuality, national policies, and transnational solidarity. Yet instead of being a disadvantage, such diversity actually spurs innovative and politically radical approaches in the field. The multiplicity of feminisms theorised in this issue allows us to challenge patriarchal ideologies and structures on myriad fronts, both on the African continent and beyond.
>
> (Alicia Decker and Gabeba Baderoon 2018: 219)

African feminisms, then, while inclusive of developmental feminisms, are more than this. By suturing together African women's liberation history, concrete examples of women's critical symbolic political work, and African feminist theoretical frameworks, together with feminist institutionalism, we see the emergence of a more nuanced, complicated space (Adeleye-Fayemi 1999). A space where one size fits all, gender essentialized approaches are rejected in favour of intersectional approaches that complicate and historicize gender and leadership, along with other significant identities.

Conclusion

In a 2012 *Pambazuka News* article about whether or not women in Africa are now occupying new movements, the author pinpoints the sense of shock uttered by many people that women play such a large and visible role in the many recent acts of mass civil resistance. According to Executive Director of the Association of Women's Rights in Development (AWID) Hakima Abbas, even though women have been widely involved in past liberation struggles, what is consistently disputed is the participation of women in acts of civil resistance and while the question of role is posed, an important question of power remains. In the age of Twitter, Facebook and rapid diffusion of images around the world, *the participation of women on the front lines of protest and in acts of mass civil resistance can no longer be disputed.* (emphasis ours). (2012, https://thefeministwire.com/2012/06/are-women-occupying-new-movements/)

While the above quote references the proliferation of social media in documenting women's participation in local and global efforts to make change, we have argued throughout this chapter that women have been involved in this work all along and there is evidence of this work. If we extend consideration to the making, wearing and using of *khangas* as a localized form of knowledge and visual culture diffusion, we can then view use of social media as an extension of prior acts of visibility. In 2015, more than 1,039 Tanzanian women ran for office. This is in addition to the reserved seats – 30 per cent in which political parties, based upon proportional representation, appoint women. It is exciting to see more women than ever claiming their space, contesting in their own right through their constituencies. However, many of the NGOs involved in supporting women's political participation are unaware of this early history and are often not linked to feminists on the ground. The feminism that is espoused by these organizations and within the current feminist institutionalism literature presents feminism as a global phenomenon originating in the West. While we agree that there are shared structures and ideologies that link us as women, the priorities of feminists, as represented in many NGOs and in the feminist institutionalism literature, are a narrow version of feminism that is widely contested. For example, Amina Mama argues that feminism originated in Africa, by way of African diasporic women. Mama also contends that because there are so many nations and nationalities on the African continent, feminism in Africa is inherently transnational. Because of this, African feminist thinking is useful to any project that seeks to understand and overcome 'gender blindness' of existing scholarship and therefore 'gendering' the field of NI, as well as to find substantive ways to include women as political actors in the political process, and to move forward a research agenda that considers the interplay between gender, race, sexuality, class (and other identities) within the operation and effect of nationalist political institutions.

It is our contention that 'forgetting' women's early contributions to liberation not only erases their political agency but also impacts possibilities for acknowledging the achievements of women in the future (Jaksch 2014). Culture is a common source of wealth and a tool for advancing women's equality. Representation and equality achieved through policy and gender quotas must be undergirded by allowing people to actively draw on symbols cultural identity, history and heritage. As we have argued throughout this chapter in order for feminist institutionalism to be relevant to women in Africa, there needs to be an expansion of approaches that includes women's history and African feminist perspectives (Arnfred and Ampofo 2009). The historical accounts, theoretical frameworks and symbolic work documented here point to the foundations of an African feminist institutionalism that may have more success in challenging normative erasures, distortions, exclusions, as well as ways forward.

Note

1   Tanzania's 333 parliamentarians hold either constituent or special seats. There are approximately 140 women in parliament. As many as 79 per cent of women in parliament hold special seats, which means they have been elected to seats only open to women. There are only thirty women who hold constituent seats. While the creation of 110 special seats might imply a progressive approach by ensuring one-third of parliament consists of women, it is also important to ask questions about (1) whether this might be a form of tokenising and (2) why it is women not elected to the regular constituent seats.

References

Abbas, H. (2012): *Are Women Occupying New Movements?* https://thefeministwire. com/2012/06/are-women-occupying-new-movements/.

Achebe, N. (2005): *Farmers, Traders, Warriors, and Kings: Female Power and Authority in Northern Igboland, 1900-1960*. Portsmouth, NH: Heinemann.

Adeleye-Fayemi, B. (1999): *Feminist Leadership in Africa into the 21st Century: Report of the Third African Women's Leadership Institute. February 6th–26th 1999, Entebbe, Uganda: Regional Networking, Training and Information Forum for African Women.* London: Akina Mama wa Afrika.

Alexander, M. J. and Mohanty, C. T. (2010): 'Cartographies of Knowledge and Power: Transnational Feminism as Radical Praxis', in A. L. Swarr and R. Nagar (eds) *Critical Transnational Feminist Praxis.* Albany: SUNY Press.

Arnfred, S. and Ampofo, A. A. (2009): *African Feminist Politics of Knowledge: Tensions, Challenges, Possibilities.* Uppsala: Nordiska Afrikainstitutet.

Babeiya, E. (2011): 'Multiparty Elections and Party Support in Tanzania', *Journal of Asian and African Studies,* Vol. 47, No. 1, 83–100.

Bauer, G. (2008): 'Reserved Seats for Women MPs: Affirmative Action for the National Women's Movement or the National Resistance Movement?', in M. Tremblay (ed.) *Women and Legislative Representation: Electoral Systems, Political Parties, and Sex Quotas.* New York: Palgrave Macmillan.

Berger, I. (1976): 'Rebels or Status-seekers? Women as Spirit Mediums in East Africa', in Nancy J. Hafkin and Edna G. Bay (eds) *Women in Africa: Studies in Social and Economic Change.* Stanford, CA: Stanford University Press.

Berger, I. (2003): 'African Women's History: Themes and Perspectives', *Journal of Colonialism and Colonial History,* Vol. 4, No. 1.

Bold, C., Knowles, R. and Leach, B. (2002): 'Feminist Memorializing and Cultural Counter Memory: The Case of Marianne's Park', *Signs: Journal of Women in Culture and Society,* Vol. 28, No. 1, 125–48.

Bourdieu, P. and Passeron, J. C. (1990): *Reproduction in Education, Society, and Culture.* London: Sage.

Bourdieu, P. and Thompson, J. B. (1991): *Language and Symbolic Power.* Cambridge, MA: Harvard University Press.

Coombes, A. E. (2003): *History after Apartheid: Visual Culture and Public Memory in a Democratic South Africa.* Durham, NC: Duke University Press.

Daniels, J. (2016): 'The Trouble with White Feminism: Whiteness, Digital Feminism, and the Intersectional Internet', in S. U. Noble and B. M. Tynes (eds) *The Intersectional Internet: Race, Sex, Class and Culture Online.* Digital Formations, Vol. 105. New York, NY: Peter Lang Publishing.

Decker, A. D. and Baderoon, G. (2018): 'African Feminisms: Cartographies for the Twenty-First Century', *Meridians,* Vol. 17, No. 2, 219–31.

Geiger, S. (1996): 'Tanganyikan Nationalism as "Women's Work": Life Histories, Collective Bibliography and Changing historiography', *The Journal of African History,* Vol. 37, No. 3, 465–78.

Geiger, S. (1997): *TANU Women: Gender and Culture in the Making of Tanganyikan Nationalism, 1955-1965.* Portsmouth, NH: Heinemann.

George, A. (2018): 'Conversation: Each Generation Writes Its Own History of Generations', *The American Historical Review,* Vol. 123, No. 5, 1514–15.

Hanson, H. (2002): 'Queen Mothers and Good Government in Buganda', in J. Allman, S. Geiger and N. Musisi (eds) *Women in African Colonial Histories.* Bloomington: Indiana University Press.

Hodgson, Dorothy Louise (2001): *Once Intrepid Warriors: Gender, Ethnicity, and the Cultural Politics of Maasai Development*. Bloomington: Indiana University Press.

Hodgson, Dorothy Louise. (2005): *The Church of Women: Gendered Encounters between Maasai and Missionaries*. Bloomington: Indiana University Press.

Hodgson, Dorothy Louise. (2017): *Gender, Justice, and the Problem of Culture: From Customary Law to Human Rights in Tanzania*. Bloomington: Indiana University Press.

Ibrahim, J. (2004): 'The First Lady Syndrome and the Marginalisation of Women from Power: Opportunities or Compromises for Gender Equality?', *Feminist Africa*, Vol. 3, 46–69.

Issa, A. A. (2016): 'Women, Kanga and Political Movements in Zanzibar, 1958–1964', *JENdA: A Journal of Culture and African Women Studies*, No. 28. https://www.africaknowledgeproject.org/index.php/jenda/article/view/3022. Accessed 8 January 2018.

Jaksch, M. (2013a): 'Mapping Differential Geographies: Women's Contributions to the Liberation Struggle in Tanzania', in A. Oberhauser and I. Johnston-Anumonwo (eds) *Global Perspectives on Gender and Space: Engaging Feminism and Development*. New York: Routledge.

Jaksch, M. (2013b): 'Feminist Ujamaa: Transnational Feminist Pedagogies, Community, and Family in East Africa', in T. Jenkins (ed.) *Family, Community, and Higher Education*. New York: Routledge.

Jaksch, M. (2014) *Mapping Differential Geographies: New Media, The Virtual Freedom Trail, and the Politics of (Re)-Telling African Women's Contributions to the Liberation Struggle in Tanzania, in Global Perspectives on Gender and Space: Engaging Feminism and Development* A. Oberhauser (ed.). Ibipo Johnston-Anumonwo.

Lal, P. (2010): 'Militants, Mothers, and the National Family: "Ujamaa," Gender, and Rural Development in Postcolonial Tanzania', *The Journal of African History*, Vol. 51, No. 1, 1–20.

Lal, P. (2012): 'Self-Reliance and the State: The Multiple Meanings of Development in Early Post-Colonial Tanzania', *Africa: Journal of the International African Institute*, Vol. 82, No. 2, 212–34.

Lal, P. (2015): *African Socialism in Postcolonial Tanzania: Between the Village and the World*. New York: Cambridge University Press.

Links, G. (2015): *SADC Gender protocol: 2015 Barometer. Johannesburg: Southern Africa Gender Protocol Alliance*. http://www.genderlinks.org.za/page/sadc-research

Linnebuhr, Elisabeth. (1992): *Kanga: Popular Cloths with Messages*. W. Graebner (ed.). Amsterdam: Rodopi.

Mackay, F. and Krook, M. L. (2015): *Gender, Politics and Institutions: Towards a Feminist Institutionalism*. New York: Palgrave Macmillan.

Mackay, F. and Waylen, G. (2009): 'Feminist Institutionalism', *Politics & Gender*, Vol. 5, No. 2, 237–80.

Mackay, F., Kenny, M., and Chappell, L. (2010): 'New Institutionalism through a Gender Lens: Towards a Feminist Institutionalism?', *International Political Science Review* Vol. 31, No. 5.

Mama, A. (2001): 'Talking about Feminism in Africa', *Agenda*, Vol. 50, 58–63.

Mama, A. (2004): 'Demythologising Gender in Development: Feminist Studies in African Contexts', *IDS Bulletin*, Vol. 35, No. 4, 121–24.

Mbilinyi, M. (2015): 'Transformative Feminism in Tanzania: Animation and Grassroots Women's Struggles for Land and Livelihoods', in R. Baksh and W. Harcourt (eds) *The Oxford Handbook of Transnational Feminist Movements*. New York: Oxford University Press.

McFadden, P. (2005): 'Becoming Postcolonial: African Women Changing the Meaning of Citizenship', *Meridians*, Vol. 6, No. 1, 1–18.

McFadden, P. (2018): 'Contemporarity: Sufficiency in a Radical African Feminist Life', *Meridians*, Vol. 17, No. 2, 415–31.

Miller, K. (2009): 'Moms with Guns: Women's Political Agency in Anti-Apartheid Visual Culture', *African Arts*, Vol. 42, No. 2, 68–75.

Miller, K. (2011): 'Selective Silencing and the Shaping of Memory: The Case of the Monument to the Women of South Africa', *South African Historical Journal*, Vol. 63, No. 2, 295–312.

Mohanty, Chandra Talpade, Ann Russo, and Lourdes Torres (1991): *Third World Women and the Politics of Feminism*. Bloomington: Indiana University Press.

Mosha, A. A. and Johnson, M. (2004): *Promoting Women's Access to Politics and Decision-Making: the Role of TGNP and other Advocacy Groups in the 2000 General Elections*. Dar es Salaam, Tanzania: Gender Networking Programme.

Mulligan, K. (1999): 'Africa: Review', *Journal of the International African Institute*, Vol. 69, No. 3.

Mulligan-Hansel, K. (1995): 'Tanzanian Women's Movement Challenges Structural and Cultural Limitations', *Feminist Voices*, Vol. 8, No. 2. https://search-proquest-com. ezproxy.bucknell.edu/docview/212977315?accountid=9784. Accessed 10 February 2018.

Musisi, N. (1992): *'Transformations of Baganda Women: From the Earliest Times to the Demise of the Kingdom in 1966'*, Unpublished PhD Dissertation, University of Toronto.

Musisi, N. (1996): 'A Personal Journey into Custom, Identity, Power and Politics: Researching and Writing the Life and Times of Buganda's Queen Mother Irene Drusilla Namaganda (1896-1957)', *History in Africa*, Vol. 23, 369–85.

N.A. (2012): *Building Inclusive Democracy: Gender and Political Decision-Making in Tanzania (Meeting summary)*. London: Chatham House. https://www.chathamhouse. org/publications/papers/view/181679.

Ndziku, T. (1994): 'Tanzanian Women's Roles in Decision Making Policy', *Women in Action*, Vol. 1.

Nieves, A. D. (2008): 'Introduction: Mapping Geographies of Resistance along the 16 June 1976 Heritage Trail', in A. K. Hlongwane (ed.) *Footprints of the 'Class of 76': Commemoration, Memory, Mapping and Heritage*. Johannesburg: The Library.

Nieves, A. D. (2009): 'Places of Pain as Tools for Social Justice in the "New" South Africa: Black Heritage Reservation in the "Rainbow" Nation's Townships', in W. Logan and K. Reeves (eds) *Places of Pain and Shame: Dealing with Difficult Heritage*. New York: Routledge.

Nnaemeka, O. (2004): 'Nego Feminism: Theorizing, Practicing, and Pruning Africa's Way', *Signs*, Vol. 29, No. 2, 357–85.

Nsekela, A. J. (1984): *Time to Act*. Dar es Salaam: University Press.

Nyerere, J. (1967): *The Arusha Declaration and TANU's Policy on Socialism and Self Reliance*, Published by the Publicity Section, TANU, Dar es Salaam, Tanzania.

Oyěwùmí, O. (2002): 'Conceptualizing Gender: The Eurocentric Foundations of Feminist Concepts and the Challenge of African Epistemologies', *JeNDA*, Vol. 2, No. 1. https://www.africaknowledgeproject.org/index.php/jenda/article/view/68. Accessed 1 February 2019.

Oyěwùmí, O. (2003): *African Women and Feminism: Reflecting on the Politics of Sisterhood*. Trenton, NJ: Africa World Press.

Perter, C. M. and Tenga, N. (1996): 'The Right to Organize as the Mother of all Rights: The Experience of Women in Tanzania', *The Journal of Modern African Studies*, Vol. 34, No. 1, 143–62.

Pitcher, A. M. (2006): 'Forgetting from above and Memory from below: Strategies of Legitimation and Struggle in Postsocialist Mozambique', *Africa*, Vol. 76, No. 1, 88–112.

Ryan M.M. (2017): 'A Decade of Design: The Global Invention of the Kanga, 1876-1886', *Textile History*, Vol. 48, No. 1, 101–32.

Sadie, Y. (2005): 'Women in Political Decision-Making in the SADC Region', *Agenda*, Vol. 65, 17–31.

Salo, E. and Mama, A. (2001): 'Talking about Feminism in Africa', *Agenda: Empowering Women for Gender Equity*, Vol. 50, No. 50, 58–63.

Schoenbrun, D. L (1998): *A Green Place, a Good Place: Agrarian Change, Gender, and Social Identity in the Great Lakes Region to the 15th Century*. Portsmouth, NH: Heinemann.

Seppänen, M. and Virtanen, P. (2008): *Corruption, Poverty and Gender: With Case Studies of Nicaragua and Tanzania*. Helsinki: Ministry for Foreign Affairs of Finland. http://formin.finland.fi/public/default.aspx?contentId=130591&nodeId=15445&contentlan=2&culture=en-US.

Shetler, J. (2015): *Gendering Ethnicity in African Women's Lives*. Madison, WI: University of Wisconsin Press.

Strachan, J. J. (2015): 'Narratives of Difference and Sameness: Original Research', *Verbum Et Ecclesia*, Vol. 36, No. 2, 1–8.

Swai, E. V. (2010): *Beyond Women's Empowerment in Africa: Exploring Dislocation and Agency*. New York: Palgrave Macmillan.

Tenthani, K., Kafuko, B. and Madsen, H. L. (2014): *Women in Political Parties: WIP Approach and Experiences*. Copenhagen: Danish Institute for Parties and Democracy. http://dipd.dk/dipdpublications/.

Tamale, Sylvia.(2020): *Decolonization and Afro-Feminism*. Ottawa: Daraja Press.

Tripp, Aili Mari (2009): *African Women's Movements: Transforming Political Landscapes*. Cambridge: Cambridge University Press.

Tripp, A., Konaté, D. and Lowe-Morna, C. (2006): 'Sub-Saharan Africa: On the Fast Track to Women's Political Representation', in *Women, Quotas and Politics*. London: Routledge.

Tripp, A. M. and Kang, A. (2008): 'The Global Impact of Quotas: on the Fast Track to Increased Female Legislative Representation', *Comparative Political Studies*, Vol. 41, No. 3.

Wang, V. and Yoon, M. Y. (2018): 'Recruitment Mechanisms for Reserved Seats for Women in Parliament and Switches to Non-Quota Seats: A Comparative Study of Tanzania and Uganda', *The Journal of Modern African Studies*, Vol. 56, No. 2, 299–324.

Willis, R. G. (1981): *A State in the Making: Myth, History, and Social Transformation in Pre-Colonial Ufipa*. Bloomington, IN: Indiana University Press.

Wright, M. (1990): 'Chieftainess Ngalu under Attack, 1927, in Colonial Tanzania', Unpublished Paper.

Yahya-Othman, S. (1995): 'Aren't You Going to Greet Me? Impoliteness in Swahili Greetings', *Text*, Vol. 15, No. 2, 209–28.

Yegenoglu, M. (1998): *Colonial Fantasies: Towards a Feminist Reading of Orientalism*. New York: Cambridge University Press.

Yahya-Othman, S. (1997): 'If the Cap Fits: 'Kanga' Names and Women's Voice in Swahili Society', *Afrikanistische Arbeitspapiere: Schriftenreihe Des Kölner Instituts Für Afrikanistik*, No. 51, 135–49.

Yoon, M. Y. (2008): 'Special Seats for Women in the National Legislature: The Case of Tanzania', *Africa Today*, Vol. 55, No. 1, 60–81.

Yoon, M. Y. (2011): 'More Women in the Tanzanian Legislature: Do Numbers Matter?', *Journal of Contemporary African Studies*, Vol. 29, No. 1, 143–9.

Yoon, M. Y. (2013): 'Special Seats for Women in Parliament and Democratization: The Case of Tanzania', *Women's Studies International Forum*, Vol. 41.

6

Experiences of gender equality legislation in Kenya: The role of institutions and actors

Shillah Sintoyia Memusi

Introduction

It has been widely stated that gender equity, especially in politics and policymaking, is crucial for economic growth and genuine democracy. Redressing gender inequality is therefore crucial in paving the way for women's increased involvement in public institutions. In this discussion, gender equality is understood as 'a deliberate move to reforming or eliminating past and present discrimination using a set of public policies and initiatives designed to help on the basis of gender' (Kaimenyi et al. 2013: 91). In Kenya, this is aptly addressed in Article 27 (8) of the 2010 Constitution, which provides for affirmative action where the state is required to take legislative and other measures to ensure that not more than two-thirds of members in elective or appointive bodies are of the same gender.

Like in many other jurisdictions, Kenya's dedication to improve women's representation in the sphere of politics and public service is founded on the argument that the presence of women as elected representatives legitimizes their concerns and promises a broader recognition of their interests (Lovenduski and Norris 2003). This recognition notwithstanding, the presence of women remains substantially low in governance structures globally, as Table 6.1 demonstrates regarding the number of women in national parliaments. Except for the Nordic countries, women's representation in global politics remains at less than 30 per cent. From a critical mass standpoint therefore, this under-representation means that these women are limited in their efforts 'to "make a difference" in gendered policy debates' (Childs and Krook 2008: 734).

In Kenya's current 12th national assembly, women account for only 76 out of the total 349 representatives. Of the seventy-six, forty-seven were elected through the special seat of a Women Representative for each county, meaning that without the provision for this under Article 97 (1) (b) of the Constitution, only twenty-nine women would be present in the assembly, a mere 8.3 per cent. Kabeer (2005) points out that such underrepresentation is not so much a result of conscious discrimination, but due to various forms of bias in civil society

Table 6.1 Women in National Parliaments as of 1 January 2019

REGIONAL AVERAGES			
	Single House or Lower House	**Upper House or Senate**	**Both Houses Combined**
Nordic countries	42.5%	---	---
Americas	30.6%	31.6%	30.7%
Europe (Nordic countries included)	28.6%	28.0%	28.5%
Europe (Nordic countries included)	27.2%	28.0%	27.4%
Sub-Saharan Africa	23.9%	22.2%	23.7%
Asia	19.9%	17.4%	19.6%
Middle East and North Africa	19.0%	12.5%	18.1%
Pacific	16.3%	36.0%	18.4%

Source: http://archive.ipu.org/wmn-e/world.htm

institutions and the political sphere whose operations exclude women. As this discussion will demonstrate, this exclusion is founded on 'long-standing patterns of traditional socialization that associate men with the public realm and women with the private' (Krook 2010: 709).

The impact of this gendered role definition is that institutional arrangements manifest gendered power relations, which extend beyond 'formal "public" structures – politics and paid work – to include "private" structures, such as the family' (Kenny 2007: 94). Evidence of this is in Paul Spencer's *Time, Space and the Unknown: Maasai Configurations of Power and Providence* for example, where he describes Maasai women as 'passive bystanders, commodities owned by men, with little power in the face of the patriarchal principles that structure Maasai social organization' (Hodgson 2005: 350). The agency of women in this community is therefore heavily determined by the power they are 'allowed' to wield in both private and public realms. Seeking to improve the equality status of women in this and similar setups thus requires institutional reforms that would ensure gender justice.

In line with this, there is a global trend towards constitutional and legislative amendments to increase the representation of women in the public sphere. In 2005 alone, more than forty countries introduced electoral quotas by amending constitutions or introducing different types of legislation (Dahlerup 2005). Krook (2008) posits that this can be accredited to the realization by states that incorporating women in public life through political institutions is strategic for improving their socio-economic wellbeing. These efforts have however been accompanied by allegations of focusing on the rhetoric of women empowerment, gender equality and mainstreaming as a political tool, without honest commitment to real institutional transformation.

Kenya's National Gender and Equality Commission has admitted failure to implement affirmative action, with compliance being pushed to the 2022 election cycle, to fulfil a constitutional requirement ratified in August 2010. Nonetheless, we must acknowledge that the country has made significant strides in achieving gender equality in the political realm, at least descriptively. This is the outcome of reform processes that gained momentum in the 1990s, through increased participation by women in national politics after the introduction

Table 6.2 Women representation in Kenyan parliament, 1963–2017

Term	Period	No. of constituencies	Elected		Nominated		Total		Total
			Men	Women	Men	Women	Men	Women	Total
1st	1963–9	158	158	0	2	0	158	2	160
2nd	1969–74	158	157	1	10	1	167	2	169
3rd	1974–9	158	154	4	14	2	168	6	174
4th	1979–83	158	154	4	11	1	165	5	170
5th	1983–8	158	156	2	9	1	165	3	168
6th	1988–92	188	186	2	10	0	196	2	198
7th	1992–7	188	182	6	12	1	194	7	201
8th	1997–2002	210	206	4	9	5	215	9	224
9th	2002–7	210	200	10	4	8	204	18	222
10th	2007–13	290	194	16	6	6	200	22	222
11th	2013–17	290	274	63[a]	7	5	281	68	349
12th	2017–22	290	267	70[a]	6	6	273	76	349

Source: Author's compilation.

[a]Forty-seven of whom are elected as Women Representatives for each county.

of multiparty politics (Nzomo 1997). The current status of representation, as shown in Table 6.2, is therefore a mark of progress, demonstrating that legislative amendments are indeed useful in the quest for gender parity.

To investigate the role of actors and institutions in the gender equality debate in Kenya, I adopt a feminist institutionalist framing. This is because feminist institutionalism provides a lens through which 'constitutive gendered power relations and the processes that support and undermine them' are made visible, allowing for the modelling of causality in analysing institutional change (Lovenduski 2011: x).

The chapter begins by summarizing the gender equality debate in Kenya. Following this is a brief background on the politics of space and equality among the Maasai who predominantly inhabit Kajiado and Narok counties where this study was carried out. Known for its patriarchal social organization (Coast 2001; Hodgson 2001; Kibutu 2006; Llewelyn-Davies 1981 among others), the Maasai community provides an informative lens on the reception and effect of formal state norms in environments where informal norms dictate gender roles in public affairs.

Among the Maasai, gender relations are interactive, defined along socio-economic factors such as age, wealth and leadership skills (Coast 2001; Hodgson 2001). Social organization is therefore hinged on age and gender, as these define the rules of engagement and the logic of appropriate conduct. Under this system, men are *de facto* leaders, a position they have managed to maintain in the formal political realm. As the discussion will shortly demonstrate, this has been strengthened by the colonial and immediate post-colonial state-making processes. In the case of political participation therefore, even though it is, by principle, a right to be enjoyed by everyone, Maasai men have the historically advantaged position of having been the key political actors in the community. Maasai men are therefore better positioned to navigate formal processes to their own benefit, unlike women who have to play catch-up due to their limited political efficacy.

This reality is however not unique to the Maasai. Kimani (2014) points out that the poor performance of Kenyan women in the political arena can be attributed to the country's patriarchal culture and the electoral system. He explains that the country's politics rely heavily on social capital; yet, the processes of accumulating economic, cultural and political capital continue to be more favourable to men than women irrespective of men's demographic characteristics. I however focus on the Maasai, as a case study approach enables 'a full appraisal of the complex policy process and multiple actors involved in contesting, negotiating and delivering substantive gains for women' (Mackay 2008: 128). Kenny (2014: 682) explains that single case studies enable feminist institutionalists to identify causal mechanisms of power, continuity and change by shedding light on 'the ways in which the gendered rules of the game (both formal and informal) play out on the ground'.

This book chapter investigates the relevance of Kenya's new Constitutional provision on attitudes and behaviour in public participation, a platform for the promotion of women's political agency. A brief discussion of the findings from the case is detailed in the next section, which is then followed by the conclusion. Findings presented here were collected through participant observation, citizen focus group discussions and interviews with administration officers from both counties over seven months in 2016 and 2017.

Framework for gender equality in Kenya

Chapter 4 of Kenya's 2010 Constitution details equality and freedom from discrimination as fundamental rights per the Bill of Rights. The constitution additionally established the Kenya National Human Rights and Equality Commission under Article 59, with the mandate to promote gender equality and equity, as well as coordinate and facilitate gender mainstreaming in national development. The National Gender and Equality Commission was also established by an act of parliament in 2011, with the promotion of gender equality and freedom from discrimination as its core objectives. Furthermore, under Article 97(b) of the Constitution, the descriptive representation of women was increased through the creation of the 'Women Representative' position in all forty-seven counties. These efforts have contributed to a significant increase in the number of women in the assembly after the 2013 and 2017 elections as Table 6.2 demonstrates.

The position of Women Representatives for each of the forty-seven counties has also had unintended negative consequences, as women limit themselves to these positions, as they are regarded to be the only guaranteed winning spots (Maina 2013). Brownsell (2013) argues that this is a result of the nature of Kenyan politics, which not only requires a lot of financial resources, but is also ruled by a male-dominated patronage. These conditions thus limit the capacity of women, and especially those with limited economic and social capital, from fully engaging in party politics and legislation in general. By not pursuing other elective positions therefore, the political environment continues to be dominated by men. This dominance has become the most significant barrier to legislative reforms. For instance, the Constitution Amendment Bill (No. 4) of 2015, which sought to ensure that the National Assembly and the Senate would comprise a membership that is not more than two-thirds of either gender, failed to muster the required two-thirds of the National Assembly's votes. This occurred despite extensive lobbying by the Kenya Women Parliamentarians Association, civil society organizations and calls for support by the executive and opposition leaders. In explaining his boycott, one member of parliament (MP) argued that the amendment was just a way of giving free tickets to people's girlfriends[1] even though the proposed nomination of women was supposed to be a competitive process. Such attitudes and approaches thus continue to hinder proposals presented to rectify the underrepresentation of women. They also validate arguments that male resistance to women's participation and political structures and processes have made the biggest contribution to the underrepresentation of women in decision-making processes and positions (Nzomo 1997). Another parliamentary debate on 28 November 2018 also failed, forcing a postponement to February 2019. This was not successful either, once again due to a lack of quorum.

These efforts imply that a lot of work is ongoing to get women represented in politics in a meaningful way, but with little success. Understanding this requires a historical look into the gendered nature of the public sphere in Kenya, and how this has influenced the underrepresentation of women.

The institutionalizing of gender disparity in Kenya

The reality of women's political marginalization in Kenya is shaped by patriarchal structures that concentrate authority on the men, with women expected to be submissive to this authority. Nzomo (1997) notes that with perpetuation over time, the constellation of gender stereotypes, male resistance to the political participation of women, limited resources, and political structures and processes have significantly contributed to the underrepresentation of women.

A look into Kenyan women's political participation therefore involves the unravelling of a complexity rooted in state structures, both historical and contemporary, 'informed as much by colonialism, autocratic rule and recent democratic politics, as by social and cultural values steeped in patriarchy' (Wambui 2016: 2). These factors have continually shaped and reshaped power relations to magnify gender inequalities. Perhaps a most informative starting point of evidence is the institutional structures of colonialism. The indirect rule applied by the British colonial government allowed local male leaders to redefine relationships and roles at the domestic level, especially concerning the role and place of women. Wambui (2016) points out that in their position as local leaders, men facilitated the passing of discriminative laws which not only excluded women from the political space, but also subordinated them in the domestic realm. With power over the adjudication of customary laws, local chiefs and elders redefined customs to their advantage, especially in matters of gender roles, sexuality, marriage, divorce, adultery and property rights among others.

Gender relations among the Maasai were not exempt from these reconfigurations. Customary rules of civic engagement and separation of powers in the community can be traced to the incorporation of subjects into the state system under colonial administration. The pre-existing complementary, interconnected responsibilities of men and women were divided into 'spatially separated, hierarchically gendered domains of "domestic" and "public/political" and the consolidation of male control over cattle through the commodification of livestock, monetization of the Maasai economy and targeting of men for development interventions' (Hodgson 1999: 43).

Male political authority and economic control were thus reinforced through the expansion of bases of power and the introduction of new forms of property relations. For example, communal land tenure was replaced through the provision of title deeds to male household heads, reflecting effects of policies such as the 1954 Swynnerton Plan aimed at intensifying the development of cash crop agriculture. Hodgson (1999) reiterates that this led to the curtailment of access and participation in political decision-making processes for women, relegating them to the domestic concerns of home and homestead. Men's political authority intersected with the advantaged economic position and patriarchal influences to perpetuate the disadvantaged status of Maasai women. Colonialism replaced the multifaceted property systems with a homogeneous system of private property among the Maasai (Hodgson 2001). A lack of direct access to resources thus affected the freedoms of expression and socio-economic development for women, limiting their capacity for action. Similar observations can be made among the Yoruba of Nigeria, where Oyewumi (1997) reports that the colonial system undermined the property rights of women and ignored their pre-existing role in public political decisions, as ownership rights shifted from being communal to private, and under male authority. In addition to not earning wages, women lost an avenue for wealth accumulation, spearheading present-day gendered politico-economic gaps.

Furthermore, the codification of customary law perpetuated and protected by the Native Authorities and Native Authority Courts emphasized the authority of men and powerlessness of women (Wambui 2016). This process disregarded pre-existing socio-political structures and women's positions in them, while at the same time ignoring challenges introduced by the colonial state structures. Oyewumi (1997) explains that there was nothing customary in the creation of customary law since the British colonial government was ultimately the source of the codified customary law. Colonial administrators sought to develop a rational legal model guided by neutrality and consistency, by searching for 'rules in each "culture" which they could learn, record, and then apply to the specifics of the various cases' (Hodgson 1996: 109). These rules were determined by elderly men, in their capacity as authority figures, and would then be acknowledged or denied depending on the colonial administrators' intentions.

The imposition of taxes forced men to seek jobs in settlers' farms and urban areas, and women had to remain at home and take care of domestic needs by concentrating on human reproduction and subsistence farming to feed their families. While this made them *de facto* household heads, it further relegated them to the domestic space, subjecting them to the challenge of time constraints on political participation as will be discussed shortly. On the other hand, men got exposure to urban environments and, with it, increased socio-political awareness that facilitated their dominance in decision making. Oyewumi (1997) explains that steady income from wage employment contributed to the valuing of men's labour while the contribution of women became underrated. This was so, she explains, even though the wage earned by men was insufficient to meet all needs, and women were therefore responsible for ensuring the stability and continuity of their communities. This laid the groundwork for change in the socio-economic and cultural position of women in society, not only marginalizing them, but leaving them subject to state and patrilineal interests. The result of this reorganization of gender roles was that patriarchy within traditional cultures reinforced the negative influence of colonialism.

The indirect colonial rule groomed a generation of very powerful individuals who sought to centralize state power in the post-colonial African states (Wambui 2016). Wambui expounds that the rationale behind this was to homogenize the ethnically and religiously plural societies that characterized the demographics to fit into the European idea of nation states. Kenya was therefore administratively subdivided into provinces, under which came districts, divisions, sub-divisions, locations and sub-locations in descending order. These post-independence political structures continued the entrenchment and legitimization of patriarchal norms in a manner that curtailed the political leadership of women. This was made possible by the male dominance of the political space and one whose quest for hegemony informed the propagation of women's subordination as a unifying factor. The adoption of patrimonial politics reinforced this, reflecting what Oyewumi (1997) describes as the hallmark of the colonial era – a public sphere where only men could participate. Women were thus relagated to wifehood and motherhood at the expense of other socio-cultural and economic roles.

This system dominated the Kenyan political sphere until the early 1990s. The awakening of the fight for political empowerment by Kenyan women coincided with the international movement for women's empowerment, giving a positive impact on the equality struggle by Kenyan women. The women's movement in Kenya therefore made use of international conventions on equality to advance their agenda, and the increased consciousness among women on their socio-economic and political rights added momentum to the fight for equality. In 1992 the National Council of Women of Kenya (NCWK) and the Africa Women's Development and Communication Network (FEMNET) organized a National Women's Convention to discuss how women could access political power. The convention focused on establishing an 'institutional framework for gender mainstreaming and resulted in the establishment of the National Gender Commission, a ministry in charge of women affairs, children and social services, a presidential directive for 30 per cent women's representation in public service, establishment of women's fund and publication of the Sexual Offences Act, among many other gains' (Kabira and Kimani 2012: 843). These efforts were followed by gender mainstreaming in public institutions to de-masculinize and make them more democratic and responsive to women's needs (Kanyi 2016).

A motion was tabled in parliament in 1997 to increase the number of women in decision making at parliament and local government to 33 per cent. The motion failed, with some of the arguments against it being that men represented all citizens, the Constitution did not stop any woman from going to parliament, and most importantly, that there was already a woman heading the Ministry of Culture and Social Services (Kanyi 2016). These challenges notwithstanding, there was a lot of mobilization by women groups, involving grassroots organizations and making affirmative action a national movement. When the ruling party – KANU – won the 1997 elections despite strong opposition, the debate on reviewing the Constitution began. Women lobbied to be part of the negotiations under the Women's Political Caucus, where they negotiated for inclusion in drafting the law to review the Constitution. The constitutional review process kicked off in 1998 courtesy of The Constitution Review of Kenya Act, 1998.

While the review was ongoing, another affirmative action motion was presented in 2000, seeking a 30 per cent representation of women in parliament, and it was a success. In 2001, another motion was tabled, seeking representation of marginalized groups and women. The Attorney General amended the bill to have its contents reviewed by the Constitution of Kenya Review Commission (CKRC), which then convened a conference to draft the Constitution in April 2003. The drafting continued to April 2004. Throughout, women were able to make contributions, as well as monitor the progress, with key players such as the Federation of Women Lawyers (FIDA) Kenya, Kenya Human Rights Commission (KHRC), League of Women Voters, and the Institute for Education and Democracy paying scrutiny (Owuor 2016). The 2005 draft Constitution was however rejected, with gender being one of the nine contentious issues (Kameri-Mbote 2016). The constitutional review process resumed in 2006, with the promise that the new Constitution would address the adequate representation of women in parliament and local government. Women therefore followed the constitution review process very closely to ensure that their needs were prioritized. Extra effort was required to counter the lack of support for the rights of women due to the patriarchal stereotypes of empowered women. In the end, affirmative action was successfully integrated into the draft by the Constitution's committee of experts. When the Constitution was brought to a referendum on 4 August 2010, it was overwhelmingly voted for and subsequently promulgated on 27 August 2010.

Engagement, equality and authority in public participation

Discussing impediments to the political participation of women in Kenya, Kivoi (2014) points out that their marginalization is the result of perceptions, stereotypes and traditional beliefs that depict women as inferior to men. This is part of a 'globally pervasive ideology of male superiority' that has shaped the structures and processes that uphold women's marginalization (Peet and Hartwick 2009: 267–8). It is therefore important to understand how these beliefs, perceptions and stereotypes are reproduced to shape male dominance in the public sphere.

Generally, attitudes towards the political agency of women and the equality agenda are based on the interests of an individual, as well as their levels of exposure to different norm environments (Bolzendahl and Myers 2004). This exposure could be from personal experiences, as well as contextual realities. An interest-based approach is influenced by whether individuals stand to gain from a feminist agenda while exposure to feminist ideology, through either education, personal experience or socialization, is what determines the attitude of an individual towards the same (ibid).

A push for gender equality, in this case through the incorporation of Maasai women in political affairs, holds a lot of promise for women, which is evidently why most of them support it. For most Maasai men however, the engagement of women denotes reduced influence on their part, with a provision such as the two-thirds gender rule making it possible that in some instances, men could be the minority. As a respondent succinctly put it:

> On political matters, just like in development, women should be involved and in equal measure as men. Women could take up the Women Rep and Councillor positions. But not that women should take up all positions and leave out men. It should be 50/50. Just as we agree at home, so should it be in government – we should be equals. That is all I would add.
>
> (Male Respondent, Ewuaso Kedong Ward – Kajiado West, 24.03.2016)

This denotes an openness to gender equality, but one that is clouded in fear of what the implication of this would be on the dominant position of men. This fear is arguably informed by the lack of exposure to female leadership within the community. As Banaszak and Plutzer (1993) argue, resistance, or the reluctance to support the elevation of women in the political space, can be because of a status disconnect that happens when certain individuals react negatively to contexts they deem hostile to their status. The lack of exposure to female leadership in this case presents itself as a risk to the dominance of men. Men with exposure have differing opinions, acknowledging the unfair male dominance, welcoming the engagement of women and even offering support to promote the same. This is evident in the discussions on the involvement of women in the management of communal land through group ranches. The system is currently run by men, with women having no voting rights or other decision-making authority. As a member of one group ranch pointed out:

> I wanted to mention that women are not allowed to be in the group ranch committees. Women do not appear anywhere, there is no one to represent them and the women depend on the men's decisions whether or not to give them any land. The committee is the men's.
>
> (Male respondent, Keekonyokie Ward – Narok East, 20.04.2016)

It is very telling that such a practice prevails even in a space where the involvement of women would benefit their families as singular units of society. In addition, such attitudes symbolize the strong reluctance to accept the position of women as equals. As the comments by the respondent in the excerpt below however show, there are those that are of a contrary opinion. They also happen to be young, confirming arguments that the youth are more inclined towards gender equality (Kenny and Patel 2017).

> On our side as young men, we are now one with the women unlike it was with the older generation. In our times, the fights that existed between men and women have reduced because things have changed and we discuss everything together. We take women as adults unlike before. We cooperate; when you want to do something at home, you have to involve her so things have become easier. There is more understanding and we stay together.
>
> (Male respondent, Ewuaso Kedong Ward – Kajiado West, 25.03.2016)

Unfortunately, such men are evidently in the minority and lacking political influence, as they would otherwise have successfully engineered change. This points to a probable influence of other factors on individuals' attitudes towards agency in the public space. Specifically, the socialization background of an individual influences their political socialization and, with it, approaches to equality agenda. This is in accordance with social context theory whereby the attitudes of an individual are influenced by their environments (Banaszak and Plutzer 1993).

In situations where the authority of women is limited to domestic affairs, as is the case with the Maasai, there are significant socio-economic consequences. This is because, in playing this role, the hypothesis of men as providers continues to be supported and even strengthened. Besides, the exposure of women continues to be limited by the duty of care, as men continue to interact with the socio-political and economic environments. Among the Maasai, therefore, the transformative effect of public participation is curtailed by culturally mediated politics of presence, and the changing socio-political and economic contexts in Kenya.

For instance, Wangui (2008) reports that development interventions have resulted in a fundamental shift in gender roles in livestock production – the key economic activity of the Maasai. She notes that even though women's contributions to livestock production outweigh those of men, modernization efforts in the sector are causing women to lose control over milk resources, making them more vulnerable. Her findings echo Kipuri's (1990) reflection that women are losing control over the products of their labour, even though they remain active producers. An explanation for this is in the observation that the expansion of state administration, especially through the commercialization of the pastoral economy, has contributed to men's firm control over family resources (Talle 1987). The position of Maasai women is thus tied to development agenda and the class formations that ensue, which have gradually pushed them to the periphery in the socio-political and economic realms (Kipuri 1990). The political agency of Maasai women therefore reflects the historical masculization of the Kenyan public sphere detailed in the previous section.

In the examination of Maasai women's experiences in the complexity of literacy, Taeko (2014) notes that women's voices are heard and have an impact on the implementation of projects within their created space of women groups, but have almost zero effect on the community's decision-making processes. This, she explains, is because they rarely attend political initiatives which would not only provide opportunities for political consciousness, but also act as platforms to challenge discrimination and prejudice. Characteristic of this patriarchal setup, considerations for age and paternity play a significant role in establishing power relations. At the core of it, Maasai women are supposed to respect men and do their best to avoid confrontations in both private and public spheres. Rooted in *enkanyit* (respect), Llewelyn-Davies (1981) explains that this moral value calls for courteous behaviour towards others, in a measure appropriate to their social position. As subordinates, therefore, women are expected to exhibit courtesy and respect for men in all situations, and not voice opposition even in the face of injustice.

Lack of *enkanyit* invites physical abuse in the domestic front and public shaming or shunning. Therefore, even when women have reasonable cause to disagree with men, they exercise caution in doing this openly. This behaviour points to an operating logic of appropriateness when it comes to public engagement. Chappell (2006) explains that a logic of appropriateness exists where there is a perpetuation of certain types of behaviours and the discouragement of others.

In a system upheld by actors who dictate the acceptability of 'masculine and feminine forms of behaviour, rules, and values for men and women within institutions' (Chappell 2006: 226), a Maasai woman is encouraged not to argue against men in public forums. This emboldens the dominance of positions that do not oppose the views of men. Respondents in the focus group discussions reported that widespread fear of curses from men pervades, and it is believed that the curses affect not just the woman in question, but her future generations. With a Christianity dominance, most do not believe in the power of these curses but would still avoid contradicting and confronting men publicly as this would taint their image and soil their family name – a social cost too high to bear. In discussing how culture inhibits the implementation of women's rights in Anglophone sub-Saharan Africa, Howard (1982) explains that individuals place a high value on beliefs and practices, even when outsiders may regard these as irrational.

The effect of notions of appropriateness contributes to the limiting of women's freedom to participate and contribute to decision making in public affairs. Instead, most women choose to complain in the safe spaces of women group meetings, with the hope that their opinions will reach the decision makers through a woman or two among them who can openly discuss such matters with her husband, and the husbands will then have the matter addressed at an appropriate avenue. It is however important to note that this system was, and remains, unfair as far as public awareness on development matters is concerned. Using husbands as proxies presupposes equality in access to information. As respondents however reported, men are not always keen to share the details and outcomes of their deliberations.

> If it is a meeting that does not discuss deep secrets, women are involved but when the meeting is about hot topics that require a lot of deliberations, women are sent away. They are told that the men have a private meeting. We are only invited to general conversations ... When he comes home, and you ask him what was being discussed, he cannot tell you ... But as women, we do talk because if he were to ask me, I would tell him. But the men would never discuss what their private meeting was about ... He would tell you that the discussions were men's affairs.
>
> (Female Respondents, Ewuaso Kedong Ward – Kajiado West, 23.03.2016)

Despite the passing of time and availability of policies that support equal participation, the reliance on men by most women is reminiscent of the traditional political organization where sons and husbands were the voices of Maasai women's political interests (Hodgson 1999). This system cemented a gendered separation of authority which saw women largely excluded from political affairs.

Notably, there is only one Maasai woman elected to parliament in Kenya today – Ms Peris Tobiko – even though the dominantly Maasai counties of Kajiado and Narok have a total of eleven parliamentary seats. She is also the first Maasai female MP in the country's history, and to achieve this, she is reported to have overcome threats, alienation and curses from Maasai elders for 'trying to be a man'.[2] This analogy once again points to the association of the political sphere with men, and the presence of women as out of order. Mackay (2008: 130) explains that this is made possible through the reinforcement of masculinist ideologies, which are regarded as 'ostensibly gender neutral' in public institutions and political life. The effect of this is that the absence of women in public and political institutions is normalized, causing efforts by women to seek leadership in these spaces to be regarded as disruptive and out of order.

All these notwithstanding, evidence from this research shows that while the women may be powerless, they are certainly not passive (as reported by Spencer 2003). Any perceptions of passivity can be argued to be resulting from the lost will to fight losing battles against the dominant male authority. Many Maasai women rely on the courage of the outspoken women who, mainly with the support of their husbands, can speak out in public and engage with men without fear. These women therefore become the mouthpieces for the many who cannot raise their voices in public. Most of these outspoken women have gained experience from working with non-governmental organizations, mainly as community mobilizers, and therefore enjoy a legitimacy informed from their actions as key players in community development.

Nevertheless, the Maasai social structure and power relations have retained a stronghold in the community, especially in rural areas. The influence of gender and age in shaping roles, responsibilities and power relations within the community is still persistent in present-day politics in the community, confirming that internalized informal rules are very effective in shaping institutional arrangements (Mackay et al. 2010). In its design, the finality of male authority in structuring the community contributes to denying women freedom and justice. This is especially made evident when matters reported to the Chiefs, or even the police, fall through the cracks. Cases involving the unfair sale of land and livestock, female circumcision and early child marriages are therefore not properly dealt with, as they are mostly orchestrated and resolved by and among men. By opting to settle such matters with male leaders, Chiefs contribute to the obstruction of justice. In the case of an old man being reported to the authorities for marrying an underage girl, for example, a respondent reported:

> He can speak to the chief and explain that they are of the same age set and stuff like that and next thing you know, he has been released.
>
> (Female Respondent, Ewuaso Kedong Ward – Kajiado West, 23.03.2016)

The influence of traditional structures and pervasion of patriarchal considerations even at the civic public sphere inhibit women's access to fair recourse on private and domestic disputes. Unsurprisingly therefore, and as Taeko (2014) reiterates, most Maasai women remain dormant on matters relating to public engagement, which leaves them increasingly unaware of social and political injustices due to the limited exposure to engagement and acting upon solving community problems. How does this play out under the new legislative framework?

Commitment to the process and belief in the value of public input

Respondents made it clear that the biggest problem lies in the inability to assert influence, rendering them helpless within the male-dominated socio-political structure that mostly disregards their input. All together, these conditions exacerbate the socio-economic underdevelopment of Maasai women and are made worse by reports that silence is sometimes due to concerns about their security in the community (Taeko 2014). This assertion is reiterated by Parsimei (2013) who notes that male family heads and other male relatives can become oppressors and exploiters within Maasai families, leading to an inferiority complex in most women. The absence of Maasai women from the political space therefore becomes a result of both choice and the lack of it, conditions that have promoted a culture where Maasai women remain subordinated in power structures, with very limited chances of being uplifted to an equal status of influence as men.

The 2016 County Public Participation (CPP) guidelines point out that proponents of public participation must be willing to obtain and consider public input in decision making and to ensure that public participation works. This is necessary to minimize decoupling in change processes (Meyer and Rowan 1977). While checking commitment levels can be difficult to ascertain, the participant observation technique adopted in the study was instrumental in checking on the consideration for public input.

At only two hours, the time allocated to discuss the development needs in the 2017–2022 Kajiado County Integrated Development Planning forum in Loitokitok was clearly insufficient. Coupled with the lack of access to information regarding the issues to be discussed, one can argue that the discussion was more of an information and verification exercise, instead of being genuinely deliberative. To further this argument, I will use the example of a youth group that was represented in the forum on December 4 2017. Having informed themselves of the upcoming meeting, a group of youth came together to discuss and articulate development issues they wanted to have addressed. Their action conforms to the principle of inclusion that is at the heart of pro-participation arguments, in addition to supporting the argument that participation allows problem definition by key stakeholders, and the consequent development of home-grown solutions (Gaventa 2002). Unfortunately, the representative was not allowed to present the group's agenda, since, to paraphrase the forum's coordinator, the youth were part of the general public whose development needs had been presented in the general discussions. He therefore argued that allowing the youth to present their agenda would be repetitive and time consuming. This argument prevailed, disregarding the CPP guidelines' allowance for the formation of groups to represent special interests in public deliberation exercises.

Such instances of questionable commitment to public participation strengthen the argument that public participation is not really a platform for inclusion (Hanna 2000). Instead, it is used to create the illusion of inclusion, as governments and public institutions seek to legitimize their governance approaches. As platforms for gender mainstreaming, these participation exercises are instead contributing to the 'repeated exclusion of women' through their rules and routines which further render women and their interests invisible (Chappell and Waylen 2013: 602). As a requirement for meaningful engagement, due consideration for public input results in better decision making and improved governance. The output of a public participation exercise would therefore have a genuine impact on policy. Most importantly, the fulfilment of this condition ensures that there is an alignment between input and policy relevance for the public. Involvement of all stakeholders is therefore argued to be the most effective way to ensure that policies reflect actual needs of the affected public. Cornwall and Jewkes (1995) point out that by its very nature, participation emphasizes a bottom-up approach that is focused on locally defined priorities and perspectives for the generation of knowledge for action. Public involvement thus provides room for the emergence of alternative interpretations of needs, resulting in alternative policy solutions (Cornwall and Gaventa 2000). It is these alternatives that reflect the needs of the public as deliberated upon in participation exercises. This is however not a guaranteed outcome in the Kenyan case.

One respondent reported that despite endlessly requesting better roads, her village continues to get more boreholes. She is therefore surrounded by five water projects, but a poor road that makes transport, trade and medical emergencies a nightmare. The government does not seem intent on listening to what the needs of the citizens are, relying instead on informants seeking to benefit from tendering processes.

> They don't care about coming to the people, they get information on development needs from a few men with whom they eat and drink. Sometimes they carry out simple projects like drilling boreholes and find ways to misappropriate funds ... Presently, because 2017 is nearing, we are important stakeholders, we have started being invited to meetings.
>
> (Female Respondent, Loitokitok – Kajiado South, 03.03.2016)

Elsewhere, another respondent argued that men are in a better position to understand community needs since women are mostly holed up at home taking care of household chores. This reinforces observations that the Maasai woman's sphere of influence remains the homestead, while the man deals with public affairs and political matters (Hodgson 1999). These informal and cultural dictates on gender roles are still powerful, and as respondents from Ewuaso Kedong Ward pointed out, some women are resigned to having no influence on decision making.

> A lot of things are decided by men and as women, we only get to hear that decisions have been made. It is very hard for us women to be involved and our opinions sought. They believe they are knowledgeable enough and we just act on their decisions because we cannot refuse as we have no authority to do so. We agree with their decisions and see them fit for the whole community.
>
> (Female Respondent, Ewuaso Kedong Ward – Kajiado West, 23.03.2016)

The attitude reflected here points to internalized dependence and subordination as effects of a socialization process that informs the avoidance of conflict (Moglen 1983), maintaining an institutional environment that perpetuates male dominance. The influence of traditional gender roles means that participation forums limit not only the input by women, but also opportunities for them to gain knowledge, skills and confidence in their ability to influence decisions that affect their daily lives. This lack of engagement in decision making strips them of the opportunity to exercise their power to challenge the boundaries to their participation; benefits Dworski-Riggs and Langhout (2010) point out may be gained from participation, even if limited.

The role of county governments is therefore brought to question, as their influence in public participation processes appears to be absent. An explanation for this can be found in arguments on inadequate resources to enable the government agencies fulfil their brief. This discussion was prevalent in the discussions with both citizens and economists from Kajiado and Narok counties. Considering the economic challenges discussed earlier, more women than men are subjected to economic marginalization which further limits their political engagement (Mackay 2008). The inability of the government to ensure breadth and depth of outreach means that there is no foreseeable remedy for this.

A Narok County Budget Officer reported that his office did not have enough resources to facilitate participatory budgeting as provided for in the Public Finance Management (PFM) Act. As a result, the county has resorted to carrying out the annual budgeting exercises in twelve locations within the county that are easily accessible to the officers. This process leaves out many residents who cannot reach these locations, while at the same time making the twelve areas the entire county's mouthpiece.

Resources do provide a constraint to the successful realization of public participation, with Jütting et al. (2005) pointing to the reality that local governments may sometimes lack the human and financial resources to effectively implement decentralization. This is well captured in the reflection of the Narok County Chief Officer in charge of Gender, Youth, Sports and Culture. She notes that due to the limited financial resources, there are no efforts to promote women's political empowerment, with focus being on economic empowerment through women groups instead.

Now, my office is not focusing much more on the political space for women … it is more about economic empowerment, other than political.

It's not like a human rights aspect whereby we want women to be participating politically ... we have never really developed a program that is targeted on the political aspect or even one that encourages women to participate in politics.

(Chief Officer – Gender, Youth, Sports and Culture – Narok County, 20.02.2017)

The same strategy is employed in the women empowerment programme administered by the gender department in Kajiado County. Even though the economic empowerment objective is also valuable, its preconditions lock out most women, especially the illiterate. This is because women groups need to fulfil criteria that involve reading, writing and arithmetic, to be considered for such programmes. The inability of these programmes' benefits to be more inclusive and widespread becomes disempowering for the non-beneficiaries, as there is no due consideration for the socio-economic dimensions of class and poverty that affect them.

From her study on the empowerment of factory workers in Malaysia, Miles (2016) finds evidence that redressing gender inequality requires not so much a focus on the economic integration of women, but the redistribution of power so that social relations, processes and structures can be transformed. Putting these into consideration would require that relevant agencies find ways of reaching to all people. In the context of this study, financial constraints faced by the county governments merge with the logistical and socio-economic challenges the citizens must deal with, making it increasingly difficult to ensure a resource input that would result in widely inclusive participation forums whose outcomes not only reflect public needs, but provide women with the opportunity to improve their political efficacy.

Law as a tool for transformation?

The study sample included community activists, village leaders, ordinary farmers, business owners and government officials. Highlights used to reinforce arguments herein are therefore not wholly representative of the views held or practised by the entire community. Even among those involved in the study, opinions differed, with some men agreeing that there is need to change attitudes towards women in the community.

Evidence however shows that policy decisions in the Maasai community remain in the hands of an elite few, predominantly men. This is especially perpetuated by informal laws that govern gender roles within the community. Majority of the citizens therefore remain unaware of their rights, and the reported desire by county governments to reach out and engage is curtailed by the financial constraints. These findings illustrate a lack of commitment to institutional reform in general, signifying failure in addressing gender equality through public participation forums. There is arguably little in the way of benefits for the Maasai community, and specifically women, from the provisions of gender equality and public participation legislation.

This points to a gap between expectations and reality in the application of this legislation in the community; that citizens can now influence policy processes has not resulted in any tangible empowerment outcomes. As Hanna (2000) explains, control and empowerment are not equivalent, and sometimes co-option might be the unforeseen outcome. In reiterating the observation by Bruce Stiftel, he highlights that "[e]ven the most well-developed participation program cannot ensure that it will significantly influence a decision. The provision or non-provision of participation events, or dialogue, is a sparse measure of participation and the reasons for its influence" (Hanna 2000: 400). Public participation as described in the case herein demonstrates the fulfilment of legal requirements, without necessarily engaging with power relations that necessitate institutional reforms.

The case clearly depicts the shortcomings of using law as a transformation tool in the pursuit of gender equality. In any democracy, choice architecture exists in a form that helps the definition and constitution of self-governance (Sunstein 2015). A Constitution can therefore be seen as a social engineering tool. This holds a lot of promise in the case of gender equality among the Maasai, as the 2010 Constitution of Kenya sets out to undo norms that perpetuate inequality. As 'a highly specialized form of social control in a politically organized society', the law is systematically applied in the maintenance of order and aimed at inducing patterns of behaviour conducive for prosperity (McManaman 2013: 15). The success of this process thus requires careful balancing of competing individual and public interests to achieve the common good. In the case of Maasai, the law as a transformative tool cannot be seen to be achieving this goal, thanks largely to the lack of commitment to the common good or the protection of the interests of special interest groups such as women.

There is recorded evidence by several scholars that 'the informal can work to undermine, replace, support, or work in parallel with the formal institutions of the state' (Chappell 2013: 606), which this discussion has highlighted using the case of the Maasai. Such conditions therefore call for the alignment and realignment of laws to the needs of a society. Adoption of alternative engagement processes would be a more promising pathway towards gender equality in this case, to avoid stirring conflicts within the community and undermining the equality objective. This is especially important, considering the role men – as cultural gatekeepers in the community – play and could play, in opening the space for the effective engagement of women in the public sphere.

The experiences captured here thus reiterate that institutional reforms must be accompanied by policies and grassroots processes that examine how communities can operationalize the same in a manner that is both objective and respectful to local and cultural realities. This is crucial if legislative reforms are to be truly transformative and especially in the quest for matters such as gender equality as a pathway to wellbeing and overall socio-political and economic development. However, this is practically unattainable in situations where traditional rules of engagement and elite capture are just as powerful, if not more powerful, than statutory law, as the case in the Maasai community demonstrates.

Conclusion

Changes to formal rules will not guarantee the implementation of these changes in society. As has been noted, governance is a matrix of rule sets that reflect power relationships that exist in historical and spatial contexts (Lowndes 2005). These affect the interpretation, adaptation and implementation of rules as influenced by power relations and positions of authority.

The empirical analysis herewith demonstrates that as transformative as the new Constitution may be, local realities have a strong influence on its implementation and can very well be barriers. It is crucial therefore that such realities are taken into consideration to enable constructive confrontation of socio-political and economic inequities. Cultural norms and gendered separation of the domestic and the public among the Maasai continue to strongly dictate engagement in public affairs and politics. Unfortunately, they do very little, if anything at all, to promote gender equality due to their heavily patriarchal inclination.

As Naila Kabeer illuminates, 'Institutional transformation requires movement along a number of fronts: from individual to collective agency, from private negotiations to public action, and from the informal sphere to the formal arenas of struggle where power is legitimately exercised' (Kabeer 2005: 16). This discussion thus demonstrates gender equality outcomes as derived from the interdependence between gender norms and institutional settings. At the same time, it calls for the understanding of political institutions in both their formal and informal guise if envisioned gender equality outcomes are to be realized. It is therefore imperative that the adoption of legal instruments in reforms is accompanied by the incorporation of new methods and engagement techniques for interaction. Most importantly, these need to be founded upon a proper understanding of the challenges brought about by the intersectionality of formal and informal institutions and the actors therein.

Notes

1   Why Kenyan MPs shot down gender bill, https://www.standardmedia.co.ke/ article/2000200820/why-kenyan-mps-shot-down-gender-bill (accessed 6 May 2016).
2   How Peris Tobiko escaped child marriage, Maasai curses to be MP, https://www.the-star.co.ke/news/2017/10/24/how-peris-tobiko-escaped-child-marriage-maasai-curses-to-be-mp_c1657699 (accessed 24 October 2017).

References

Balassa, L. and Plutzer, E. (1993): 'Contextual Determinants of Feminist Attitudes: National and Subnational Influences in Western Europe', *American Political Science Review*, Vol. 87, No. 1, 147–57.

Bolzendahl, C. and Myers, D. (2004): 'Feminist Attitudes and Support for Gender Equality: Opinion Change in Women and Men, 1974–1998', *Social Force*, Vol. 83, No. 2, 759–89.

Brownsell, J. and Gatabaki, P. (2013): 'Kenyan Women March towards Political Equality'. Retrieved from http://www.aljazeera.com/indepth/features/2013/03/201338111 54329530.html. Accessed 12 August 2015.

Chappell, L. (2006): 'Comparing Political Institutions: Revealing the Gendered "Logic of Appropriateness"', *Politics and Gender*, Vol. 2, 223–35.

Chappell, L. and Waylen, G. (2013): 'Gender and the Hidden Life of Institutions', *Public Administration*, Vol. 91, 599–615.

Childs, S. and Krook, M. L. (2008): 'Critical Mass Theory and Women's Political Representation', *Political Studies*, Vol. 56, No. 3, 725–36.

Coast, E. (2001): *Maasai Demography*, PhD Thesis. London: LSE Research Online. Retrieved from http://eprints.lse.ac.uk/264/1/Maasai_Demography_PhD.pdf

Constitution of Kenya (2010). Retrieved from http://www.kenyalaw.org/lex/actview. xql?actid=Const2010

Cornwall, A. and Gaventa, J. (2000): 'From Users and Choosers to Makers and Shapers: Repositioning Participation in Social Policy', *IDS Bulletin*, Vol. 31, No. 4, 50–62.

Cornwall, A. and Jewkes, R. (1995): 'What Is Participatory Research?' *Social Science and Medicine*, Vol. 41, No. 12, 1667–76.

Dahlerup, D. (2005): 'Increasing Women's Political Representation: New Trends in Gender Quotas', in J. Ballington and A. Karam (eds) *Women in Parliament: Beyond Numbers*. Retrieved from https://www.idea.int/sites/default/files/publications/women-in-parliament-beyond-numbers-a-revised-edition.pdf. Accessed 12 February 2015.

Dworski-Riggs, D. and Langhout, R. D. (2010): 'Elucidating the Power in Empowerment and the Participation in Participatory Action Research: A Story about Research Team and Elementary School Change', *American Journal of Community Psychology*, Vol. 45, No. 3–4, 215–30.

Gaventa, J. (2002): 'Exploring Citizenship, Participation and Accountability', *IDS Bulletin*, Vol. 33, No. 2, 1–18.

Hanna, K. S. (2000): 'The Paradox of Participation and the Hidden Role of Information: A Case Study', *American Planning Association*, Vol. 66, 398–410.

Hodgson, D. L. (1996): '"My Daughter … Belongs to the Government Now": Marriage, Maasai and the Tanzanian State', *Canadian Journal of African Studies*, Vol. 1, No. 30, 106–23.

Hodgson, D. L. (1999): 'Pastoralism, Patriarchy and History: Changing Gender Relations among Maasai in Tanganyika, 1890–1940', *Journal of African History*, Vol. 40, 41–65.

Hodgson, D. L. (2001): *Once Intrepid Warriors: Gender, Ethnicity, and the Cultural Politics of Maasai Development*. Bloomington: Indiana University Press.

Hodgson, D. L. (2005): 'Time, Space, and the Unknown: Maasai Configurations of Power and Providence by Paul Spencer', *African Affairs*, Vol. 104, 349–51.

Howard, R. (1982): 'Human Rights and Personal Law: Women in Sub-Saharan Africa', *A Journal of Opinion*, Vol. 12, No. 1/2, 45–52.

Jütting, J., Corsi, E., Kauffmann, C., McDonnell, I., Osterreider, H., Pinaud, N. and Wegner, L. (2005): 'What Makes Decentralization in Developing Countries Pro-Poor?' *The European Journal of Development Research*, Vol. 17, No. 4, 626–48.

Kabeer, N. (2005): 'Gender Equality and Women's Empowerment: A Critical Analysis of the Third Millennium Development Goal 1', *Gender & Development*, Vol. 13, 13–24.

Kabira, W. M. and Kimani, E. N. (2012): 'The Historical Journey of Women's Leadership in Kenya', *Journal of Emerging Trends in Educational Research and Policy Studies*, Vol. 3, No. 6, 843–9.

Kaimenyi, C., Kinya, E. and Chege, S. M. (2013): 'An Analysis of Affirmative Action: The Two Thirds Gender Rule in Kenya', *International Journal of Business, Humanities and Technology*, Vol. 3, No. 6, 91/97.

Kameri-Mbote, P. (2016): 'The Quest for Equal Gender Representation in Kenya's Parliament: Past and Present Challenges', in J. Biegon (ed.) *Gender Equality and Political Processes in Kenya. Challenges and Prospects*. Nairobi: Strathmore University Press, pp. 39–65.

Kanyi, W. M. (2016): 'Kenyan Women's Journey in Their Quest for Affirmative Action. The Walls We Can't See: Public Policy Lethargy on Women's Political Participation in Kenya'. Retrieved from https://ke.boell.org/sites/default/files/uploads/2016/06/gender_briefs_-_wambui_kanyi.pdf

Kenny, C. and Patel, D. (2017): 'Gender Laws, Values, and Outcomes: Evidence from the World Values Survey', Center for Global Development Working Paper. No. 452. Retrieved from https://ssrn.com/abstract=2956405

Kenny, M. (2007): 'Gender, Institutions and Power: A Critical Review', *Politics*, Vol. 27, No. 2, 91–100.

Kenny, M. (2014): 'A Feminist Institutionalist Approach', *Politics & Gender*, Vol. 10, No. 4, 679–84.

Kibutu, T. N. (2006): 'Development, Gender and the Crisis of Masculinity among the Maasai People of Ngong, Kenya'. Retrieved from http://ethos.bl.uk/OrderDetails. do?uin=uk.bl.ethos.431354

Kimani, K. (2014): 'The Gender Rule Quagmire: Implementing the Two-Thirds Gender Principle in Kenya'. Retrieved from http://iedafrica.org/index.php/policy-legal-reforms/143-the-gender-rule-quagmire-implementing-the-two-thirds-gender-principle-in-kenya

Kipuri, N. N. O. (1990): 'Maasai Women in Transition: Class and Gender in the Transformation of a Pastoral Society. *Dissertation Abstracts International*', A, *Humanities and Social Sciences*, Vol. 51, No. 3, 910.

Kivoi, D. L. (2014): 'Factors Impeding Political Participation and Representation of Women in Kenya', *Humanities and Social Sciences*, Vol. 2, No. 6, 173–81.

Krook, M. L. (2008): 'Quota Laws for Women in Politics: Implications for Feminist Practice'. Retrieved from http://www.mlkrook.org/pdf/social_politics_2008.pdf

Krook, M. L. (2010): 'Beyond Supply and Demand: A Feminist-institutionalist Theory of Candidate Selection', *Political Research Quarterly*, Vol. 63, No. 4, 707–20.

Llewelyn-Davies, M. (1981): 'Women, Warriors and Patriarchs', in S. B. Ortner and H. Whitehead (eds) *Sexual Meanings. The Cultural Construction of Gender and Sexuality*. Cambridge: Cambridge University Press.

Lovenduski, J. (2011): 'Foreword', in M. L. Krook and F. Mackay (eds) *Gender, Politics and Institutions: Toward a Feminist Institutionalism*. Basingstoke: Palgrave Macmillan.

Lovenduski, J. and Norris, P. (2003): 'Westminster Women: The Politics of Presence', *Political Studies*, Vol. 51, 84–102.

Lowndes, V. (2005): 'Something Old, Something New, Something Borrowed ... How Institutions Change (and Stay the Same) in Local Governance', *Policy Studies*, Vol. 26, 291–309.

Mackay, F. (2008): "'Thick' Conceptions of Substantive Representation: Women, Gender and Political Institutions', *Representation*, Vol. 44, No. 2, 125–39.

Mackay, F., Kenny, M. and Chappell, L. (2010): 'New Institutionalism through a Gender Lens: Towards a Feminist Institutionalism?', *International Political Science Review*, Vol. 31, No. 5, 573–88.

Maina, E. (2013): 'Female Participation in the Kenyan Political Process'. http://internationalpoliticalforum.com/female-participation-in-the-kenyan-political-process/. Accessed 12 August 2015.

McManaman, L. J. (2013): 'Social Engineering: The Legal Philosophy of Roscoe Pound', *St. John's Law Review*, Vol. 33, 1–47.

Meyer, J. W. and Rowan, B. (1977): 'Institutionalized Organizations: Formal Structure as Myth and Ceremony', *American Journal of Sociology*, Vol. 83, No. 2, 340–63.

Miles, L. (2016): 'The Social Relations Approach, Empowerment and Women Factory Workers in Malaysia', *Economic and Industrial Democracy*, Vol. 37, No. 1, 3–22.

Moglen, H. (1983): 'Power and Empowerment', *Women's Studies International Forum*, Vol. 6, No. 2, 131–4.

Nzomo, M. (1997): 'Kenyan Women in Politics and Public Decision Making', in G. Mikell (ed.) *African Feminism: The Politics of Survival in Sub Saharan Africa*. Philadelphia: University of Pennsylvania Press.

Omwami, E. M. (2011): 'Relative-change Theory: Examining the Impact of Patriarchy, Paternalism, and Poverty on the Education of Women in Kenya', *Gender and Education*, Vol. 23, 15–28.

Owuor, E. (2016): 'Women and Political Inclusion in Kenya: A Historical Overview, 1963–2016', in J. Biegon (ed.) *Gender Equality and Political Processes in Kenya. Challenges and Prospects*. Nairobi: Strathmore University Press.

Oyewumi, O. (1997): *The Invention of Women. Making an African Sense of Western Gender Discourses*. Minneapolis: University of Minnesota Press.

Parsimei, E. (2013): 'The Maasai Women: Childhood to Womanhood'. Retrieved from http://web.education.unimelb.edu.au/UNESCO/pdfs/maasai.pdf. Accessed 12 October 2015.

Peet, R. and Hartwick, E. (2009): *Theories of Development, Second Edition: Contentions, Arguments, Alternatives*. New York: Guilford Press.

Spencer, P. (2003): *Time, Space, and the Unknown: Maasai Configurations of Power & Providence*. London: Routledge.

Sunstein, C. (2015): 'The Ethics of Nudging', *Yale Journal on Regulation*, Vol. 32, 413–50.

Taeko, T. (2014): 'The Complexity of Literacy in Kenya: Narrative Analysis of Maasai Women's Experiences', *Compare: A Journal of Comparative and International Education*, Vol. 5, 826–44.

Talle, A. (1987): 'Women as Heads of Houses: The Organization of Production and the Role of Women among Pastoral Maasai in Kenya', *Ethnos*, Vol. 52, No. 1–2, 50–80.

Wambui, J. (2016): 'Neo-Patrimonialism, Patriarchy and Politics of Women's Representation in Kenya', in *The Walls We Can't See: Public Policy Lethargy on Women's Political Participation in Kenya*. Retrieved from https://ke.boell.org/sites/default/files/uploads/2016/06/gender_briefs_-_jane_wambui.pdf.

Wangui, E. E. (2008): 'Development Interventions, Changing Livelihoods, and the Making of Female Maasai Pastoralists', *Agriculture and Human Values*, Vol. 25, No. 3, 365–78.

7

Women's political representation and institutionalism in Nigeria – historical perspectives

Monica Adele Orisadare

Introduction

The importance of women's representation in decision making at the level of governance – a prerequisite for gender equity, equality and sustainable development – has been undermined continually in Nigeria by the absence of women's critical mass in politics at a time when most regions of the world have shifted their thinking to increasing women's effectiveness in politics. There is historical evidences depicting women representation in politics en mass in Nigeria as respectively women leaders, party supporters, dancers and singers during political party meetings, rallies and election campaigns and as voters during elections, while their participation as decision makers remains low. With the clamour for more women's participation in politics as decision makers – a major prerequisite to closing the gender gap and achieving the sustainable development goals (SDGs) – one would expect that the number of women would have increased because of lessons learnt from best practices around the world. However, two decades after the return to democratic rule from military rule in Nigeria, the number of women in politics still remains meagre and has even gone lower in recent times. This worrisome development needs attention. A lack of women's critical mass in politics – a lacuna that can deprive appropriate voice to, lobby and advocate in favour of women's issues into government agenda has been an issue for concern in Nigeria. The present situation makes the popular slogan 'beyond numbers' a non-issue and non-pressing for the case of Nigeria, where a critical mass of women is non-existent. While several sub-Saharan Africa countries are making progress in their efforts at increasing women's political participation using several strategies including electoral quotas, etc., and have moved ahead to tackle women political effectiveness, Nigeria, the giant of Africa, remains far behind. While few women have always featured in position of power when compared to the number of men, this number in recent times has reduced, and attempts at increasing the number are yet to yield fruit. This calls for a concern and the need for further investigation of the possible explanations for this.

Empirically, there is no conflicting evidence on the effects of women's representations in politics as several studies have affirmed the important role of women political participation in nations' economic development. As highlighted by some scholars (Celis et al. 2008; Dahlerup 2010; Lovenduski and Norris 2004; Philips 1995; Tolleson-Rinchart 2001), the achievement of a gender balance in national government can affect immensely the quality of policymaking, in relation to both women's specific needs and the policymaking process more generally. The visibility of women in politics has also been theorized to have a symbolic effect, potentially increasing women's status and reducing societal gender inequalities more broadly (Paxton and Hughes 2007 among others). It has also been argued among scholars that gender parity in politics is among the most important changes required to produce a system of gender equality in the society (Moore and Shackman 1996). Several factors (e.g. persistent cultural stereotype, abuse of religious and traditional practices, etc.), limiting women participation in politics and hence the low representation of women in politics, have been identified by authors (e.g. Agbalajobi 2010; Kira 2003). Some authors have linked the persistent underrepresentation of women in politics in recent times with the diagnosis of the problem, that is, how the problem of women's underrepresentation is perceived and understood. Following the thought of Dahlerup's argument, the Policy and Legal Advocacy Centre (2018) also stated that Nigeria's inability to resolve the problem of women's political underrepresentation, despite the several measures put in place, is a result of an inappropriate diagnosis of the problem and consequently wrong application of therapy. The recent concern in the unsatisfactory level of development indicators performance brought about a rethink in the academic sphere across disciplines on how global development problems are conceptualized, birthing the inclusion of institutions as an intervening variable and a major subject of social science research. Although the study of institutions has a long history, its reappearance and interest in it beginning from the early 1980s followed a familiar pattern – a reaction to dominant strands of thought that neglected institutions, historical context and processes in favour of general theorizing.

The importance of institutions was reinforced with the emergence of the methodological approach known as new institutionalism, and its intellectual streams, including rational choice institutionalism, historical institutionalism, normative institutionalism and sociological institutionalism. Institutions have been recognized to matter in the affairs of human life beyond simply reflecting or codification of the power structure of the international system. In addition, they can have a major impact on political processes and outcomes.

Thus, institutions as opined by March and Olsen (2011) can empower and constrain actors differently, and make them more or less capable of acting according to prescriptive rules of appropriateness. March et al. (2011) observed that institutionalism comes in many flavours, but they are all perspectives for understanding and improving political systems. The 'basic premise of new institutionalism is that institutions do matter' (Kenny 2007). Institutionalism is the study of the origins, effects and potential for reform of institutions. North (1990) stated that many Third World countries today, as well as much of world's economic history, are a function of institutional frameworks. Supporting this view, Mabogunje (2000) also observed that, although formal rules may change overnight because of political or judicial decisions, informal constraints are impervious to deliberate policies. Because they are usually cultural in form and essence, informal constraints not only connect the past with the present and future but also provide a key to explaining the path of historical change. Similar to Mabogunje, Mandani (2001) also observed that colonization as an institution marked the beginning of a history for African societies culturally, economically and politically. According to the author, the struggle to decolonize contributed to the reinforcement of neo-colonialism for according to him there is no way colonial legacies can be addressed without reproducing the past. He went further to describe modern-day political identities as a consequence of the history of state formation. The understanding of how power and inequality are produced and reproduced through governmental and non-governmental structures and processes has long been a preoccupation of feminist political scientists.

A wave of feminist institutionalism looks at the operation of gender norms within institutions, and how institutional processes construct and maintain gender/power dynamics. Feminist institutionalism focuses on how institutions are gendered, and how their formal and informal rules play a part in shaping political life (Kenny 2014). Feminist institutionalism as a new institutionalism approach suffers from a lack of serious attention. Very little about the workings of state institutions and policy machinery is documented in literature. However, in recent times there is a growing attention to the exploration of feminist institutionalism as an analytical framework. Unfortunately, empirical work on the examinations of social reproduction, state institutions and women's political representation is relatively rare at this time. The Feminist Political Economy (FPE) literature examining women representation and governance through the dynamic of social reproduction using the historical institutionalism approach is underdeveloped and is at present scarce, hence the attempt by this present study to examine representation and governance through the dynamic of social reproduction in Nigeria. This study, therefore using explorative method by carrying out a document analysis from a feminist institutionalism lens, explores the participation of women in decision making in governance during the periods – pre-colonial, colonial and post-colonial to date – in an attempt to understand the low level of representation of women in politics and the influence of institutional frameworks in Nigeria.

Literature on women's political representation and institutions

In order to understand the framework for women's political representation and institutions, this section reviews theoretical and empirical literature. Institutions are a set of formal rules, informal norms or shared understandings that constrain and prescribe political actor's interaction with one another. There are three perspectives of institutions – institutional, rational actors and cultural community – that are not exclusive. Most political systems can be interpreted as functioning through a mix of organizing principles. Within neo-institutionalism, as observed by scholars (Krook and Mackay 2011; Lovenduski 2011), there are theoretical and methodological divisions. At least four different forms of institutionalism with which feminists are engaging include rational choice, sociological institutionalism, discursive institutionalism and historical institutionalism. The rational choice institutionalism explains the origins and outcomes of institutions at the macro-level with a focus on the behaviour of micro-level actors. Here, institutions are evaluated in terms of the incentives created for cooperation or competition. Sociological institutionalism has to do with organizational theory focusing mainly on institutions critiquing and the Weberian bureaucracy processes. This variant moves between the micro- and macro-level, challenging the notions of institutional rationality and efficiency by uncovering the myths, cultural norms, symbols, interest and social context that work to legitimize institutions (Mackay et al. 2009). Discursive institutionalism on the other hand spans from the micro- to the macro-level. It is fixated on the influence of ideas and discourses on actors, institutions and power relations. Discursive institutionalism is viewed by Kulawik (2009) as a bringing together of historical institutionalism and discourse analysis.

Historical institutionalism, more generally, follows the research programme of Max Weber in understanding economy, politics and society in terms of historically contingent, particular developmental paths, whose meanings depend upon the subjective interpretations of human actors. In this regard and in relations to the African society-historical materialism, social classes and the relationship between them, along with the political structures and ways of thinking in society, are founded on and reflect contemporary economic activity (Fromm 1961). For instance, according to Byfield (2012) during the colonial era in Nigeria, the system of governance introduced by the colonial administration in Abeokuta, Nigeria, was the main proponent behind all oppressions towards African women. All powers resided in the hands of the traditional rulers and local elites, where women were entirely excluded from Nigerian governance – which meant no female participation in communal affairs or Nigerian politics.

Mabogunje (2000) noted that gender organization in African societies is often seen in the context of the gender division of labour. In most of these societies, apart from their reproductive roles, women are seen as farmers, traders and artisans. Because of the segmented nature of activities in these their different roles, women are hardly conceived of as central to any major societal institutions. However, whenever opportunities do present themselves, such as among trading women in societies in Ghana and Nigeria, their ability to organize themselves, develop a hierarchy of authority, and insist on transparency and accountability of their officers has always been impressive.

Based on the assumption that 'the role of actors within a political system can be understood only by investigating, over time, the nature of the institutions within that system' (Chappell 2002), the historical view shared by classical authors, such as Georg Friedrich Hegel, sees traditions, customs, norms, laws and institutions as inheritances that have achieved legitimacy (if they have indeed achieved it) by standing the test of time. Waylen (2011) posits that historical institutionalism is best able to advance our understanding of structure and agency, and to explain why changes occur. The concept of path dependency, from historical institutionalism, has resonated with many feminist political scientists, interested in how initial choices about policy affect future ones and how policy legacies affect policy change for women (Chappell 2002; Krook and Mackay 2011; Kenny 2007). Some of the central features of a historical institutionalism approach are that it disaggregates the state, takes a broad definition of political institutions, studies the interaction between institutions, and takes an 'embedded and dynamic view of state' (Chappell 2002). In addition, according to Chappell (2002) one of its main strengths is its ability to comprehend social behaviour by examining institutions over time. While Smith (1999) adds that historical institutionalism views state institutions, as well as state policies, as potentially independent variables that structure political conflict and shape the mobilization of social forces. Some other authors disagree about whether all of these are equally promising; some prefer a synthesis (Krook and Mackay 2011), but many others show an affinity for the historical variant (Lovenduski 2011; Waylen 2011). Scholars (e.g. Chappell 2002; Lovenduski 2011) have appreciated the expansive definition of institutions, the focus on the ways institutions shape political behaviour, and the importance of comparing institutions across time and place.

Kenny (2007) points to several ways in which neo-institutionalism and feminist political science share a number of common preoccupations: Firstly, there is an understanding that seemingly neutral institutional processes and practices are in fact embedded in hidden norms and values, privileging certain groups over others. Secondly, both are centrally concerned with explanations of institutional creation, continuity, resistance and change. Thirdly, there is the emphasis on the *historicity* of power relations, opening up the possibility of institutional resistance and power reversals. Despite this commonality among scholars, however, Kenny (2007) and Lovenduski (2011) have also stressed that neo-institutionalism, as it currently stands, is inadequate, as it does not account for the gendered nature of institutions. Thus, Lovenduski (2011) concludes that neo-institutionalism much more should learn from feminist political science, which demonstrates that institutions are not neutral – they have a normative element.

Waylen (2008) recognized that the overall approach and underlying assumptions of historical institutionalism make it potentially more open to incorporating gender into its frameworks than other forms of institutionalism. However, Chappell (2006) pointed out that although historical institutionalism approaches can be useful in explaining how particular gender regimes arose and why it is often so difficult to change them, it is also important to be able to explain how and why institutions can or cannot be renegotiated in different contexts. This includes a focus on both its formal and informal variants and the ways in which institutions have gendered norms and logics (Chappell 2006).

According to feminist institutionalism establishes some foundational premises from which to examine institutions, the foremost being that all institutions are gendered – meaning that gender is present in the processes, practices, images and ideologies, and distributions of power within that state. The author concludes that institutions matter as stressed by historical institutionalism and at the same time make a stronger case for feminist institutionalism that they matter quite differently for women. However, historical institutionalism scholars have recognized for some time the need to not only better our understanding of institutional change but also improve our understanding of how that change is gendered (Mahoney and Thelen 2010; Waylen 2017). The fact remains that mainstream institutional scholars have largely neglected the gendered dimensions of institutional dynamics resulting into gender blindness of most new institutionalism research.

This study is an attempt to understand the nature of women participation in decision making in politics, the causes of low women participation in decision making in politics and the influence of institutional framework in Nigeria. I carry out an examination of women representation in decision making in politics and how institutional frameworks have influenced women participation in decision making in Nigeria using the historical institutionalism approach with a focus on the periods: pre-colonial, colonial and post-colonial period to date. In this study, existing literature and data were explored and reviewed. The study hinges on the feminist historical institutionalism framework to explore the participation of women in decision making in governance from the pre-colonial, colonial and post-colonial to date (2018). Particular attention is paid to the colonial era when the indirect rule of British government had the most obvious negative impact on Nigeria. Its effect on women's political representation during this period was particularly devastating as Nigerian men have little relevance in governance, but the women were totally excluded. To put this study in perspective, three types of institutions were examined during the periods under review – social institutions, constitutions and regimes – which refer to the process of giving something the character of an institution.

Historical context of women's political representation and institutions in Nigeria

The role of women in Nigeria has been one of dynamic development since the periods – pre-colonial, colonial and post-colonial to date. Nigeria, a multicultural nation with diverse cultures and people, scattered in the thirty-six states of the federation and a federal capital Abuja north-west of Nigeria, with different cultures having their own laws, norms and customs concerning women's political representation. Women's rights to represent in politics in Nigeria still lie on the culture of its society irrespective of the concern for women by the international society.

Pre-colonial era, women political representation and institutions

In pre-colonial indigenous Nigerian societies, *the ideal* traditional role of women included providing for her family by means of financial support; therefore, her traditional responsibility required her financial independence. Furthermore, many members of the extended family helped to rear the children, not only the mother. Concerning politics, women in pre-colonial Nigeria were an integral part of the political set of their communities. Often, they carried out separate functions from the men and these functions were fully complementary and power in the society during this period was based on seniority rather than gender (Rojas 1994). Women rulers in various kingdoms were common during this period and some women functioned as warriors and even spies. Several women in the pre-colonial era were rulers for their communities. From account of pre-colonial Bomu, women played active role in the administration of the state; they held very important offices in the royal family, including the offices of the Megira (the Queen mother) and the Gumsu (the first wife of the Mai or King). In Zaria, women also played a very significant role in its political history. Examples of women rulers during the pre-colonial era included: Luwo Gbadiaya of Ife, Iyayun of Oyo, Queen Amina of Zaria, Queen Idia of Benin and Queen Kanbasa of Bonny (see Table 7.1).

Table 7.1 Women political representation during the pre-colonial era

S/N	Name	Town/ Village	LGA	State	Type of rule	Date
1	Luwo Gbadiaya	Ife	Ife Central L.G.	Osun	Ooni of Ife	Pre-colonial days
2	Iyayun	Oyo	Oyo	Oyo	Alaafin	Pre-colonial era
3	Orompoto	Oyo	Oyo	Oyo	Alaafin	Pre-colonial era
4	Jomijomi	Oyo	Oyo	Oyo	Alaafin	Pre-colonial era
5	Jepojepo	Oyo	Oyo	Oyo	Alaafin	Pre-colonial era
6	Queen Amina of Zaria		Zaria	Old Northern states	Emir	Pre-colonial era
7	Daura	Daura	Daura Emirate	Katsina	Queen	Pre-colonial era
8	Kofono	Daura	Daura Emirate	Katsina	Queen	Pre-colonial era
9	Queen Idia of Benin	Benin	Benin	Benin	A great warrior who provided an effective military bastion for her son, Oba Esigie of Benin	1504 to 1550
10	Eye-moi	Akure	Akure	Ondo	Regent-Monarch	Pre-colonial days 1705–35 AD
11	Ayo-Ero	Akure	Akure	Ondo	Regent-Monarch	Pre-colonial days 1850–1 AD
12	Gulfano	Daura	Daura Emirate	Katsina	Queen	Pre-colonial era
13	Yawano	Daura	Daura Emirate	Katsina	Queen	Pre-colonial era
14	Yakania	Daura	Daura Emirate	Katsina	Queen	Pre-colonial era
15	Walsam	Daura	Daura Emirate	Katsina	Queen	Pre-colonial era
16	Cadar	Daura	Daura Emirate	Katsina	Queen	Pre-colonial era

S/N	Name	Town/ Village	LGA	State	Type of rule	Date
17	Agagri	Daura	Daura Emirate	Katsina	Queen	Pre-colonial era
18	Queen Kanbasa	Bony	Bony L.G.	Rivers	Queen	Pre-colonial era

Source: Kolawole et al. (2012).

A woman called Bakwa Turuku in the first half of the sixteenth century founded the modern city of Zaria in the present Kaduna state. Bakwa had a daughter called Amina who later succeeded her as Queen. Queen Amina was a great and powerful warrior who built a high wall around Zaria to protect the city from invasion and extended the boundaries of her territory beyond Bauchi. Queen Amina transformed Zaria into a very prominent commercial centre. The people of both Kano and Kastina paid tribute to her. Through Queen Amina of Zaria's story of bravery and exemplary leadership in the fourteenth century, Nigerian women became aware of the roles they could play assisting the men in politics. Thus, a new role for political participation was defined for women. The story is also similar in ancient Yoruba land as accounted for by Omu and Makinwa (1976) where the Oba (King) ruled with the help of a number of women known as ladies of the palace, consisting of eight titled ladies of the highest rank. Notably, there are prominent women such as Moremi of Ile-Ife, Emotan of Benin and Omu Okwel of Ossomari whose significant role in the history of Nigeria politics cannot be ignored. Both Moremi and Emotan were great amazons who displayed tremendous bravery and strength in the politics of Ife and Benin respectively, while Omu Okwel dominated commercial scene of Ossomari in the present-day Delta State.

In the traditional Igbo culture, there was a balance of power between men and women. Men decided on issues relevant to them through consensus. In a similar manner women run their own affairs through the women's town meeting on matters such as trade, farming and family relationship and arrived at a conclusion through a consensus. In the situations, where the decision of the women was not accepted by the men, a group action of publicly berating the men is tagged, or beating on his house until he repented, or conducting a village-wide cooking strike if the men refuse to clear the bush paths leading to the market. During this period, the men in the community viewed this form of collective group action as legitimate. During this period, women were elected leaders of the community and this in a way complements the governance of the people.

Colonialism and women representation

Authors (e.g. Mandani 2001) have opined that colonialism was more about the institutions they created than just about the identities of who ruled. Colonialism changed greatly the ideas of the appropriate social role for women from the traditional role of women in indigenous Nigerian societies. The ideas of the colonizers resembled the patriarchal European assumption that women belonged in the home, engaged in child rearing as an exclusively female responsibility and other domestic chores. The colonizers expected African societies to consider women as subordinate to men just like the Europeans. They thought that if a woman obtained financial independence, she might not give her husband and his family their entitled respect. The introduction of the assumptions of European patriarchy into Nigerian society by the Colonial administrators and Christian missionaries placed restrictions on women that changed the position of women in indigenous societies. Legislation restricting women was passed by the colonial state, indirectly preventing them from performing their duties towards their families. The extent of the changes inspired many Nigerian women to hold a series of protests throughout the colonial period against particular colonial policies and against colonialism, itself set the stage for women politics representation. Prominently, it was the Aba women riot, which dates back to 1928, which was a period of unrest in British Nigeria. It was a strategically executed anti-colonial revolt organized by women to redress social, political and economic grievances. The protest was against the Warrant Chiefs, whom they accused of restricting the role of women in the government. It was organized and led by the rural women of Owerri and Calabar provinces. During the events, many Warrant Chiefs were forced to resign and sixteen Native Courts were attacked, most of which were destroyed. The result of the protest was that women were appointed to serve on the native court. Similarly, in 1948, from the account of Ayobami (2010) the Abeokuta Women's Union (AWU) under the leadership of Funmilayo protested against the patriarchal structure of the colonial rule to end the unfavourable taxation regime against the women and argued for women representation in local government. After weeks of persistent protest and petitions by the AWU, the Alake (King of Egba land) abdicated from the throne and as a result, the Egba Interim Council emerged, which included four women representing the four sections of Abeokuta town.

The AWU emerged as one of the first proto-nationalist feminist activist groups in Nigeria (Byfield 2012). Moreover, since then Nigerian women have delved into different aspects of partisan politics first by campaigning for men as husbands or as candidate of their choice. It is quite easy to use women as campaign tools because they can pull crowd through the different women grassroots groups, for example, market women associations and women religious groups. Women play a critical role in marketing and have established quite formidable organizations to this end. Similarly, in some societies, especially those where women enjoy a substantial degree of economic independence, a parallel but complementary institution of governance for women has evolved over time (Mabogunje 2000).

Colonialism affected Nigerian women adversely as they were denied the right to vote and very few of them were offered any political or administrative appointments. During this period, the country could not boast of any prominent female nationalist leaders as the women's wings of political parties possessed very little functional relevance and women's representation in government was rare (Attoe 2002). From account, it was not until the 1950s that women in the South were granted the right to vote while women from the North were still denied the right to vote or be voted for until 1978. In addition, at the height of the clamour for independence three women, namely, Chief (Mrs) Olufunmilayo Ransome-Kuti (appointed into the western Nigerian House of Chiefs), Chief (Mrs) Margaret Ekpo and Janet Mokelu (both appointed into the Eastern Nigeria House of Chiefs), were appointed into the House of Chief. These women were appointed to represent their constituencies by the ruling government.

Post-colonial to date

The post-colonial era heralded women playing active role in various aspects of nation's development again. Although the role of women in the period immediately after the post 1960 in politics was not sufficiently reflected, in terms of appointments and election to policymaking post, very few women were part of the government at that time. This was in spite of the massive support given to women organizations. This was because women were only allowed to vote and be voted for just at about this time, the aftermath effect of colonialism on women participation in politic, as well as the deeply rooted patriarchal, cultural and religious bias against women participation in decision making. Nevertheless, it was an improvement over the pre-colonial and colonial periods, especially the colonial period. Women in southern Nigeria by 1960 already had the franchise, so they could vote as well as contest election; Mrs Wuraola Esan from western Nigeria was voted for to become the first female member of the Federal Parliament. In 1961, Chief (Mrs) Margaret Ekpo contested in Aba Urban North constituency under the National Council of Nigerian Citizen (NCNC) platform and also won, becoming a member of the Eastern Nigeria House of Assembly until 1966. Mrs Janet N. Mokelu and Miss Ekpo A. Young also contested elections, won and became members of the Eastern House of Assembly. However, during the same period the women in northern Nigeria were still denied the franchise even after independence, because of the strict Islamic beliefs of the people. As a result, prominent female political activists like Hajia Gambo Sawaba could not vote nor be voted for. It was only in 1979 that women in northern Nigeria were granted franchise, following the return to civilian rule. Table 7.2 shows some women representation in politics during this period.

After independence, Nigeria witnessed series of military rule with partial civilian government between 1967, 1979 and 1983. Socio-cultural factors such as patriarchy and religion as well as colonial influence prevailed affecting the level of women participation (Rojas 1994). This is despite the fact that the Nigerian constitution at this time, that is, 1979 guaranteed women's rights and generally prohibited any form of discrimination based on gender (denoting that women have the right to vote from eighteen years of age and be voted for by twenty-one and above (Badejo 1985)). This scenario

Table 7.2 Women representation in politics in Nigeria (post-colonial era)

S/N	Name		Date
1	Christy Boyo	Political activist	Post-colonial-1978
2	Funmilayo Ransome –Kuti	Political activist in the western region	Post-colonial (1978)
3	Madam Tinubu	Lagos	She flourished in commercial venture in Lagos
4	Hajia Gambo Sawaba	Northern region	Political activist in the northern region
5	Mrs Kerry	Midwest region	First woman senator in the then Midwest region
6	Franca Afegbua	Nigeria	Second Republic Senator in Nigeria
7	Janet Akinriade	Nigeria	Minister for National Planning in the Second Republic
8	Mrs Flora Nwapa	East Central state	General Gowon regime of 1970
9	Folake Solonka	North Eastern state	General Gowon regime of 1970
10	Ronke Doherty	Oyo	General Gowon regime of 1970
11	Kofoworola Pratt	Lagos	General Gowon regime of 1970

Source: Kolawale et al. (2012).

depicts the often-discussed issue of public versus the private dichotomy of the society, which highlights the challenges of enforcing a written document on the public and private space. In the First Republic 1979–83, two women senators were nominated. During the Second Republic democratic regime, President Shehu Shagari gave meaning to what democracy is all about, by giving women a noticeable position in governance. There was one female senator and two members of House of Representatives, and two female members of the Federal Executive Council minister of national planning/ education (Mrs Oyebola, Mrs Ivase). There were also Mrs J. C. Eze of the Nigerian People's Party (NPP) who represented UzoUwani constituency in former Anambra State; Mrs V. O. Nnaji, also of NPP, who represented Isu and Mrs Abiola Babatope of the Unity Party of Nigeria (UPN) who represented Mushin Central II of Lagos State.

During the Second Republic, very few women won elections into the National, State Houses of Assembly and into the Local Councils as a whole. In addition, just as in the First Republic, the political arena remains largely male dominated especially the political parties. Although these women made a few gains as the pioneer advocates for feminine emancipation and spearheaded social movements that sought equal rights for women within political institutions and beyond in the interests of women and the nation, there are arguments that these gains were only restricted to the elites and highly inconsequential (Dibua 2006). The military coup by December of 1983 short-lived this recorded success, and this led to changes in the political structure of the country yet again (Attoe 2002; Dibua 2006; Okome 2009). The Third Republic which was aborted had a token election of one female in the ninety-one members Senate and thirteen females into the 589-member House of Representatives and two female deputy governors. Very few women were elected as councillors and only one woman (Titilayo Ajanaku) emerged as a chairperson of Local government Council in the West. Two women, namely, Mrs Cecilia Ekpeyong and Alhaja Sinatu Ojikutu, emerged as deputy governors for Cross River and Lagos states respectively.

The National Committee on Women and Development was established in November 1982 and directed that committees on Women and Development should be set up at state levels. This was in response to recommendations of the World Conference of the International Women's Year in Mexico City, 1975, and the second extraordinary session of the Assembly of Heads of State and Governments of the Organisation of African Unity in Lagos, April 1980, with a focus on the theme 'Equality, Development and Peace'. The Nigerian Federal Government established The National Committee, which is intended to increase the participation of women at grassroots, rural worker's organization/associations among others, both in decision making and in the implementation of projects that affect women (Aina 1993). According to Okwuosa (1994), the military regime of General Ibrahim Badamosi Babangida of 1983–92 took affirmative action to include women in all areas regarded as the exclusive concern of the men. For instance, the military government in December 1983 introduced the first formal quota system for the appointment of women into governance. The regime coincided with the end of the United Nations Declaration of the Decade for Women and, as such, the then military government 'flirted' with women and their issues (Oyebade 2002). The directive of the quota was that at least one female must be appointed as a member of the executive Council in every state; all states complied with the directives and some even had two or three female members. Despite the progressive steps by Babangida administration towards promoting women's participation in governance and leadership in Nigeria, the number of women in key policy positions remained low when compared with their male counterparts. Nevertheless, this act did not reflect the recommendations of equal opportunity and emancipation of women in the constitution.

The structure of the military has also made it difficult for women to be part of the defunct Supreme Military Council or the later Armed Forces Ruling Council. As related by International Centre for Investigative Reporting (2017) there are various types of commissions in the Armed Forces, namely, Regular Combatant Commission, Short Service Combatant Commission, Direct Regular Commission, Direct Short Service and Executive Commission. The Regular Combatant Commission is the only commission that can give an officer the opportunity to aspire to head any of the services or rise to become the chief of Defence Staff, while the others have limited career path. However, female officers in the Nigerian armed forces, irrespective of their competence or skill, have always been limited to non-combat duties, thereby limiting their career path for attaining higher post. Although the training of female cadets in Nigeria only commenced in 2011, this has been revised in November 2017 with a recommendation to phase out the training of female regular combatant cadet. With this, chances of a woman becoming the Nigerian chief of Army Staff (CAS) or a member of the Supreme Military Council may have been foreclosed.

By 1992, only one woman – Mrs Kofo Bucknor Akerele – won a seat in the Senate while very few emerged victorious in the National House of Assembly – less than 5 per cent (Attoe 2002). In the bid to ensure transition to civilian rule as promised by the regime, a transitional council was appointed in

January 1993, and only two of the appointees were women (Attoe 2002). This trend continued with the interim government of Ernest Shonekan, and the military regime of Gen Abacha with only few a number of female ministers at various times in his cabinet; even the transitional government (1998–9) of Gen Abubakar had only two women out of thirty-one members of the Federal Executive Council (Attoe 2002).

It is of importance to state that the country since 29 May 1999 has witnessed a steady democratic rule. Before the year 1999, statistics of the participation of women in leadership position was minimal. Its progressive increase within the period may not be unconnected with the democratic rule, which was in progress at the time as against the military era. In this era, the use of parliament (the legislative assembly and the executive) as a measure of participation in decision making reveals the fact that women participated in politics in Nigeria more within the period of 1999–2007. However, this gain in number reduced in the 2011 elections and presently averages 5.6 per cent since 2015–19, very different from averages of most other regions of the world. It is noteworthy to mention here that in the period 1999–2018, politics in Nigeria turned the most lucrative business more than ever; an average lawmaker earns more than his or her counterparts in the UK or United States. Depending on the exchange rates, Nigerian lawmakers remain among the world's top paid in recent times, receiving an annual salaries of between $150,000 and $190,000 per annum. Nigeria is a country where millions live on less than two dollars daily and minimum wage is set at $90 a month; the lawmakers' bumper pay has been described as outrageous (The Economist 2013). Due to politicians' high earnings, coupled with the high unemployment rate, many people see it as a way of making quick money. Thus, in a country where politics has become a very lucrative business, little wonder why it remains a herculean task for women to be part of politics and to vie for elective position. So far, in Nigeria no woman has won election as a governor, vice president or president. Moreover, the first and only woman in history, Mrs Patricia Etteh, who became the Speaker of the Federal House of Representatives, resigned from office. Mrs Etteh was elected to the position of speaker unanimously in June 2007 and on September

2007 faced a committee of MPs over accusations that she had authorized spending of 628 million Naira (about US$5 million) on renovations of her official residence and that of her deputy, and the purchase of twelve official cars meant for the House of Representatives. Following weeks of pressure calling for her resignation, she finally resigned her position as speaker on 30 October, although officially Mrs Etteh was not indicted until date. Several activities engaged in by male politicians, consciously or unconsciously, which included political thuggery, elimination of political opponents, incitement of ethnic and sectarian violence, vote rigging, intimidation, vote buying, propaganda and unnecessary clandestine meetings are targeted at excluding women from participating.

The structures of political parties also impede the effective participation of Nigerian women in politics and public positions. Numerous empirical studies have shown that information about politics is disseminated through channels that men have more access to, not to mention that the language of politics can appear alien to women. Furthermore, according to Alani (2006) experience during the last general elections shows that some parties had unwritten policies against female aspirants. Parties determine candidatures for elections as well as who gets to contest for what post. The party apparatus is used to enhance the ambition of selected candidates. Indeed, women continue to endure inadequate representation in political and decision making because of formidable socio-cultural determinants against women's participation in education (Nzomo 1987).

Due to socio-cultural attitudes, submissiveness, sexist stereotypes, early female marriages, motherhood, passivity, family subsistence through child labour and parental perception of education's influence on women's worldview, financial limitations and patriarchal practices, women continue to endure inadequate representation in political decision making.

Findings indicate that the present power play between men and women in the political arena is a product of a historical development of the state as well as the cultural and institutional framework. The ideal concept of what the traditional conception of the role of women should be changed drastically during the colonial era and obstructed the hitherto existing structures and institutions, which in turn affected the social order by redefining the representation of women in power. There is evidence from a historical perspective that women have been in the forefront representing women's interest as warriors, traders and economic powers in addition to their role in the household as wives and mothers from pre-colonial period to date. Structures of inequality though existed in the pre-colonial times; no doubt, they were however heightened and institutionalized as new legal structures under the colonial rule, with the creation of colonial economy. The creation of the colonial economy during the colonial era marginalized the position of the majority of women and there was evidence that existing institutional framework did not favour women in their political representation, thus perpetuating their low representation.

The colonial legacy of identity dilemma of rights and entitlements in indigeneity birthed a highly politicized indigeneity as a settler libel against the natives and as a native self-assertion (Mamdani 2001). Thus, rights and entitlement were subject to indigeneity and became a litmus test under the post-colonial state as under the colonial state. The foundation built turned indigeneity into a fertile land for justice, and thus entitlement under the post-colonial state – a situation described as a reproduction of dual legacy of colonialism by Mandani. This trend continued during the post-colonial period, where the existing colonial economy was extended – the prolonged military rule in Nigeria, which never had any women in its Supreme Council. Nigeria is lagging behind in the implementation of the mandate of international framework/policies of gender equality. In recent times, the monetization of politics, which has made election to political post a do or die affair, has contributed greatly to the exclusion of higher representation of women in political decision making.

Conclusion

The study influenced by the feminist historical institutionalism explored the participation of women in decision making in governance from different periods in the history of Nigeria – the pre-colonial, colonial and post-colonial to date, in an attempt to understand the low level of representation of women in politics and the influence of institutional frameworks in Nigeria. From the findings of the study, the history and the institutional frameworks in Nigeria over time play a key role in shaping the level of women representation in decision making that we have today. Drawing from the writings of on state production and reproduction of unequal gender and class relationship, the study concludes that the Nigerian state does not relate to all people(s) equally, and as far as it relates to women at all, it tends to treat women as quantitatively aberrant and qualitatively homogeneous. Thus, the study establishes that institutions do matter in determining women representation in politics in Nigeria for the periods under review and play a major role in the present low level of women representation in the political arena. While some of these institutions especially the traditional role of women in the pre-colonial setting encouraged women participation in decisions both at the household and in the community, the Victorian style of the colonial era limited women representation in decision making, especially in the public sphere. Similarly, the civilian/democratic rule in the post-colonial era encourages more women political representation as compared to military rule. However, the case for understanding the low level of women representation in decision making during the military era is an opportunity for further study.

There is no doubt that the present number of women representation in politics is low and a far cry away from the affirmative action recommendation, and that this trend may continue unless there is a major rethinking on the role of women in the society away from the colonial patriarchal legacy to change the extant status quo. The commitment of all stakeholders – the Government, Women's group/movement, CSOs and CBOs are paramount at this time and especially raising a critical mass of women in governance. The study therefore concluded by suggesting that learning from best practices from around the world and an adaptation of same to local reality will go a long way in correcting the situation. However, beyond that a concerted effort on the part of government in honouring international mandates and agreements, in order to achieve the country's gender equality agenda of global sustainable development goals, should be a top priority.

References

Agbalajobi, D. T. (2010): 'Women's Participation and the Political Process in Nigeria: Problems and Prospects', *African Journal of Political Science and International Relations*, Vol. 4, No. 2, 75–82.

Aina (1993): 'Mobilizing Nigerian Women for National Development: The Role of the Female Elites', *African Economic History*, Vol. 21, 1–20. University of Wisconsin Press.

Associated Press. 'Nigeria's Parliamentary Speaker Quits over Corruption Scandal', *Associated Press*, 30 October 2007.

Attoe, E.S. (2002): 'Women in the Development of Nigeria since pre-colonial time'. http://www.onlinenigeria.com/links/adv.asp?blurb=150#ixzz2xd6UxI3c.

Badmus, I. A. (2006): 'Political Parties and Women's Political Leadership in Nigeria: The Case of the PDFD, the ANPP, and the AD', *Ufahamu: A Journal of African Studies*, Vol. 32, No. 3.

Badejo, O. (1985): Education, Women and Society. A Paper Presented at the Departmental Seminar University of Maduguri, Nigeria.

Bannerji, H. (1996): 'On the Dark Side of the Nation: Politics of Multiculturalism and the State of Canada', *Journal of Canadian Studies*, Vol. 31, No. 3 (Fall), 103–24.

Birrell Gray Commission (1929): 'Public Records Office, CO583/169/3, Sessional Paper No. 12', p. 43.

Byfield, J. (April 2012): 'Gender, Justice, and the Environment: Connecting the Dots', *African Studies Review*, Vol. 55, 1–12 – via JSTORE.

Celis, K., Childs, S., Kantola, J., and Krook, M. L. (2008). 'Rethinking Women's Substantive Representation', *Representation*, Vol. 44, No. 2.

Chappell, L. (2002): *Gendering Government: Feminist Engagement with the State in Australia and Canada*. Vancouver: University of British Columbia Press.

Chappell, L. (2006): 'Comparing Political Institutions: Revealing the Gendered Logic of Appropriateness', *Politics and Gender*, Vol. 2, No. 2, 223–35.

Dahlerup, D. (2005): 'Strategies to Enhance Women's Political Representation in Different Electoral Systems'. *Paper to the Conference 'Women Shaping Democracy'. Progressive Politics Ten Years after the World Conference on Women in Beijing* Manila, Philippines, 24–25 October.

Dahlerup, D. (2010): 'From a Small to a Large Minority: Women in Scandinavian Politics', in M. Krook and S. Childs (eds) *Women, Gender, and Politics: A Reader*. New York: Oxford University Press, pp. 225–30.

Dibua, J. I. (2006): *Modernization and the Crisis of Development in Africa: the Nigerian Experience*. Aldershot: Ashgate, Volume 77, Issue 3, August, pp. 472–3.

Driscoll, A. and Krook, M. L. (2009): 'Can There Be a Feminist Rational Choice Institutionalism?', *Politics & Gender*, 18 Vol. 5, No. 2, 238–45.

The Economist (2013): '*A Comparison of Lawmakers' Pay*', Rewarding work. The Economist Jul 15.

Fromm, E. (1961): 'Marx's Historical Materialism', in *Marx's Concept of Man*. New York: Frederick Ungar Publishing.

International Centre for Investigative Reporting (2017): 'Why Women May Not Become Military Chiefs in Nigeria', International Centre for Investigative Reporting, 13 November.

Kira, S. (2003): *Political Knowledge and Gender Stereotypes. American Politics Research.* November 1.

Kenny, M. (2007): 'Gender, Institutions and Power: A Critical Review', *Political Science Association*, Vol. 27, No. 2.

Kenny, M. (2014): 'A Feminist Institutionalist Approach', *Government and Opposition*, Vol. 10, 679–84. Doi: 10.1017/s1743923x14000488 (https://doi.org/10.1017%2Fs1743923x14000488).

Kolawole, T. O., Abubakar, M. B., Owonibi, E. and Adebayo, A. A. (2012): 'Gender and Party Politics in Africa with Reference to Nigeria', *Online Journal of Education Research*, Vol. 1, No. 7, 132–44.

Krook, M. L. and Mackay, F. (2011): 'Introduction: Gender, Politics, and Institutions', in M. L. Krook and F. Mackay (eds) *Gender, Politics and Institutions: Towards a Feminist Institutionalism.* Basingstoke: Palgrave Macmillan, pp. 1–20.

Kulawik, T. (2009): 'Staking the Frame of a Feminist Discursive Institutionalism', *Politics & Gender*, Vol. 5, No. 2, 262–71.

Lovenduski, J., and Norris, P. (2004): 'Westminster women: The Politics of Presence', *Political Studies*, Vol. 51, No. 1, 84–102.

Lovenduski, J. (2011): 'Foreword', in M. L. Krook and F. Mackay (eds) *Gender, Politics and Institutions: Towards a Feminist Institutionalism.* Basingstoke: Palgrave Macmillan, pp. vi–xi.

Mabogunje, A. L. (2000): 'Institutional Radicalization, the State, and the Development Process in Africa', *Proceedings of the National Association of Sciences of the United States of America*, Vol. 97, No. 25, 5 December 2000, pp. 14007–14.

Mackay, F., et al. (2009): 'The Feminist Potential of Sociological Institutionalism', *Politics and Gender*, Vol. 5, No. 2, 253–62.

Mahoney, J. and Thelen, K. (eds) (2010): *Explaining Institutional Change: Ambiguity, Agency, and Power.* Cambridge: Cambridge University Press.

Mamdani, M. (2001): 'Beyond Settler and Native as Political Identities: Overcoming the Political Legacy of Colonialism', *Comparative Studies in Society and History*, Vol. 43, No. 4 (October, 2001), 651–64. Cambridge University Press.

March, J. G. and Olsen, J. P. (2011): 'Elaborating the "New Institutionalism"', in Robert E. Goodin (ed.) *The Oxford Handbook of Political Science.* June. Doi: 10.1093/oxfordhb/9780199548460.003.0001.

Moore, G. and Shackman, G. (1996): 'Gender and Authority: A Cross-national Study', *Social Science Quarterly, Vol. 77, No. 2*, 273–88.

North, D. C. (1990): *Institutions, Institutional Change, and Economic Performance.* Cambridge: Cambridge University Press.

Nzomo, M. (1987): 'Women, Democracy and Development in Africa', in Walther O. Oyugi, A. Odhiambo, M. Chege and A. Gitonga (eds) *Democracy Theory and Practice in Africa.* Nairobi: Heinemann, pp. 111–13.

Obi, M. A. (2007): 'Women's Participation in Democratic Governance and Leadership in Nigeria', *International Journal of Studies in the Humanities*, Vol. 4.

Okome, O. (2009): *Popular Culture in Africa: The Episteme of the Everyday*. S. Newell (ed.). Routledge.

Okwuosa, A. (1994): 'Women in Democratization Process in Nigeria: Gains and Limitations', in Omoruyi et al. (eds) *Democratization Nigerian Perspectives*, Vol. 2. Benin: Hima and Hima Press.

Olusola, A. (2010): 'The Abeokuta Women's Revolt'. Home. N.p., 13 April, Web, 5 March 2013.

Oyebade, A. (ed.) (2002) *The Transformation of Nigeria: Essays in Honor of Toyin Falola*. Trenton, NJ: Africa World Press. Volume 73, Issue 3, pp. 478–9.

Paxton, P. and Hughes, M. M. (2007): 'Women, Politics, and Power: A Global Perspective', in *Sociology for a New Century Series*. United States: Sage.

Philips, Anne. (1995): *The Politics of Presence*. Oxford: Clarendon Press.

Policy and Legal Advocacy Centre (2018): 'Women's Political Representation in Nigeria: Why Progress Is Slow and What Can Be Done to Fast-track It', Policy and Legal Advocacy Centre (PLAC).

Robertson, C., Iris Berger, I. and Staudt, K. (1986): *Women and Class in Africa*. C. Robertson and Berger I. Iris (eds). New York: Africana.

Rojas, A. M. (1994): 'What It's Like to Be Hispanic in the Workplace', *International Society for Performance Improvement*, April. Vol. 33, No. 4, 25–6.

Smith, L. T. (1999): *Decolonizing Methodologies. Research and Indigenous Peoples*. London, UK: Zed Books (and Otago University Press).

Smith, M. (2010): 'Federalism and LGBT Rights in the US and Canada: A Comparative Policy Analysis', in M. Haussmann et al. (eds) *Federalism, Feminism and Multilevel Governance*. Burlington, VT: Ashgate, pp. 97–110.

Staudt, K. (1986): *Women and Class in Africa*. C. Robertson and Berger I. Iris (eds). New York: Africana.

Tolleson-Rinehart. (2001): 'Do women leaders make a difference? in S. Carrol (ed.) *The Impact of Women in Public Office*. Bloomington: University of Indiana Press, pp. 149–65.

Waylen, G. (2008): 'What Can Historical Institutionalism Offer to a Comparative Politics of Gender?' *Paper Prepared for the ECPR Joint Sessions in Rennes 11–16 April 2008 Workshop 12: Gender, Politics and Institutions: Towards a Feminist Institutionalism?*

Waylen, G. (2011): 'Gendered Institutionalist Analysis: Understanding Democratic Transitions', in M. L. Krook and F. Mackay (eds) *Gender, Politics and Institutions: Towards a Feminist Institutionalism*. Basingstoke: Palgrave Macmillan, pp. 147–62.

Waylen, G. (2017): 'Gendering Institutional Change', in *Oxford Research Encyclopedia of Politics*. USA: Oxford University Press 2019.

8

Affirmative action in Ghana? Patriarchal arguments and institutional inertia

Diana Højlund Madsen

Introduction

Affirmative action in the form of adoption of gender quotas has been sweeping over the African continent with 'first-wave' sub-Saharan countries such as Rwanda and South Africa related to post-transition or post-conflict changes.[1] Currently, Rwanda has the highest representation of women in parliament in the world with 68 per cent. The 'second-wave' is composed of sub-Saharan countries such as Kenya and Senegal where the adoption of affirmative action has been achieved as a part of broader constitutional reform processes and the national women's movements have been promoting a higher representation of women in politics. However, Ghana is not on the 'fast-track' (Dahlerup and Freidenvall 2003) to more women in politics and is falling behind other countries with (only) 13 per cent women in parliament. Paradoxically, Ghana was the first sub-Saharan country to introduce a quota with ten reserved seats for women as an acknowledgement of their contribution to the struggle for independency led by Kwame Nkrumah[2] as CPP (Convention People's Party) passed the Representation of the People (Women Members) Act in 1959. This is despite the fact that Ghana has adopted a range of instruments such as CEDAW (Convention of the Elimination of All Kinds of Discrimination against Women), BFA (Beijing Platform for Action), SDG (Sustainable Development Goals) with goal number 5 on gender equality, The African Charter on Human and People's Rights and The Maputo Protocol. Furthermore, in 2017 the current Ghanaian President Nana Akufo-Addo from NPP (New Patriotic Party) has been appointed as 'African Union's Gender Champion' linked to a gender programme, which includes a focus on women's political representation.[3]

Ghana is formally a multi-party system but in reality a two-party system. In the latest 2016 election power shifted, as the current ruling party NPP gained 53.8 per cent of the votes against 44.4 per cent for NDC (National Democratic Congress) and John Mahama and only 0.24 per cent for the more 'women-friendly' CPP (http://ghanaelections.peacefmonline. com/pages/2016/). Ghana is ranked number 80 (out of 115) on political empowerment (Global Gender Gap Report 2020) and with a female-to-male ratio on 0.15 per cent for women in parliament and slightly higher for women in government, 0.33 per cent (with one being equal). Data illustrates that most women are nominated in Greater Accra, Central, Eastern and Ashanti and least in Upper West, Northern, Volta and Western regions (Ghana Electoral Commission 2019), indicating some difference between the south and the more underdeveloped north. The nominations influence the actual elections as most female members of parliament (MPs) were elected in the region of Greater Accra (ten), Eastern (eight), Central (six) and Volta (five). Although the number of women nominated in the Volta region is relatively low, it is considered NDC 'safe seats'. Generally, 11.9 per cent of the nominated parliamentary candidates are women indicating that when women contest they do win. The total number of female MPs is 37 (including one elected in a by-election) out of 275.

The book chapter aims at explaining the reasons for the low representation of women in politics and the delaying in introducing an affirmative action bill in Ghana inspired by a feminist institutionalist perspective. The main focus will be on how the formal and informal institutions interact and influence women's political representation and the introduction of the affirmative action bill? And in which ways these formal and informal institutions are gendered? And to which extent do the feminist institutional spaces at the state level work to promote a gender agenda in the form of affirmative action? The book chapter unveils how informal institutions are working against more women in politics in Ghana and how the feminist institutional spaces within the state are not working effectively to promote a gender agenda and the introduction of the affirmative action bill in Ghana. The book chapter is based on data collection from fieldworks in Ghana in 2016, 2018 and 2019 in the form of qualitative interviews (thirty-one) with female and male MPs, women's organizers, the Committee on Gender, Children and Social Protection, representatives from the party leaderships, the national gender machinery, UNDP and women's organizations working with this area. In addition, I am drawing on gender-differentiated election data and readings of party manifestos from 2016 as well as participant observation in fora on gender/politics.

Firstly, the approach of feminist institutionalism is introduced. Secondly, the historical background for affirmative action and the recent attempts for the introduction of affirmative action will be debated. Thirdly, the informal institutional barriers are identified – a politics of insults, ridicule and rumours and the monetarization of Ghanaian politics. Fourthly, the feminist institutional spaces designed to promote women's rights and gender equality within the state are analysed – the Committee on Gender, Children and Social Protection and the Ministry for Gender, Children and Social Protection. Fifthly, the patriarchal arguments against affirmative action are debated and finally the insights from the Ghanaian case are used to point towards an African feminist institutionalism.

Feminist institutionalism – institutional change or inertia?

Feminist institutionalism sees institutions as gendered norms, rules and processes defining institutions as 'rules and procedures (both formal and informal) that structure social interaction by constraining or enabling actors' behaviour' (Waylen 2014: 214 with reference to Helmke and Levitsky 2004). Feminist institutionalism analyses how formal and informal institutions interact in complex ways and how they shape actors' strategies and preferences. Hence, there is a need to uncover the 'hidden life' of institutions. Informal institutions are defined as 'socially shared rules, usually unwritten, that are created, communicated and enforced outside of officially sanctioned channels' in opposition to formal institutions defined as 'rules and procedures that are created, communicated and enforced through channels which are largely official' (ibid). In aiming to explain why informal rules exist, 'some hypothesise that informal rules emerge when formal institutions are incomplete; when actors prefer but cannot achieve, a formal institutional solution; or when actors are pursuing goals that are not publicly acceptable, either because they are unlikely to stand the test of public scrutiny, or will attract international condemnation' (Krook and Mackey 2011: 11). Informal rules will often work against or parallel with formal rules as they often serve to preserve the status quo and maintain existing power structures. Different versions of feminist institutionalisms coexist, and the book chapter has a more eclectic approach mainly drawing on organizational and sociological as well as historical institutionalisms. The first mentioned has a focus on the meso-level in the form of political parties and the national gender machinery. Here institutions are seen as 'formal rules, procedures and norms, as well as symbol systems, cognitive scripts, and moral templates that provide the "frames of meaning" guiding human behaviour' (Krook and Mackay 2011: 9). However, the book chapter also draws on historical feminist institutionalism with its focus on the development over time in political representation and historical female political icons.

As institutions can be gendered, they can also be re-gendered. The book chapter debates if or how gender and institutional change takes place in a Ghanaian context with respect to women's political representation(?) According to Mahoney and Thelen (2010) four types of institutional change can be identified – 'layering', 'displacement', 'drift' and 'conversion'. Layering occurs when new rules are attached on top of existing ones in the form of revisions, attachments and amendments and is therefore a less radical model of change. Displacement refers to the replacement of existing rules with new ones. Losers of the old system often introduce new institutions. If the supporters of the old system are unable to defend it, a gradual version of displacement may take place. Drift involves when rules remain the same but their impact changes due to external factors. Conversion occurs when rules remain but institutions designed with one set of goals in mind are redirected to other ends.

Strategies of layering and conversion are more likely to be successful for promoting gendered institutional change compared to displacement and drift. The argument is that the strategy of displacement may not have sufficient power as it relies on weak veto possibilities and 'gender equity actors rarely have sufficient power to achieve wholesale displacement in the absence of strong opponents' (Waylen 2014: 218). She also argues that drift is unlikely to be an effective strategy for promoting gender equality as it is a rather 'slow' way of introducing change relying on external changes instead of changes in formal rules (Waylen 2014). In opposition to this layering and conversion are more common for bringing about change in the right gendered direction as 'they are gradual, endogenous and potentially more achievable when actors have sufficient power to create some new rules or use existing rules in creative ways, but not enough to displace these existing rules' (Waylen 2014: 219). Thus, gender actors have to manoeuvre strategically to promote institutional change.

However, even processes of introducing new institutions may result in either change or inertia depending on their orientation towards something 'old' or something 'new' (Mackay 2014). With her concept 'new nestedness' she (ibid) underlines how institutional changes can be 'actively resisted or passively neglected: "remembering" the old and 'forgetting the new' (Mackay 2014: 550–1) and as such is embedded in the existing institutional arrangements. She also emphasizes how 'remembering' can be linked to 'reincorporating the old' and 'borrowing' from alternative institutional arrangements (ibid; 555). Drawing on the thinking of gender and institutional change or inertia I turn to the Ghanaian case study and the background for affirmative action.

Affirmative action in Ghana

In pre-colonial times, political structures existed giving prominence to the complementarity of both female and male political powers. According to Prah (2005), the matrilineal Akan women had considerable independence and exercised political influence, whereas the ethnic groups with patrilineal descent like Konkomba, Kusase, Ewe and Dagomba had more limited powers. Even before colonial times in the eighteenth and nineteenth centuries these complementary structures were weakened (Manuh 1991). However, with colonization women became more marginalized with the introduction of Victorian ideas and indirect ruling with a focus on chiefs at the expense of queen mothers. In the northern part of Ghana, a position of Magazia was created who was supposed to organize women for forced communal labour (Manuh 1991). However, women also organized against the colonial powers, for example, the iconic queen mother Yaa Asantewaa from Ejisu who organized 40,000–50,000 to fight against a siege in Kumasi. She is said to have spit in the face of the British officer who arrested her (Vidrovitch-Coquery 1997).

With Kwame Nkrumah and CPP women had a platform for fighting for independence – especially the women traders who were against the monopolization of European firms in trading with goods and as result organized 'cocoa hold-ups' (Prah 2005). Manuh (1991) and Tsikata (1989) describe how a 'women's section' of CPP was formed and how women like Mabel Dove Danquah and Akua Asabea Ayisi worked alongside Nkrumah on writing articles on independence just like some went to prison for the sake. In 1951 CPP appointed four women as propaganda secretaries (Ama Nkrumah, Hanna Cudjoe, Leticia Quaye and Sophia Doku) who travelled all over the country to recruit supporters for CPP. As a sign of his recognition of the role the women had played in the fight for independence, Nkrumah ensured the passing of the representation of the People (Women Members) Act in 1959 where ten women should be part of parliament.[4] However, Manuh (1991) records how a (then) male member of the opposition party[5] referred to these ten new female MPs as 'lipstick and pancaked faces of doubtful utility to the deliberations of the House' (Manuh 1991: 115). Table 8.1 illustrates the development in women's political representation over time.

Table 8.1 Female MPs in Ghana 1960-2016 (independence and onwards)

Year	1960	1965	1969	1979	1992	1996	2000	2004	2008	2012	2016
Number of seats	114(10)[a]	198[2b]	140	140	200	200	200	230	230	275	275
Men	104	179	139	135	184	181	181	205	210	244	238
%	91.2	90.4	99.3	96.5	92	90.5	90.5	89	91.3	88.7	86.5
Women	10	19	1	5	16	19	19	25	20	31	37
%	8.8	9.6	0.7	3.5	8	9.5	9.5	11	8.7	11.3	13.5

Data from Frempong (2015): *Elections in Ghana 1951–2012* and www.ghanaweb.com.
The table includes women elected in by-elections.

[a] In the 1960 election Nkrumah appointed 10 women to parliament.
[b] In the 1965 election the number of parliamentary seats increased to 1998 in line with the CPP policy of making each constituency coterminous with a local council (Frempong 2015).

However, this affirmative action initiative died with the overthrow of Kwame Nkrumah. The period from 1966 to 1981 was characterized by a series of military coup d'états (only with civilian government in the years 1969–72 and 1979–82). This phase has been characterized as 'The apolitical phase' (Tsikata 1989) and 'The period of democratic disengagement' (Prah 2005) indicating that women's rights including political representation and affirmative action in this period have rather been characterized by a setback. The presence of the military in itself rather re-enforced male-dominated structures with few women in the ranks and there is no indication of women being appointed to high-ranking positions in this period (Prah 2005). The following period has been characterized by the dominance of the thirty-one. December Women's Movement (31. DWM) chaired by the then first wife Nana Konadu Agyeman-Rawlings and named after the date of the coup d'état of Flight Lieutenant Jerry Rawlings and PNDC (Provisional National Defence Council). The 31. DWM is mentioned by many written sources (e.g. Aubrey 2001; Fallon 2008; Madsen 2010; Manuh 1993) and mostly in critical terms for its close linkages to the state level and access to resources, marginalization of other women's organisations and for the (ab)use of the organization as a platform to mobilize women in the elections 1992 and 1996. Although the concept of 'First-Lady syndrome' originates from Nigeria, it also applies to the Ghanaian context implying that the leadership has been decided on the basis of personal ties to the leaders or as co-optation by elite women of the women's organizations and the gender agenda. However, most of the female MPs in the democratic and free election in 1992 had a background in the 31. DWM (Allah-Mensah 2007; Madsen 2019; Prah 2005).

In 1998 under the ruling of Rawlings, an administrative directive[6] was adopted by Cabinet based on the recommendations from the then national gender machinery the National Council on Women and Development (Tsikata 2009). A part of the directive was to equip the National Electoral Commission to encourage all the political parties to present more women candidates to achieve a target of at least 40 per cent. However, this directive has not been implemented even though both the major parties in their 2016 manifestos have made promises to remedy the low representation of women in parliament – NDC with a reference to the ongoing work on an affirmative action bill and NPP with an ambition to have a critical mass of 30 per cent women in all appointments. Currently, the work on an affirmative action bill is ongoing. However, this work was initiated in 2011 with a roundtable on how the 1998 affirmative action policy could be revised and with a focus on inputs for a future affirmative action bill. Since then a draft bill has been approved by Cabinet and the Attorney General and debated by a technical committee with numerous comments delaying its presentation in parliament and actual adoption. Currently, the draft affirmative action bill has been presented (again) for the Cabinet with the hope that it will be presented before parliament soon.[7]

However, in the 2015 primaries NPP embarked on an affirmative action initiative with the attempt to introduce women's seats implying that only women could contest in the constituencies where a woman was elected (sixteen). However, the initiative was soon withdrawn as it created a lot of turmoil within the party (see also Madsen 2019). Firstly, the initiative was based on a fragile alliance between the flagbearer and a fraction of female parliamentarians and as a result was 'sneaked in through the backdoor' without the proper groundwork in the party. Secondly, the initiative created a lot of male resistance – especially in the affected constituencies – just before the elections and with some threatening to run as independent candidates. Thirdly, in some constituencies the question of 'ethnicity' was more important than 'gender', for example, in the Ablekuma West where the female candidate was not from the old ethnic group in Accra the 'Ga'. Fourthly, the female MPs in NPP were told not to celebrate too much and as a result the women's organizations had not been mobilized for support. However, some organizations like WILDAF (Women in Law and Development in Africa) and FIDA (International Federation of Women Lawyers) issued a press statement in support of the NPP affirmative action initiative. Nevertheless, the consideration for the party to be united before the upcoming election seemed to be more important than the considerations for more gender equal representations. The NPP affirmative action initiative backfired as a number of the more experienced female MPs lost their primaries, but due to the general positive election results new ones were elected in the 2016 election. The following section focuses on informal institutions undermining women's political representation and the introduction of the affirmative action bill in Ghana.

Politics of insults, ridicule and rumours

> Somebody called me a political terrorist who does not want to be criticised. It is not because I do not want to be criticised, but I am doing my best. If you have ideas bring them to the table. But when you start to insult me and talk about my make-up instead of focusing on the issues, I get emotionally affected.
>
> (interview female MP, NDC, April 2019)

Several of the female MPs account of how they are under more scrutiny than their fellow male MPs and are attacked based on their gender and sexuality. Some female MPs are attacked on their appearances, for example, with the focus on make-up and how they are 'old' women and do not look like the picture on their posters (interview female MP, NPP, April 2019). Other female MPs are attacked based on accusations of their inability to take care of their children in a society where motherhood is highly valued or is labelled as prostitutes bearing in mind the focus on women as moral guardians in Ghana. One female MP accounts how the male opponent brought forward three guys who all claimed to have slept with her on a platform at her constituency shouting to the crowd 'Do you want a prostitute?' and they said 'No' (interview female MP, NDC, February 2016/April 2019). A number of other female MPs tell similar stories about the labelling as a prostitute due to their involvement in politics. However, one female MP also brings forward how she has been associated with supernatural powers and the devil by a political opponent who claimed that anybody who shakes her hand should wash it with seawater (interview, female MP, NDC, February 2016) – an accusation that could potentially put her into danger in a country where beliefs in witchcraft still prevail. A study on women's political representation at local level in Malawi accounts of similar gender-based defamation by political competitors resulting in a toxic political climate where women are accused of 'sleeping around' and being 'witches' (Clayton et al. 2020: 619). In addition, Tamale states on Uganda that 'women spent a great deal of campaign time convincing the electorate of their moral aptness to stand for political office instead of articulating political issues … Women encountered slurs regarding their marital status, sexuality and infidelity' (Tamale 1999: 93). Other studies confirm that 'socio-cultural perceptions' of women play a role for the low representation of women in politics in Ghana (Bawa and Sanyare 2013: 286) and that politics is a 'dirty game' with the 'mudslinging' preventing many women from engaging in it (Darkwa 2015: 255). This has been labelled as a 'politics of insults' by a high-ranking member of the party leadership (interview, male member of party leadership, NDC, April 2019) elaborating that women do not want this 'name tagging' (ibid). Many of the female MPs account how their families have tried to influence them to step down due to the 'politics of insult' that affect not only the women themselves but also their families. A few are mentioning that they are themselves considering giving up politics due to the insults and labelling as, for example, 'small girls', 'girlfriends' or 'wives' downplaying their professional competences (interviews, female MPs NDC & NPP February 2016). However, some of the women from 'political' families have been prepared by their relatives for these discriminatory informal 'rules of the game', which are actively preventing women from seeking office.

As a part of the 'politics of insults', some female MPs and women at the party level are being ridiculed. Some of the female MPs who are outspoken, assertive, relative powerful and strong gender advocates account of how they are being portrayed in cartoons and associated with masculine traits aiming at undermining and excluding women from the political sphere (interviews, female MPs, NPP, February 2016). This is in line with the use of the wording 'Yaa Asantewaa' which is 'used, often mockingly, to refer to a woman who shows strength and power in ways normally associated with men' (Manuh and Nayidoho 2015: 21). A former female MP and now part of the party leadership refers to how references are done mockingly to the 'Beijing conference' whenever a gender issue is being brought up. According to Manuh and Anyidoho, the word 'Yaa Asantewaa' is mostly used to refer to individual empowerment whereas 'Beijing' is related to collective empowerment. They state: 'Thus, when a man jokingly exclaimed, "The Beijing women are coming!"

at the sight of a gender activist entering the room, the statement would be tinged with alarm at the possibilities of the collective will of women gathered behind the cause of women's empowerment' (Manuh and Nayidoho 2015: 23). The 'Beijing conference' has made an impact in the Ghanaian context and influenced the gender norms in the society to the extent that some feel threatened by it.

Another aspect of the 'politics of insults' is that female MPs are exposed to rumours, when they are in positions where there interact with men. However, most of the female MPs have mostly men in their networks, as they have to rely on male MPs for access to instrumental resources such as resources (network and economic) for their political work and potential achievements, whereas men can rely solely on homosocial networks (Bjarnegård 2015). However, female MPs also use these instrumental resources strategically to establish alliances when a pro-gender equal law, policy or statement will be put up. A female MP states the following about a male MP talking 'that women ought to be in the kitchen or women ought to dress in a certain way, then you know those guys are not going to cooperate … But when you see those that are nice to you, saying look my mother raised me, then you see, he is a good ally and you can lobby him' (interview, female MP, NDC, February 2016). This underlines the emphasis on 'motherhood' in the Ghanaian context, but also questions if fellow colleagues do not deserve the same respect. In addition, the women have to rely on external economic support for campaigning – sometimes in the form of gifts – often with the assumption that exchange of sexual favours has taken place. Such rumours have been associated with Charlotte Osei, former chairperson of the Electoral Commission, who was said to be literally 'in bed with government' implying the former president and one of the (then) female MPs who was accused of having an affair with the party leader (interview, female MP, NPP, February 2016). In this way, women are trapped in a catch twenty-two where on the one hand they need to establish networks with men for access to instrumental resources and as potential allies, but on the other hand based on rumours run the risk of condemnation in the public sphere and jeopardizing their family life. Consequently, rumours play a significant role as a weapon to exclude women and expose their vulnerabilities as a part of the 'politics of insults'. In a report on 'Violence against Women in Politics' (Westminster Foundation for Democracy 2018) encompassing psychological, physical, sexual and economic violence Ghana is referred to[8]. A survey conducted revealed that political violence of different forms negatively impacts on women in politics and their ability to win elections and that those women who actually won 'had their confidence eroded' or that it 'nearly caused their withdrawal' (Westminster Foundation for Democracy 2018: 10).

Monetarization of Ghanaian politics

The greatest problem we have in politics is that we do not have anything like appointments or quotas for parliament. What we have is that you must contest and this is money – you need funds. When I say resources, it is not just workshops but funding is a very deep issue. This is one of the things I wish that if anybody want to help women to be represented in politics, this would be it.

(interview female MP, NDC, February 2016)

The female MP continues to list all the expenses related to becoming an MP and campaigning such as T-shirts with the picture of herself as the candidate, economic support for vehicles/motorbikes and fuelling of these and catering for party workers and volunteers, etc. All the female MPs' interviews underline the importance of economic resources as an important factor for the low representation of women in politics. Furthermore, costs are increased by the nature of politics in Ghana characterized by clientelistic relations between the national and local level in the absence of well-functioning state structures. In a report (Westminster Foundation for Democracy 2018), it is documented that the expenditures on parliamentary election on average have increased 90 per cent from the 2012 to the latest 2016 election.[9] Bauer and Darkwah describe how the party primaries have been labelled as 'the cocoa season' (Bauer and Darkwah 2019: 139) by the people represented in the electoral colleges in compensation for their votes (potentially around 500 people). One female MP pinpoints:

Our selection process have become frightfully expensive and so many women, who cannot match the spending of it, may lose, because the team selecting does not understand what is at stake and would choose the highest bidder or the best spender and biggest payer and vote for them. So if we do not build up women's financial muscle as well it will be difficult for them to compete.

(interview female MP, NPP, February 2016)

Generally, women spent less than men (50,000 cedis) on three of the four parameters mentioned in the report (Westminster Foundation for Democracy 2018) – campaigning, donations and party workers – and more on media/advertising. Women (often) have a more disadvantaged economic position and have to negotiate with their husbands over the use of income. Women use their family and professional networks for fundraising and they also receive gifts – often with the expectation that they 'deliver' once they become an MP. Others have obtained loans to be able to finance the campaigning as one MP states, 'I lost this primary because of lack of funds. I did not have enough money and my bill is big so I could not go in for more loans' (interview female MP, NPP, February 2016). Another study also underlines (a lack of) economic resources as an important factor women for women being 'hesitant to run for political office' (Bawa and Sanyare 2013: 287) emphasizing that (women's) appointment to high public offices also depends on the economic contributions to the political party – the plural majority system where 'the winner takes it all' is making it harder for 'newcomers' and does not work in favour of women. A study emphasizes that 'competitive elections tend to be capital intensive' and that '[Women] do not have the latitude to take risks with their resources' (Darkwa 2015: 255) as they do (often) not have the same decision-making powers as men over economic resources in the family.

In the 2012 election, the major political parties (NDC and NPP) have introduced an affirmative action initiative to half the filing fees for women. However, this initiative is far too little, as the big spending takes place during campaigning as mentioned earlier. However, the initiative somewhat acknowledges women's (often) disadvantaged economic position, but fails to address the underlying economic unequal structures. As such, it can be characterized as a general informal rule, which can easily be changed and either abolished or become a formal rule – most likely the latter – as no party would like to be framed as less 'women-friendly'. It is a strategy of 'layering', which does not undermine men's political overrepresentation. In opposition to this, the introduction of the NPP affirmative action initiative with the women's seats could be labelled as a strategy of (sudden) 'displacement' challenging political gender/power structures and as a result was met with fierce resistance.

Feminist institutional spaces – potential for change?

'The affirmative action is a book that we open once in a while, it has created dust and been shelved' (interview, member of the party leadership, NDC, April 2019).

'It is time for us to be serious … and if the women are there and can decide with the men, then we can move and have sustainable development in Ghana. Let us stop toying with it, the Ministry of Gender, Children and Social Protection is leading the process, please stop sleeping: wake up' (Joana Opare, Executive Director of Gender Planning Consults at engagement on the bill, Tuesday 18 June 2019).[10]

Parallel with the informal institutions working against more women in politics, formal institutional spaces at the state level are put in place to address feminist claims within a patriarchal state structure. In a Ghanaian setting the national gender machinery in the form of the Ministry of Gender, Children and Social Protection and the Committee on Gender, Children and Social Protection is the main institutional spaces with the mandate to promote the adoption of the affirmative action bill. The following section of the book chapter explores if and how these institutional spaces work as enabling or constraining for the promotion of women's political representation and empowerment.

President Kufuor from NPP established the Ministry of Gender, Children and Social Protection (MOGCSP) in 2001 (then MOWAC – Ministry of Women and Children) against the wishes of the national women's organizations fearing 'ghettoisation' of women's issues. It was a further institutionalization of the National Council on Women and Development (NCWD) established in

1975, the year of the UN conference on women in Mexico City and marking the beginning of the UN decade for Women. NCWD lived a turbulent life as it has undergone 'state capture' orchestrated by the (then) first lady Nana Konadu Agyeman-Rawling who replaced its board with a management committee including prominent members of the 31. DWM and took over the NCWD making the national women's organizations shy away from it. Although MOGCSP was (probably) set up to please the national women's organizations and demonstrate the commitment of the new government towards international gender norms, it has been hampered in doing so by several factors (Tsikata 2000).

Firstly, the national gender machinery has been characterized by the lumping together of 'gender, children and social protection' somewhat linking 'gender' to questions of care work (only). Secondly, MOGCSP suffers from a long to-do list linked with many expectations; meanwhile, it is suffering from serious underfunding and staffing. Thirdly, recently (2018) the minister has been replaced with Cynthia Morrison (NPP) apparently based on internal power struggles in the ministry and perhaps the inability of the former minister to deliver on the promises to ensure the adoption of the affirmative action bill as promised by the President Nana Akufo-Addo. MOGCSP does not seem to be in favourable position for spearheading the affirmative action bill as its ability to work effectively and efficiently is constrained and the process (so far) with the affirmative action bill characterized as a bureaucratic 'back and forth' process. However, the new minister has expressed her commitment towards getting the process back on track and ensuring the adoption of the affirmative action bill. However, in her statement Joana Opare does not only encourage the Ministry of Gender, Children and Social Protection to 'wake up' but also states that 'it is time for advocacy, so we will not be like ostriches, we are going to say it as it is. So please when you (the delegation of the MOGCSP) go, tell them, that we are disappointed that they are not here. I was expecting to see my leaders here, that is my first disappointment' (Joana Opare, Executive Director of Gender Planning Consults at engagement on the bill, Tuesday 18 June 2019 – see earlier footnote).

The parliamentary Committee on Gender, Children and Social Protection has an important role in preparing the ground for the affirmative action bill and the oversight responsibilities of MOGCSP. The committee is chaired by a male MP from the ruling party NPP as the party leadership wants to signal that 'gender' is not related to women (only) and with the rationale that if men are considered 'the stumble block' they should be sensitized and not left out of all debates on gender (interview, representative of the party leadership NPP, April 2019). However, the committee is balanced in complementary power structures with a female MP from NPP as vice-chair as well as female MP ranking member and a male deputy-ranking member from NDC. Although the Committee on Gender, Children and Social Protection is a forum with possibilities for establishing alliances across party divisions, it is a partisan institution with marked differences between the assessment of the work of the committee between most of the members of the ruling party (NPP) and the opposition party (NDC). Some of the NDC party leadership members and committee members put forward that the 'committee should be more assertive' and that there are 'leadership issues' (interview, male MP, NDC, April 2019). However, on the affirmative action bill the committee has commented on a draft version, but does not seem to monitor the process closely as there is no clear picture about its status in the committee leadership. A number of committee members emphasize the need for 'capacity-building' within the committee (interview female MP, NDC, April 2019) as not all its members have expertise within the area of gender and the 'institutional memory' of the committee can easily be lost due to shifting of members (interview, male MP, NDC, April 2019). Many of the committee members emphasize the 'empowering effect' at a personal level of being part of the committee and the related exposure to gender issues and international gender norms and fora strengthening their capacity to act as 'gender ambassadors'. In sum, the Committee on Gender, Children and Social Protection is also constrained but individual members are strong advocates for the affirmative action bill and the leadership expressed a will to monitor MOGCSP and its adoption more closely.

The lack of strong feminist institutional spaces seems to be part of the reasons for the delaying of the affirmative action bill and its 'shelving'. However, in the latest draft of the affirmative action bill, it is suggested to establish a committee to monitor the implementation of the bill in practice linked to the MOGCSP.[11]

Patriarchal arguments against affirmative action

You can hear people debate certain aspects of the bill and then we read the bill you take out some aspects which makes it affirmative. Most of the male MPs support it – I do not know if they are scared or what (?) They are not stable in their support. They always find a way to take out some parts. It will be passed but when (?).

(interview female MP, NPP, April 2019)

The quotation indicates that some of the male MPs are merely paying lip service to the affirmative action bill. At a forum on 'Strengthening advocacy for the passage of an affirmative action bill in Ghana' on Tuesday 18 June 2019 the CPP chairperson stated: 'I think the agenda should be such that, we get more men who are gender sensitive like the men in this room', Hajia Hamdatu Ibrahim (see earlier footnote). The process of introducing the affirmative action bill is characterized by a strategy of delaying. In its current form the affirmative action bill is designed with periodic targets increasing the representation of women in parliament over a longer time span – a form of gradual displacement. However, these periodic targets are put in an appendix to the currently draft bill and in the latest version the focus is more rhetorically on equity leaving it to the political parties to include specific measures in their manifestos (for at 2016 status see Ministry of Gender, Children and Social Protection 2016).[12] In addition, it is suggested that women should be put in place in the 'safe seats' for NDC (Volta region) and NPP (Ashanti) and/or that the number of parliamentarians should be increased and the additional seats reserved for women.[13] The 2016 NPP affirmative action initiative to introduce women's seats was taken off the table based on a list of patriarchal arguments. Firstly, it was stated that some of the female MPs were unpopular in their constituencies (despite the fact that other female candidates could potentially contest the seat). Secondly, there was a fear that it would become a permanent measure from the aspiring candidates in the affected constituencies. Thirdly, as the initiative was only designed for NPP, it was indicated that the opposition party (NDC) could potentially put up a strong male candidate (assuming that he would overrule a female NPP candidate). Fourthly, some felt that the upcoming female candidates would be handed their positions as potential MPs on a silver platter compared to other female MPs. Lastly, as the 2016 parliamentary election was approaching the main concern for the party was that it should be united before the elections – not gender equality. Some of these arguments are also part of the debate against the affirmative action bill, but with the adoption of a cross-party solution some of the arguments are not valid and the parties would be on an equal footing in ensuring the actual implementation of the bill. However, the actual implementation of the affirmative action bill will rely on the political parties. Currently, the major political parties (NDC and NPP) are male dominated apart from the positions as women's organizers and they have failed to address the underlying patriarchal structures working against more women in parliament as indicated in the sections on the 'Politics of insults, ridicule and rumours' and the 'Monetarisation of Ghanaian politics'. Even though the current focus is on the adoption of the affirmative action bill, there is a need to move beyond and address the underlying informal institutions working against more women in parliament. The 'institutional nestedness' of the affirmative action bill will determine the orientation of the bill towards either something 'old' or a 'new' direction for a more gender equal political representation in Ghana.

Concluding comments

In Ghana, there is a lack of political will for a 'fast-track' model for women's political representation. Processes of gender and institutional change are slow, gradual and pragmatic. Feminist institutionalism has proven useful as an overall framework for analysing formal potential feminist institutional spaces, the informal institutions hampering women's political representation and the institutional nestedness as a future perspective. From the Ghanaian case study different conceptual and methodological aspects emerge pointing towards an African feminist institutionalism. Firstly, the case illustrates the development of African concepts on politics based on the empirical realities on the ground. One example is the First-lady' syndrome (although this is originally coined in Nigeria) referring to the dominant role of one of the former First Ladies in Ghana based on the personal ties and networks with powerful men rather than own merits and the state capture of feminist institutional spaces. Another example is the identification of a 'Politics of insults, ridicule and rumours' encapsulating the informal institutions working against more women in politics in Ghana pinpointing the importance of verbal abuse. Secondly, the case study emphasizes the role of historical perspectives in taking into account the trajectories from the precolonial, colonial and post-colonial past in trying to understand the present and the acknowledgement of the role of female political icons including Yaa Asantewaa.

On a short term, the national women's moment is strongly advocating for the adoption of the affirmative action bill with a re-introduction of the women's manifesto in 2016 of the original 2004 version with a focus on women's political representation and updated targets – inspired by gender equality reforms in other African contexts. The national women's organization Abantu for Development is spearheading a project on advocacy for the passage of the affirmative action bill including the earlier mentioned session and marching in Accra and Tamale in support of the affirmative action bill. Furthermore, a national coalition for Affirmative action has been formed. A civil society group labelled 'Cluster on Decentralisation and Citizen Participation' has urged MOGCSP to put the affirmative action bill before the parliament before the election campaigning for 2020 starts. This provides some hope for the future as the renewed mobilization spurred by the process of advocating for the adoption of an affirmative action bill may also affect the actual implementation and effectiveness of the affirmative action bill beyond its adoption. However, the functioning of the institutional spaces within the state questions to which extent they can be labelled as 'feminist' as they do not seem to be working effectively as spaces where women can insert their claims.

Nevertheless, on a longer term the political parties have to address the informal institutions working against more women in politics and provide specific measures to achieve the targets set up in the affirmative action bill, once it is adopted, to ensure that women do not remain at the margins of politics in Ghana. In parallel, a need to reform the political parties in a more gender-sensitive direction has been identified to ensure an orientation towards something 'new' and a 'gender inclusive nestedness'.

Notes

1   Firstly, a post-conflict situation is characterized by a political vacuum, which creates windows of opportunities to advocate for the adoption of affirmative action to promote more women in politics. Secondly, women's organizations often had an (informal) role during and in the aftermath of conflicts and as such promote affirmative action. Thirdly, after a conflict international gender actors will be present and international gender norms will be promoted. Fourthly, changes in gender relations take place at micro-level and women are forced to take upon themselves tasks formerly reserved for men.

2   Ghana gained independence in 1957. Kwame Nkrumah was the first president of Ghana (1960 until 1996) but was overthrown by a military coup d'état. This initiative died with his overthrow.

3   However, the president states at www.ghanaweb.com on 19 July 2017 that he has not asked for the reasons for this award and that 'I think, it is as area that I could still do much better than I have done so far'.

4   These women were Susanna Al-Hassan, Lucy Anin, Regina Asamany, Comfort Asamoah, Grace Ayensu, Ayanori Bukari, Sophia Doku, Mary Koranteng, Victoria Nyarku and Christiana Wilmot.

5   With a swift reply from one of the new female MPs he was soon forced to apologize for this comment (Manuh 1991).

6   This directive is the second generation of affirmative action. The first generation included the reservation of ten seats under Nkrumah as well as measures for boards, professions at the labour market and education. Apart from the focus on women in parliament, the second generation also pointed out that 50 per cent of the appointed district assembly members should be women and affirmative action within education (Tsikata 2009).

7   However, observers describe this as rather unlikely due to the forthcoming budget negotiation and the election in 2020 and related campaigning activities.

8   Psychological violence refers to 'verbal and emotional abuse and acts intended to undermine a person's sense of worth and/or personal behaviour and safety and security', for example, name-calling as witches. Physical violence refers to 'injuries inflicted directly on women, as well as bodily harm against their relatives', for example, the documented assault on NPP candidate Ursula Owusu Ablekuma West in the 2012 election. Sexual violence refers to 'sexual acts and attempts of sexual acts by coercion or force, as well as unwanted sexual comments or innuendo, and sexual harassment', for example, bringing men up at a platform stating they have slept with the female MP. Economic violence refers to 'coercive and forceful behaviour to control access to economic resources', for example, if economic support for female MPs depends on sexual favours (Westminster Foundation for Democracy 2018: 6–7).

9   However, in the report it is mentioned that there are unaccounted 'other costs' related by some to 'giving gifts' or 'expressions of gratitude'.

10 See following link: https://www.ghanaweb.com/GhanaHomePage/NewsArchive/Stop-toying-with-the-Affirmative-Action-Bill-Gender-advocate-to-Government-756128

11 Consequently, the budget for its work will be allocated through MOGCSP in opposition to establishing an independent commission. The commission will include a broad representation including from civil society.

12 However, this has always been the case and has not led to any major changes as stated in the book chapter. Potentially, the Electoral Commission can provide sanctions for the political parties.

13 The current Speaker of Parliament has suggested this.

References

Allah-Mensah, B. (2007): 'Women and Politics in Ghana 1993–2003', in K. Boafo-Arthur (ed.) *Ghana: One Decade of the Liberal State*. Senegal: CODESRIA.

Asante, K. and Kunnath, G. (2018): *The Costs of Politics in Ghana*. UK: Westminster Foundation for Democracy.

Aubrey, L. (2001): 'Gender, Development and Democratization in Africa', in S. N. Ndegwa (ed.) *A Decade of Democracy in Africa*. Leiden, Boston & Köln: Brill.

Bauer, G. and Akosua, D. (2019): 'Ghana: "Some Money Has to Be Going …": Discounted Filing Fees to Bring More Women into Parliament in Ghana', in R. L. Muriaas, W. Vibeke and M. Rainbow (eds) *Gendered Electoral Financing – Money, Power and Representation in Comparative Perspective*. New York: Routledge.

Bawa, S. and Sanyare, F. (2013): 'Women's Participation and Representation in Politics: Perspectives from Ghana', *International Journal of Public Administration*, Vol. 36, No. 4, 282–91.

Bjarnegård, E. (2015): *Gender, Informal Institutions and Political Recruitment – Explaining Male Dominance in Parliamentary Representation*. New York: Palgrave Macmillan.

Clayton, A., Robinson, A. L., Johnson, M. C. and Muriaas, R. (2020): '(How) Do Voters Discriminate against Women Candidates? Experimental and Qualitative Evidence from Malawi', *Comparative Political Studies*, Vol. 53, No. 3–4, 601–30.

Dahlerup, D. and Freidenvall, L. (2003): 'Quotas as a "Fast Track" to Equal Political Representation for Women', Paper presented at IPSA World Conference, Durban, South Africa.

Darkwa, L. (2015): 'In Our Father's Name in Our Motherland: The Politics of Women's Political Participation in Ghana', in B. Y. Gebe (ed.) *Constitutionalism, Democratic Governance and the African State*. Accra: Black Mask LTD.

Fallon, K. M. (2008): *Democracy and the Rise of Women's Movements in Sub-Saharan Africa*. Baltimore: The Johns Hopkins University Press.

Frempong, A. and Duku, K. (2015): *Elections in Ghana 1951–2012*. Accra: Life 60 Publisher.

Krook, M. L. and Mackay, F. (2011): *Gender, Politics and Institutions – Towards a Feminist Institutionalism*. New York: Palgrave Macmillan.

Mackay, F. (2014): 'Nested Newness, Institutional Innovation, and the Gendered Limits of Change', *Politics & Gender*, Vol. 10, 549–71.

Madsen Højlund, D. (2010): *Getting the Institutions Right for Gender Mainstreaming – the Strategy of Gender Mainstreaming Revisited in the Ghanaian Context*, PhD dissertation, Roskilde University, Roskilde.

Madsen Højlund, D. (2019): 'Gender, Power and Institutional Change – The Role of Formal and Informal Institutions in Promoting Women's Political Representation', *Journal of Asian and Africa Studies*, Vol. 54, No. 1, 70–87.

Mahoney, J. and Thelen, K. (2010): *Explaining Institutional Change – Ambiguity, Agency and Power*. Cambridge: Cambridge University Press.

Manuh, T. (1991): 'Women and Their Organisations during the Convention Peoples' Party Period', in K. Arhin (ed.) *The Life and Work of Kwame Nkrumah*. Accra: Sedeo Publishing.

Manuh, T. (1993): 'Women, the State and Society under PNDC', in E. Gyimah-Boadi (ed.) *Ghana under PNDC Rule*. Senegal: CODESRIA.

Manuh, T. and Nayidoho, N. A. (2015): '"To Beijing and Back": Reflections on the Influence of the Beijing Conference on Popular Notions of Women's Empowerment in Ghana', *IDS Bulletin*, Vol. 46, No. 4, 19–27.

Ministry of Gender, Children and Social Protection (2016): 'Summary of Affirmative Action (Gender Equality) Bill – the Journey and Processes So Far'.

Prah, M. (2005): 'Chasing Illusions and Realising Visions: Reflections on Ghana's Feminist Experience', paper CODESRIA.

Tamale, S. (1999): *When Hens Begin to Crow – Gender and Parliamentary Politics in Uganda*. Boulder & Oxford: Westview Press.

Tsikata, E. (1989): 'Women's Political Organisation 1951–1987', in N. A. Kwame and E. Hansen (eds) *The State, Development and Politics in Ghana*. Senegal: CODESRIA.

Tsikata, D. (2000): 'Lip-service and Peanuts: The State and National Machinery for Women in Africa', National Machineries Series, No. 11, Third World Network Africa.

Tsikata, D. (2009): *Affirmative Action and the Prospects for Gender Equality in Ghanaian Politics*. Accra: Abantu, Women in Broadcasting and the Friedrich-Ebert-Stiftung.

Vidrovitch-Coquery, C. (1997): *African Women – A Modern History*. Colorado: Westview Press.

Waylen, G. (2014): 'Informal Institutions, Institutional Change, and Gender Equality', *Political Research Quarterly*, Vol. 67, No. 1, 212–23.

World Economic Forum (2020): *Global Gender Gap Report*. Geneva: World Economic Forum.

Concluding remarks

Towards an African feminist institutionalism

With all its African case studies, the book demonstrates the usefulness of adopting a feminist institutionalist lens albeit pointing out the need to adjust and adapt 'feminist institutionalism' to African realities on the ground and African conceptualizations of power, feminism and institutions. The book is a first step towards developing an 'African feminist institutionalism' based on the insights on women's political representation from Botswana, Ghana, Kenya, Malawi, Nigeria, South Africa, Tanzania and Zimbabwe. The three elements towards an 'African feminist institutionalism' will provide some guidelines for the way forward. The first element building on feminist historical institutionalism is *the re-excavating of the past moving beyond the colonial* to analyse the influence of colonial institutions and pre-colonial female icons and institutional arrangements working in a pro-women/gender-friendly direction. Thus, a number of the authors write about prominent women in the liberation struggle, for example, Tanzanian Bibi Titi Mohamed and Nigerian Queen Amina, and the need to recognize their contributions to the political shestories. The second element focuses on *the role of African feminisms in reshaping patriarchal institutions and new versions of institutionalisms* where several of the book chapters identify the African nego-feminism (negotiation/no ego) as particularly useful and a new version of 'African feminist institutionalism' is identified in the form of a 'feminist symbolic institutionalism'. The third element is *the development of specific African concepts on gendered institutions* based on the workings of gender, power and politics in different African settings. The book offers more nuanced views on African concepts such as 'Femocracy' and the 'First-Lady Syndrome' and a new focus on a 'Politics of Insults, Ridicule and Rumours' working against more women in politics. More theorizing should start from the African continent and its complex gendered institutional realities – the development of an African feminist institutionalism is a step in this direction.

African informal institutions and networks

More specifically, the focus on the role of institutions within feminist institutionalism – especially informal institutions – has proven to be useful for grasping the African realities where politics is largely characterized by informality and patronage networks. Both the chapters of 'success cases' on women's political representation (Kenya, Tanzania, South Africa and Zimbabwe) and the 'less successful cases' (Botswana, Ghana, Malawi and Nigeria) demonstrate the importance of informal institutions and how they (in most cases) work to distort, undermine or subvert existing formal rules. As such, the informal institutions effectively contribute to the exclusion of women from political spaces where they rightfully belong.

The book with all its African case studies unveils the hidden life of the informal institutions for scrutiny by policymakers and political parties who are in positions to address and counteract these informal institutions. The identification, exposure and visibility of the informal institutions and interlinked questioning are a potential first step for changing these informal institutions and either do away with them or make them work for higher representation of women in politics (see also Waylen 2017). The case study from Malawi by Chiweza highlights how male political networks from the Democratic People's Party and Malawi Congress Party hijack different stages of the candidate selection process in favour of their preferred male candidates. The case study from South Africa by Gouws illuminates how the political party African National Congress and (especially) the former president have spearheaded a form of a 'state capture' of the national gender machinery and how compliant women from the party are part of upholding the party and are helping in these processes of 'state capture'. The case study from Ghana by Madsen puts forward how women are exposed to different forms of abuse – mainly verbal abuse – in the form of insults, ridicule and rumours in a targeted way. The case study from Zimbabwe by Parichi highlights how female politicians are framed in gender stereotypical ways in the media in ways in which they are trapped in a catch twenty-two scenario with no room for alternative framings. The book therefore raises broader questions about gender and democratization such as the level of (gender) inclusion in the political system and how formal and informal institutions can be regendered to ensure gender equal representation – descriptively and substantially.

However, the case studies – especially those from the so-called 'success countries' – also demonstrate the need for not only imagining the introduction of formal institution such as a quota as solution to address all problems related to gender unequal political representation. Although quotas effectively address descriptive representation, they do not eliminate informal institutions working to distort, undermine or subvert women who are in office based on a quota and their special seats. Consequently, it is imperative that policymakers and political parties work to address these informal institutions – even in countries where quotas have been introduced. Informal institutions seem to be very 'sticky' even beyond the introduction of formal gender equality reforms.

In many of the African case studies, focus is on the role of male political networks and patronage politics with a perception of these networks and patron/client relations as negative working against more women in politics (only) (see also Waylen 2017). However, although the case studies elaborate on the mechanisms of exclusion and the 'sticky' informal institutions, more research could be done on these networks to be more specific about the operating of them in African contexts.[1] With the terminology of Bjarnegård (2015) one should rather try to understand why men are overrepresented in politics and which purposes these male political networks and patronage relations serve and through which gendered practices they are upheld. Bjarnegård refers to 'homosocial capital' (Bjarnegård 2015: 4–5) indicating the one-gendered nature of these networks and a number of the case studies illustrate how women (due to their low representation in politics) are dependent on these networks for access to instrumental resources. However, other case studies provide some nuances on the role of these networks. The South African case study by Gouws elaborates on how women are included in those network if they are compliant and vest their loyalty with the party first and foremost implying that it is not (only) a 'male' setup. The Ghanaian case by Madsen illustrates how women are also strategically forming alliances with male political networks to ensure support for pro-women/gender initiatives if they identify that their fellow colleagues are supportive towards them and their agendas. This indicates that women on their way into politics or in politics are not just victims of broad undefined 'male political networks and patronage politics' but also tactically use them to promote their own agendas.

Newer research (Valdini 2019) introduce the term 'inclusion calculation' indicating that the inclusion of women in politics by male political elites is based on calculations of costs and benefits as 'the rational opportunists party elites are being driven primarily by a desire to maximise both individual and partisan future success' (Valdini 2019: 19). In her work, she identifies five factors affecting women's possibilities for inclusion in the political sphere: the *displacement costs* referring to the 'the potential negative impact of replacing incumbents with women candidates'; the *threat costs* 'which refers to the personal fear that of the party elites that the new elected women candidates will someday undermine the power and resources of the current male elite'; the *incongruity costs or benefits* 'which concerns the potential negative electoral impact of having women on the party list due to their association with stereotypically feminine personality traits'; the *domestic responsiveness costs or benefits* 'which refers to the potential electoral punishment or reward for responding to a social movement or other societal group that is calling for increased inclusion of women'; and the *international responsiveness costs or benefits* 'which concerns the tangible benefits offered by international organisations in response to the increased presence of women in politics, as well the potential societal backlash to responding to international pressure' (Valdini 2019: 19). These five factors could be an inspiration for future research on the role of male political networks in an African context.

Training of female political candidates as a strategy for promoting political empowerment

In many African contexts, the training of female political candidates is seen as a solution to ensure higher representation of women in politics. However, the focus on trainings of individual women can also be regarded as placing the problem of women's political (under)representation in the hands of the women themselves and framing them as being in a 'deficit' situation. This is despite the role of political parties and male political networks in excluding them from politics spaces and their political accomplishments and track record. Even though training programmes are not the only solution towards higher political representation for women, the book chapter on experiences from Letsema in Botswana illustrates how training programmes for female candidates if properly designed to address the structural barriers against women's political representation can provide alternative feminist political spaces and lead to some changes.

In their book chapter, Mosime and Dikobe rhetorically ask if training workshops are useful at all, if they do not lead to a higher representation of women in parliament or the adoption of a quota system like in the case of Botswana(?) However, they argue for moving beyond not just viewing empowerment and political education as a process towards becoming candidates and being elected into political spaces but also generally strategically expanding their life choices. The non-governmental organization Letsema came into being in 2013 and has been supported by different external donors. Letsema means 'the ploughing season' but also refers to the local practice of farmers to work together as a team and take turns in working on each other's farms indicating the need for sharing resources at the farm as well as in the political life. One of the lessons learnt from Letsema is that *processes of political empowerment move beyond formal politics* and are interlinked with processes of empowerment in other spheres (social/economic). Mosime and Dikobe account of how some of the women who had attended the training workshops managed to get into politics at the community level and later used the skills acquired (networking, fundraising and media training) to embark on larger agricultural projects and mentoring other women with different backgrounds in the community. Another lesson from Letsema is that *focus should not just be on the individual woman but on collective processes of empowerment.* The training sessions are inspired by a feminist participatory action approach combining song, storytelling, social media and professional expertise. Mosime and Dikobe account of how especially the mutual mistrust between women from different political parties needed to be overcome through song and storytelling with a focus on common gendered experiences to establish 'safe places' for the female candidates. An additional value of the training workshop is the female political networks built as a basis for further collective initiatives within and outside political life. A third lesson from the work of Letsema is the *need to focus on strategies for more visibility of the female candidates.* Letsema has supported the women in the use of social media to make sure that the shestories of the candidates are being told. Furthermore, Letsema has supported the production of a common poster with female candidates with the main message 'Vote for a woman' in the 2019 election.

Consequently, designed properly training workshops can provide alternative feminist political spaces to promote women's political empowerment – a process that requires a longer time span. However, training workshops should not be regarded as a universal solution or as something to tick off the to-do list of donors, leaving political decision makers and political parties of the hook to address women's political (under) representation or perhaps rather men's overrepresentation. Political decision makers and political parties should be at the forefront of addressing the formal and informal institutions working against more women in politics.

Note

1   Even though, the theme 'Men, masculinities and institutions' was included in the call for papers for the workshop 'Gendered Institutions and Women's Political Representation in Africa', Nordic Africa Institute 12–13 December 2018, the editor did not receive any papers within this theme.

References

Bjarnegård, E. (2015): *Gender, Informal Institutions and Political Recruitment – Explaining Male Dominance in Parliamentary Representation*. New York: Palgrave Macmillan.

Valdini, M. E. (2019): *The Inclusion Calculator – Why Men Appropriate Women's Representation*. New York: Oxford University Press.

Waylen, G. (2017): *Gender and Informal Institutions*. London: Rowman & Littlefield.

Index